TRANSCENDENCE AND HERMENEUTICS

STUDIES IN PHILOSOPHY AND RELIGION

volume 2

TRANSCENDENCE AND HERMENEUTICS

AN INTERPRETATION OF THE PHILOSOPHY OF KARL JASPERS

by

ALAN M. OLSON

1979

MARTINUS NIJHOFF PUBLISHERS

THE HAGUE/BOSTON/LONDON

The distribution of this book is handled by the following team of publishers:

for the United States and Canada

Kluwer Boston, Inc.
160 Old Derby Street
Hingham, MA 02043
USA

for all other countries

Kluwer Academic Publishers Group
Distribution Center
P.O.Box 322
3300 AH Dordrecht
The Netherlands

Library of Congress Cataloging in Publication Data   CIP

Olson, Alan M
  Transcendence and hermeneutics.

  Bibliography: p.
  Includes index.
  1. Jasper, Karl, 1883-1969. 2. Transcendentalism. 3. Idealism. 4. Hermeneutics.
  I. Title.
  B3279.J34O47   193   78-31178

ISBN 90-247-2092-3

DEDICATION

To my parents, MELVIN and LUELLA OLSON
who first taught me the meaning of
Transcendence.

TABLE OF CONTENTS

INTRODUCTION

"The problem of Transcendence is the problem of our time."[1] Needless to say, Transcendence was a particularly lively issue when Karl Heim wrote these words in the mid-1930's. Within the province of philosophical theology and philosophy of religion, however, it is always *the* problem, as Gordon Kaufman has recently reminded us.[2] For the question concerning the nature and the reality of Transcendence has not only to do with self-transcendence, but with the being of Transcendence-Itself, that is to say, with the nature and the reality of God as experienced and understood at any given time or place.

Now there are those today who would claim that any further discussion of the latter half of this proposition, namely, Transcendence-Itself or God, is worthless and quite beside the point. Such persons would claim that the particular *logia* represented by the theological sciences has collapsed by virtue of its object having disappeared. Indeed, when one surveys the contemporary scene in philosophy and theology, there is a good deal of evidence that this is the case – theology of late having become something of a "spectacle," to use Fritz Buri's term. One of the reasons for this, we here contend, is that the richness and the diversity of the meaning of Transcendence has been lost. And even though we do not here intend to resolve the issue, neither do we assume that such an enquiry is either impossible or irrelevant. Viewed phenomenologically, we are saying here that the God-problem *is* the problem of Transcendence. By delineating the various operations and modalities of the *experience* of Transcendence and its relation to hermeneutics, it is our hope that what we say may *indirectly* have a bearing on the God-problem. From the outset, then, we are bold to assert that the continuing *Krisis* of Transcendence is not so much the result of a "default of the gods," as Heidegger put it so eloquently, as the consequence of theology's failure to attend care-

---

[1] Karl Heim, *God Transcendent* (London: Nesbit and Co., Ltd., 1935), p. 33.
[2] Gordon Kaufman, *God the Problem* (Cambridge: Harvard University Press, 1972).

fully to the *experience* of Transcendence. Objectifying discourse *about* Transcendence sacrifices the overplus of meaning intrinsic to the experience *of* Transcendence and easily leads to semantic confusion. On the one hand, either the meaning of Transcendence is reduced to its adjectival or adverbial significance as characterizing a peculiar form of human activity in which case the referential character of the experience of Transcendence is lost, or, on the other hand, a purely mythical referentiality is maintained in which case the symbols of Transcendence are dismissed as archaisms denoting the cosmological status of the divine as an extramental object.

This work is written with a view to the confused contemporary philosophical and theological situation and under the following theses: First, that the language of Transcendence is intrinsic to religious experience and expression because Transcendence lies at the very basis of the possibility of all experience. Secondly, that the term Transcendence and its various forms and expressions is indispensable to systematic theological and philosophical inquiry because there is no equivalent term embodying the same degree of both logical precision and existential depth. Thirdly, that the meaning of Transcendence is obscured whenever the Being of Transcendence is reduced to the act of transcending. Finally, we are suggesting that a careful analysis of the works of Karl Jaspers and recent developments in hermeneutic philosophy can be of great assistance in rehabilitating the meaning of Transcendence.

As we mentioned initially, Transcendence was the subject of diverse philosophical and theological debate during the second quarter of the twentieth century, especially in Germany and in those circles most influenced by German thought. Part of this preoccupation is no doubt attributable to the crisis of German identity following World War I and the onslaught of economic depression at a world level. Heidegger's plea to break out of the "everydayness" of mundane existence, Jaspers' invocations to "possible Existenz," and Bultmann's call for "the authentic eschatological existence," can all be viewed as various appeals for Transcendence; the early twentieth century echos, as it were, of Nietzsche's *la fin de siècle* lament. Similarly, the development of dialectical or *crisis* theology in Barth, Brunner, Gogarten, Buber and Tillich, can be viewed as the religionist's response to these and other pleas for Transcendence; responses that were tempered with warning lest the quest for Transcendence be destructive and demonic if not measured against the Unconditional Transcendence of God. With the rise of Nazism as the formula of Transcendence on a mass scale, and other forms of totalism as well, such apprehensions were obviously justified as can be seen in the political failings of Heidegger and Heim.

In the larger sense, however, the contemporary crisis is not merely the result of social, economic and political issues. These are rather surface manifestations of a much deeper problem which, we contend, has to do with the complex conceptual intertwining of religion and philosophy during the past two thousand years. Briefly stated, the current crisis is born out of three major transitional developments in the history of ideas.

The first transition has to do with the translation of the Judaic and early Christian experience of God into the thought-forms and language of Hellenistic philosophy; the effects and ambivalences of which are the perennial subject of debate among historians of dogma. While Greek thought provided an apparatus for the systematic refinement of the Christian religious experience – not least the Chalcedonian formulation of the Trinity – it simultaneously had the effect of distancing God and world. Whatever the correct interpretations of the Platonic *Idea* and the Plotinian *One* might be, the net effect of the synthesis of Christian *experience* and Greek *thought* was the development of a symbol system denoting a spatially remote deity, with images of Transcendence based, as Bultmann put it, on the mythical conception of a "three-story universe." With the development of the ecclesiastical and dogmatic structures of medieval Roman Catholicism on Ptolemaic levels, the transcendence of God as spatially "Other" was reinforced socially, culturally and legally. The experiential immediacy of Transcendence so prominent in the Judaic context of early Christianity became experience increasingly mediated by the Church with its dogmatic structure as the definitive index of mediation. Subject to the approval of orthodox interpretation, religious experience was placed into the ironclad constraints of prescribed modalities of interpretation and understanding.

The second major development has to do with the far-reaching effects of the breakdown of these constraints during the Renaissance. The skeptical mood of nominalism, the *revindication* of immediate religious experience in late medieval mysticism, and the psyche-shattering effects of the Protestant Reformation collectively subjected the veracity of all agencies of mediation other than "self" and "Holy Writ", to severe critique. Even more dramatic, of course, were the effects of the development of the natural sciences, especially cosmology. With the repudiation of the medieval, Ptolemaic conception – the "hooped universe" of Dante and its fixed astrological boundaries – the transcendence of God could no longer be viewed as a supernatural "out-there-ness." Even though such images persisted (and still persist) in popular piety, metaphorically descriptive images of a *beyond* and *otherness* after Copernicus no longer carried the weight they once enjoyed. With the advent of social and cultural pluralism and the gradual breakdown of *corpus christianum* the language of the "Beyond" was without the force of institutional infallibility which might enforce it in popular imagination and practice. The development of both pietism and deism in the seventeenth and eighteenth centuries can be viewed as alternative protests against the sedimentation of supernaturalism in the orthodox imagery of Transcendence wherein, unfortunately, "otherness" was equated with "out-there-ness."

The third development – the full implications of which are still in the making – concerns the so-called "Second Copernican Revolution" as represented in the critical philosophy of Immanuel Kant at the end of the eighteenth century. As the "transcendental turn" in modern philosophy, Kantian theory both transformed and compounded the meaning of Transcendence. Although Kant maintained belief in God as a "Transcendental Ideal," the Transcendence of God no longer had anything to do with a cosmological or ontological description of the nature and reality of God. Transcendence was identified rather with the "transcendental" or the mental operations of consciousness and understanding whereby one determined how one could come to the knowledge of anything at all. Through Kant, then, there was a radical shift of the primary meaning of Transcendence from cosmology and metaphysics to epistemology and psychology; from extra-mental to intra-mental realities. Hence the consequent compounding of meaning, for while critical philosophers and theologians since Kant have continued to regard transcendence as epistemologically descriptive and largely psychological, Transcendence still harbors a religious and even supernatural residue suggesting something about the extra-mental status of the Divine. Because of this double inference, a good many philosophers and theologians confine Transcendence to the narrowest of formal or psychological definitions, on the one hand, or reduce it to an irrational symbol or poetic metaphor, on the other. In either case the meaning of Transcendence, as in some sense equivalent to the "ancient name of Being," is lost.

In addition to compounding the meaning of Transcendence, however, the Kantian critical turn also had the salutary effect of restoring to the meaning of Transcendence its essential connection *with* experience. Even though this relationship is exceedingly complex and difficult to formalize, especially when dealing with the Judaeo-Christian experience of Transcendence, it has effected the realization that if one is to speak meaningfully of God as Transcendence-Itself such speaking must be done *within* and not *in spite of* the nature of human experience. That is to say, the critically reflective statement about Transcendence is put not on the basis of presuppositions either for or against the reality of God, but on the basis of careful reflection as to how what one *says* about Transcendence is grounded in the experience *of* Transcendence. Contrary to the contentions of pre-critical theories, Brentano, Husserl and the other pioneers of intentional psychology have shown that the meaning of experience is forged always in the dynamic crucible of *noesis* and *noema*, of the subject both constituting and constituted by meaning. Breaking with both faculty and associationist psychologies, phenomenology asserts that experience is always "experience of ... " an intended object, and judgements having to do with the veridicy of any given object, are invariably colored by "pre-understanding" (*Vorverständnis*). The positive effect of the virtually endless permutations of "Understanding understanding" by transcendental theorists after Kant is the realization that *all* experience – especially religious experience – is far more complex and profound in its consequence and meaning than heretofore recognized by either the uncritical skeptic or the naive believer.

What then of the connection between Transcendence and the "Spirit?" It scarcely needs to be mentioned that one of the principal resonances of Transcendence is *Spirit* or the *spiritual*. Thus it is not surprising that with the demise of the meaning of Transcendence in its fullness, the meaning of Spirit should have suffered a similar fate. A cursory glance at the development of pneumatology in Christian thought illustrates this demise clearly; a diminution of meaning that begins shortly after Augustine's profound writings on the Trinity, ossifies in the scholasticism after Aquinas, is momentarily revived in late medieval mysticism and the classical writings of the reformers, and is eclipsed in the scholarship of both orthodox and liberal Protestantism. Permit me to elucidate briefly.

The term *spirit* is introduced to the Tradition in the second verse of the first chapter of Genesis: " ... and the Spirit (*ru'ah*) of God hovered over the face of the deep." Here in the creation epic and throughout the Old Testament the "Spirit of God" is characterized as the life-giving source of reality; a power and a presence that is immediately present to human life and experience. Apart from the Spirit of God, human experience is unintelligible, for upon the presence of Spirit the *imago dei* and its capacity for conscious reflection and moral decision depends completely. To be "cast out" from the Spirit of the "Most High" is to be in the wilderness of non-being where "one's bones melt like wax." Therefore, the Psalmist implores, "take not thy Holy Spirit from me."

The biblical contention that intelligibility and meaning are ultimately dependent on the Spirit of God is reinforced in the New Testament, especially in the events surrounding Pentecost as reported in the book of *Acts*. Here what the Gospel of Saint John refers to as the *paraclete* is depicted as the gift of the Holy Spirit through the baptism of "tongues of fire." What had been previously a "Babel-like" state of confusion following the passion of Jesus was transformed in an archetypal Heraclitian manner through "fire" into the clear light of *logos*. What Paul Tillich refers to as the *fundamentum in re* character of the triadic or trinitarian conception, then, has a solid basis in biblical tradition, and what philosophy has subsequently referred to as the mind – body, history – nature problems are, for the Bible, problematic only if Spirit is experientially inoperative.

The Church, unfortunately, failed to recognize the value of the treasure with which it had been entrusted and to which, in fact, it owed its *raison d'être*. Experience gave way to dogma which, when combined with the native monarchism of the Western Church and the triumph of Aristotelian metaphysics, led to an hypostatization of the Trinitarian conception and the gradual displacement of pneumatology by ecclesiology. Only the Eastern Church, by dint of the iconoclastic controversy and its pro-Augustinian sentiments has given the Holy Spirit its due within the trinitarian formulations of the tradition. Resisting the subordinationist tendencies of the *filioque* clause and developing a theology of sobronost rich in the liturgical imagery of epiclesis, Orthodoxy developed pneumatology precisely with a view to "creative mystery." Nowhere is the continuing significance of Orthodoxy's intuitive grasp of the Spirit more eloquently documented than in the writings of the 20th century philosopher-theologian Nicolas Berdyaev. What the symbol "Transcendence" is to Jaspers, the "Spirit" is to Berdyaev; for Transcendence and Spirit are respectively for both thinkers the primordial antecedents of Freedom and possible Existenz.

As in the case of Transcendence, then, the Western Church slowly lost the relational-mediational character of Spirit as an intrinsic dimension of human experience and identity. The great mystics of the Rhineland and of Spain, to be sure, understood the language of Spirit. But mysticism in Roman Catholicism was tolerated only as a fringe phenomenon and never fully integrated into the life of the institution. The hierarchy viewed the language of Spirit as being synonymous with individualism whereby the mediational apparatus of the sacramental system could be bypassed through claims to spiritual immediacy. Moreover, largely confined to the "religious" living in cloistered orders, it was impossible sociologically for mysticism to make a large-scale impression on the lives of the laity.

Instigated largely by the intransigent triumphalism of Rome, the development of Protestant individualism did not, however, lead to the revival of pneumatology in any significant systematic or philosophical way. To be sure, Luther's catechetical explanations to the Third Article of the Trinity allude to the paradoxical and mysterious character of the Holy Spirit, and Luther is certainly clear regarding its mediational function in the development of faith. But Luther is rather an exception whose mystical sensibilities were quickly outstripped in the development of Lutheran Orthodoxy. In the main, Protestantism interprets "Spirit" in terms of doctrines of sanctification. In other words – and in spite of the mystical tone of Calvin's *testimonium spiritus sancti internum* – it is the *moral* and not the *mystical-experiential* dimension of Spirit that is stressed in Protestantism. Within Lutheran circles, in fact, the much disputed *usus duplex* and *usus triplex legis* serves as a sort of line of demarcation between those who lean towards Luther's paradoxical-existential understanding of "the proper distinction between Law and Gospel," within which the Holy Spirit plays such a critical role, and those who lean towards the more programmatic moral constructions of orthodox Protestantism. It was not until Kierkegaard that the paradoxical and mediational character of Spirit would be restored, and then largely as a psychological phenomenon.

The tale of Protestantism's alienation from the Spirit is told quite succinctly by William Barrett in the following quotation: "With Protestantism begins that long modern struggle, which reaches its culmination in the twentieth century, to strip man naked. To be sure, in all this the aim was progress, and Protestantism did succeed in raising the religious consciousness to a higher level of individual sincerity, soul-searching and strenuous inwardness. Man was impoverished in order to come face to face with his God and the severe and inexplicable demands of his faith; but in the process he was stripped of all the mediating rites and dogmas that could make this confrontation less dangerous to his psychic balance. Protestantism achieved a heightening of religious consciousness, but at the same time severed this consciousness from the deep unconscious life of our total human nature."[3] The loss of these agencies of mediation is

---

[3] William Barrett, *Irrational Man* (New York: Doubleday, 1958), p. 24.

precisely what leads to the eventual identification of Spirit with mind in the Enlightenment, and what is repressed progressively in the northern European religious consciousness in the dark, abysmal, apophatic character of Spirit. What emerges in its place is the lesser spirit of conquest and "mission."

The cataphatic, evangelistic pneumatology of the late eighteenth and nineteenth century Protestantism, then, is substantially different from the "Spirit" that compelled the proclamation of "Good News" in the early days of Christianity, for the evangelical spirit of the so-called "Christian Century" is indistinguishable from the wholesale exportation of Christian culture to the so-called *heathen* peoples of the world. The proclamation of the Word was not really a word of liberation but a paternalistic, culture-bound word to become mini-European Christians. Even today, with the widespread reemergence of fundamentalistic, neo-Pentecostal *ergo* "spiritually alive" Christianity, pneumatology (such as there is of it emanating from these circles) still receives its major definition in terms of the activistic, conquest-oriented spirit of nineteenth-century evangelical Protestantism. While the charismatic feature of the so-called new religious "awakening" feeds effectively on the contemporary quest for ecstatic experience, the experiential moment is quickly supplemented by the old mandate for enthusiastic proselytizing.

The triumphalist aspect of medieval Roman Catholic "ecclesial" pneumatology, then, was not really mitigated by the Protestant revolt, but subtly transformed and translated into more encompassing and technically efficient cultural and ideological forms. As Max Weber and other commentators on the secularization of the Western world have shown, the *spirit* of Protestant individualism slowly fused with a capitalist, expansionist ethic. With this fusion, the meaning of spirit as simultaneously *power* and *presence,* as in the case of the archaic religious conception of *mana* or Rudolf Otto's understanding of the Holy as *mysterium tremendum,* has been reduced to *power* conceived almost exclusively in terms of the empirically measurable result, whether individually or collectively and institutionally.[4] If then, the symbol of Transcendence is incoherent for many philosophers, the same may be said in the case of Spirit for many theologians.

There are, of course, many notable exceptions to what I have here out-

---

[4] See, for example, Hendrikus Berkoff, *The Doctrine of the Holy Spirit* (Richmond: John Knox Press, 1964). Highly acclaimed in many Protestant circles, this text was written as an attempt to reinstate and reaffirm pneumatology. Berkhoff's initial description of *Spirit* is "mission" and this is thematic throughout.

lined very briefly. Yet the progressive loss of the meaning of Transcendence and the Spirit is unmistakable. Perhaps it has been necessary to refer again to Heidegger, for us to reach the "midnight" of our "time of
need" before there can take place concerted attempts to retrieve the
meaning of symbols so fundamental to human experience. Indeed, perhaps a sign of this *midpoint* is the appearance of what Jaspers terms a
plethora of "surrogate forms of Transcendence." Such claims are surrogate in the sense that they are transparent to nothing more than the
cleverly marketed religio-economic venture and the prospect of instant
enlightenment, happiness, success and tranquility. We need not here catalogue "pop" forms of religion and philosophy, for they abound everywhere in modern consumer culture.

Thus we here make no claim to radical originality regarding the nature
and meaning of Transcendence, for the discussion, in its various forms, is
well underway. It would seem that we have finally "transcended," as it
were, what Fritz Buri termed the "puberty theologies"[5] that characterized the American scene of the 1960's, and this should give us all cause
for hope. Our purpose, then, is one of calling attention to the possibilities
of a hermeneutic philosophy of Transcendence through an analysis of
the work of Karl Jaspers, for in Jaspers we discern a treatment of this
subject that has largely been overlooked. It is, of course, the name of
Heidegger that is usually linked with a hermeneutic retrieval of the ancient name of Being. Jaspers, we contend, rehabilitates the meaning of
Transcendence in a way that parallels, in many ways, the Heideggerian
treatment of Being. And while Jaspers did not himself call his philosophy
of Transcendence *hermeneutical*, it is precisely this feature we wish to
illuminate in this study.

★ ★ ★

Before we begin, it is necessary to indicate how the term Transcendence
will be used in this book. In general Transcendence has to do with the
fundamental conviction that human beings are able somehow to grasp or
to be grasped by a reality that transcends the mere givenness of mundane
existence. Due to its inherent evanescence the experience of Transcendence has been expressed and articulated by philosophers and theologians
in many different ways: from the highly formal constructions of Aquinas
and Kant, at one extreme, to the more intuitive and metaphoric formula-

---

[5] Fritz Buri, *How Can We Still Speak Responsibly of God?* (Philadelphia Fortress Press,
1968).

tions of Bergson, Marcel, and Heidegger on the other. But regardless of the manifold forms and expressions of Transcendence, it has always denoted – directly or indirectly – an experience of God or Being-Itself, whether such experiences are natural or supernatural in their reference, theistic or atheistic in their meaning.

As we have already indicated, since the Kantian or "transcendental turn" of modern philosophy, Transcendence has been stripped increasingly of its cosmological or extra-mental reference and its meaning transformed by a host of epistemological qualifications. Consequently use of the term today is fraught with equivocation as intended meaning wavers between strict epistemological usage in which transcendence or the "transcendental" has to do with a way of understanding the nature and operations of consciousness, and usage that is metaphysical referring to a reality or entity that might be termed "Transcendence-Itself" or God. This equivocation, of course, is particularly acute in the case of theologians and philosophers of religion who have a vested interest in the more traditional cosmological and metaphysical aspect of Transcendence. Since Kant, however, religious thinkers are also obliged to speak of Transcendence qualifiedly; qualifications of such degree and moment that in many cases there is reticence to use the term at all.

In Karl Jaspers, however, we encounter a philosopher who not only uses the term "Transcendence" with all its attendant ambiguities, but considers it utterly central for "true philosophizing." Jaspers alone in modern thought devotes an entire career to the reinstatement of Transcendence in a way that will sacrifice neither epistemological clarity nor metaphysical depth. Because of the thoroughness of Jaspers' project, and because the contemporary discussion can easily profit from the critical refinements he brings to a comprehensive understanding of Transcendence, we will focus on Jaspers' position as the paradigm for this inquiry. In keeping with this focus and on the basis of my own understanding of Jaspers, we will use the term "Transcendence" in the following ways:

First, the English infinitive "to transcend" and the gerund "transcending" are understood and used with reference to an "act" by the human agent whereby one "goes beyond" or "steps over" an apparent boundary or "limit." This conforms to the meaning of the German verbs *transzendieren*, *übersteigen*, and *überschreiten,* which, as in the case of the French verbs *transcender* and *dépasser* indicate *l'action même de dépasser* or *l'opération de dépassement.* [6]

___

[6] For an extensive etymological and philological analysis of *transcendence* and its usage in the Western philosophical tradition, see "Le vocabulaire de la transcendance," in Michel

Secondly, English usage has two adjectival forms for Transcendence, "transcendental" and "transcendent." The former, "transcendental," will be used in its usual descriptive sense as it relates to epistemology. The latter form, however, will be qualified by giving it the force of the nounal form "transcendence" through the use of an upper-case "T" as in the German manner. This will reinforce the subject – object distinction so integral to the thought of Jaspers differentiating the "act" of transcending from the "object" to which this act as a metaphysical project refers, namely "Transcendence-Itself" or the "Transcendent" as in the case of the French *transcendantité* having *le caractère de transcendance absolue de Dieu*. The upper-case usage, then, will indicate that the "Transcendent" is *not* merely a descriptive term but bears within it something of the force of *das Absolute* or *das Unbedingte* which is wholly independent of the *act* of transcending but not foreign to the *experience* of Transcendence. This usage will be in close conformity to Jaspers' use of the verbal-noun *Transzendenz* which, when used within the critical framework of *mögliche Existenz*, has the quality of a substantive within which the subjective and objective aspects of *Transzendenz* coalesce experientially even though they are formally distinct. The experiential character of this substantival usage is symbolized in our hyphenated construction "transcending-thinking" (*transzendierenden Denken*). Indeed, upon a clear comprehension of both the formal and existential modalities of *transzendierenden Denken*, Jaspers' overall philosophy of Transcendence clearly rests. By this term "transcending-thinking" (which we will in all cases hyphenate in order to insist on its "lived" character) Jaspers does *not* mean "to transcend thinking" in the sense of "going beyond thinking." What is meant in each instance is "transcending *through* thinking" whereby "thinking" (*denken*) is differentiated from mere "cognition" (*Erkenntnis*), just as the medieval mystics differentiated *intellectus* from *ratio*.

Needless to say, it is the third or *substantival* form of Transcendence and its intimate relation to "transcending-thinking" that is at once the most intriguing and the most controversial feature of the Jaspersian project. Depending on the context (and the context is not always clear), Jaspers' translators render *Transzendenz* in both the lower and upper case, as is so frequently the case with English translations of *Sein*. In order to be consistent with what we believe to be the metaphysical intention of Jaspers, we will follow the above mentioned procedure. The

Piclin, *La notion de transcendance: Son sens - Son évolution* (Paris: Librairie Armand Colin, 1969), pp. 9-17.

upper-case rendering will also serve to differentiate the position of Jaspers from that of Heidegger for whom (at least in his earlier works) the "act" of transcending and the "Being" of Transcendence are one and the same. By contrast, Jaspers' Transcendence is not strictly an immanent category and for this reason he differentiates radically between Heidegger's use of *Dasein* and his own *Existenz*. As in the Platonic understanding of *thumos*, Existenz, for Jaspers, represents the mediational nexus of immanence and Transcendence and is not meant to suggest the descriptive neutrality of Heidegger's *Daseinsanalyse*. For these reasons Jaspers' method of investigation can be more easily aligned with *existential* than *eidetic* phenomenology since for Jaspers it is precisely the "mystical" character of Transcendence that cannot, as in the case of Husserl, be "rigorously excluded." At the same time Jaspers cannot simply be *identified* with an existential or *Lebenswelt* phenomenology, for the meaning of Transcendence is not discernible through descriptions of being-in-a-world alone, as in Heidegger and Merleau-Ponty. Transcendence, for Jaspers, remains always "hovering in ciphers:" it is experienced, it is known, it is real, it is transforming – but its essence is only capable of being communicated "indirectly." Because of its "indirectness" all *methode* qua *methode* can and must fail as a final and definitive way of description and elucidation. Indeed, only in the failing or "foundering" of method, as Jaspers puts it, does the metaphysical content of Transcendence "appear." At the same time Jaspers does not appreciate to the same degree as Hans-Georg Gadamer that "truth" and "method" are coordinate rather than sequential or linear realities; that method tends to emerge relative to and simultaneous with that truth or meaning being sought. There is still in Jaspers the tendency to refine first the method so that it will emerge in Truth, and about this we will have more to say in Part III.

Because Transcendence is thematic throughout the writings of Jaspers, it is also necessary here to indicate the rationale underlying our selection of material. Jaspers' first major work was the massive *Allgemeine Psychopathologie* published in 1913 when Jaspers was still practicing medicine at the psychiatric hospital in Heidelberg. This work is distinctive in representing one of the first uses of phenomenology as a tool for describing mental disorders and even today is used as a standard reference. His second major study, *Psychologie der Weltanschauungen*, published in 1919, marked Jaspers' transition from a career as a practicing physician to that of philosopher on the faculty of the University of Heidelberg. Neither of these works, together with the numerous books and articles dealing with ethics, morality and the status of German politics and culture after World War II, plays a significant role in this inquiry.

The works with which we are concerned fall into two general categories: the formally descriptive and the historically analytical, both of which, in their respective ways, contribute to what Heidegger would term a "retrieval" (*Wiederholen*) of Transcendence. The formally descriptive writings elucidate the meaning of Transcendence by delineating phenomenologically the patterns and structures of experience.Representing a *philosophische Grundoperation*, Jaspers' "periechontology" determines that Transcendence is not only present to human experience but, in fact, accounts for its very possibility. The basic features of his lifelong method of "transcending-thinking" are set forth in his first major philosophical work entitled *Philosophie*, published in three volumes in 1932, ten years after his appointment to a full chair in philosophy at Heidelberg. Since Jaspers had no formal training in philosophy, his own comments concerning the production of *Philosophie* are important, for once established he never departed from its basic principles spending the rest of his academic career refining its vision: "Replacing philosophy by an ever so extensive psychological approach and by the use of ever so interesting historical material was, after all, an evasion of the serious task of having to understand oneself, one's own existence . . . Another level of thinking had to be gained. That meant the decision to make a new start from the beginning." [7]

Between *Philosophie* and his last published work, *Chiffren der Transzendenz* (summer lectures delivered in Basel in 1961 but published posthumously in 1970) – both of which are central to this study – Jaspers' formally descriptive writings include: *Vernunft und Existenz* (1935), *Existenzphilosophie* (1938), *Von der Wahrheit* (1947), *Der philosophische Glaube* (1948), *Vom Ursprung und Ziel der Geschichte* (1949), *Einführung in die Philosophie* (1950), *Vernunft und Widervernunft in Unserer Zeit* (1950), *Die Frage der Entmythologisierung* (1954), and *Der philosophische Glaube angesichts der Offenbarung* (1962).

Although never explicitly formalized as a method of "retrieval," Jaspers' historically descriptive writings clearly intend to delineate the patterns and operations of "transcending-thinking" present to the "great philosophers" of the tradition. Jaspers, in fact, reads the history of phi-

---

"Philosophical Autobiography," in *The Philosophy of Karl Jaspers*, ed. Paul Schilpp (New York: Tudor, 1957), p. 35.

losophy as the history of *mögliche Existenz*. Even though this can be a dangerous procedure for which Jaspers, as well as Heidegger, have been severely criticized, its overall effect is constructive, for through his interpretation one not only encounters a fresh and invigorating "existential" reading of the history of philosophy, but also a means of seeing specific examples of the operative character of transcending-thinking in the voices of the past. Primary among the works important for a consideration of the historical retrieval of Transcendence and the comparative task that accompanies it are the following: *Nietzsche. Einführung in das Verständnis seines Philosophierens* (1936), *Schelling. Grösse und Verhängnis* (1955), and *Die Grossen Philosophen*, Vol. I (1956). Most of Jaspers' major writings have now been translated into English. Translations from works still available only in German are my own, including the Appendix from *Von der Wahrheit*.

Our investigation is divided into three parts. In Part I, we present Jaspers' phenomenology of the formal modalities of self-transcendence through transcending-thinking in relation to the world, the self, and God. This will include an analysis of the phenomenon of "disjointness" and its effects on consciousness, Jaspers' views on science, boundary experience and the nature of the self, freedom, historicity, and the possibilities of absolute consciousness. We will also direct our attention in this section to Jaspers' understanding of metaphysics and how the cipher is instrumental in his definition of metaphysics and the rejection of ontology.

In Part II. we attempt to locate Jaspers in the history of Western thought by focussing on four historic figures that seem to inform his philosophy at every turn, viz., Plato, Plotinus, Kant and Cusanus. We do this in order to enhance the formal dimensions of Jaspers' philosophizing, it being well understood that he has also a close relation to Nietzsche and to Kierkegaard. Indeed, it is our primary purpose in this section to bring into view the idealist underpinnings of Jaspers' thought in order to clearly indicate that he is no ordinary existentialist.

Finally, in Part III, we concentrate on the hermeneutical character of Jaspers' philosophy of Transcendence by providing a detailed examination of the nature of ciphers and their interpretation. This leads us to a synoptic presentation of Jaspers' interpretation of the cipher of God, and to a discussion of the hiatus between philosophical faith and Christian faith. Following this, and after having located what we believe is the fatal weakness in the hermeneutics of transcending-thinking, we discuss Jaspers in relation to his successors and his critics; in this case Rudolf

Bultmann, Paul Ricoeur and Hans-Georg Gadamer. In each case, we find an amelioration of the intuitive claim to immediacy as regards the nature and the meaning of Transcendence by attention to the dynamics of mediation. This, we believe, is utterly essential for the complete rehabilitation of Transcendence as a productive concept in philosophical and theological discourse, and we state our reasons why in the final chapter.

I would here acknowledge my appreciation to those who have provided guidance and inspiration during the course of this project: to Arthur Vogel who initially sparked my interest in the subject and problem of Transcendence; to Harold Oliver, Leroy Rouner, Erazim Kohák, Donald Carne-Ross, and John N. Findlay, teachers and colleagues at Boston University, who have offered critical comments and helpful suggestions along the way; and to Gershom Scholem, Paul Ricoeur, and Hans-Georg Gadamer for stimulating conversations concerning the life and work of Karl Jaspers. I would also thank Rebecca Low and Gayle Gerber Koontz for their very able assistance in the preparation of the manuscript. Finally, there is always cause for thanks beyond measure to my wife Janet, and to my daughters Maren and Sonja, for simple being who they are.

PART I

TRANSCENDING-THINKING AND ITS MODALITIES

PART I INTRODUCTION

In the introductory section of Jaspers' first major philosophical work, he established a context and method of philosophizing that remained constant throughout his career: "Awakening to myself, in my situation, I raise the question of Being. Finding myself in the situation of an indeterminate possibility, I must *search for Being* if I want to find my real self. But it is not until I fail in this search for intrinsic being that I begin to philosophize. This is what we call *philosophizing on the ground of possible Existenz*, and the method used is transcending." [1]

As this statement suggests, for Jaspers neither "Being," "Existenz" nor "Transcendence" can be objectified as things or entities, but are realities discernible only through entering into the movement or motion of "transcending." This is not to say, however, that these terms are "objectless," for without some kind of specificity any inquiry into the nature of Being or Transcendence is quite meaningless. [2] A major part of this inquiry will be the attempt to determine just what kind of objectivity Jaspers' "Transcendence" denotes. But it must also be made clear from the outset that in the philosophy of Jaspers, neither the "act" of transcending nor the "Being" of Transcendence ultimately can be separated. Therefore it is not a question of merely dissecting the method in order to arrive at some entity called Transcendence. Such a procedure would contravene directly the intent of Jaspers which is always to identify "transcending" and "true philosophizing." Jaspers insists that one does not "learn philosophy." One rather, if successful, "learns how to philosophize." Philosophy is not a familiarization with or a mastery of a collection of facts but a human event or "act" in which the personal role of the subject is affirmed absolutely.

True philosophizing, then, presupposes transcending; that is, it in-

---

[1] *Philosophy*, I, trans. E.B. Ashton (Chicago; University of Chicago Press, 1969), p. 45.
[2] This is analogous to Heidegger's observation regarding the difficulty of an adequate definition of the term "Being." Cf., *Being and Time*, trans. John Macquarrie and Edward Robinson (New York: Harper and Row, 1962), pp. 21ff.

volves a movement beyond an undifferentiated natural standpoint
through what one might call a series of conversions from constrictive to
more encompassing horizons of consciousness and thinking. Formally,
this process has three dimensions or moments, viz. *Weltorientierung, Existenzerhellung* and *spekulative Metaphysik*. Here the term "dimensions"
or "moments" is essential in order to avoid the suggestion that there is
any kind of ontological stratification between so-called levels of consciousness. Within the concrete life of a given Existenz these three
moments are in no way discrete or separate operations but are grounded
equally in the single task of "becoming" Existenz in relation to Transcendence or Being-Itself. Even though Jaspers' *Philosophie* was published in three volumes corresponding to these moments or "modalities,"
such a procedure should not be construed as indicating some kind of
a rigidly triadic formula for philosophizing. By the same token, it is almost impossible for a Western philosopher to avoid the "trinitarian"
conception when it comes to speaking about metaphysics. In the work of
Nicholas Berdyaev, for example, who during the 1930's was saying something quite similar to Jaspers, Transcendence is developed exclusively
under the rubric of the "Spirit." Berdyaev, however, maintained an open
commitment to the pneumatological tradition of Orthodoxy whereas
Jaspers expressly disavows any such dependence on Christianity. [3] For
Jaspers this division of labor follows rather from the formal necessity of
differentiating logical operations and not from the desire to stratify or
hypostatize either reality or consciousness at three discrete levels. Far
more critical questions have to do with whether Jaspers differentiates
sufficiently the modalities and sub-modalities of formal transcending,
and whether Jaspers' notion of "objectivity" is adequate to the task he
sets before him. Given the radicality of Jaspers' demarcation between the
empirically objective and the *metaphysically* non-objective, is it possible
to develop a hermeneutic of symbol that can ever communicate the Being
of Transcendence? If not, is it possible to correct Jaspers' method of transcending-thinking so that it does not become an end in itself; that is, a
lyrical and aesthetic preoccupation with something that can never be
communicated in a formal way?

Suffice it to say for the purpose of preliminary remarks that for Jaspers
the philosophical task begins from a particular situation and that situation is being-in-a-world (*in-der-Welt-sein*). It makes no sense whatsoever
to attempt to understand the nature of self-Being or Being-Itself as ulti-

---

[3] Cf., Berdyaev's *Spirit and Reality* (London: 1939).

mate reality before one becomes aware of what it means to be-in-a-world. Therefore, in Jaspers' first modality of exteriority, transcending takes place in relation to a largely undifferentiated manifold of sense data; in the second mode of interiority, the self is regarded as an alternative to the indeterminate nature of the external world; and in the third modality, thinking-itself becomes reflexively attuned to the question of Being or Transcendence-Itself through experience become "cipher." Within each of these modalities the other two are present but in differing degrees. In the case of *Existenzerhellung*, and borrowing the imagery of Whitehead, it might be said that there is a "concrescence" of the first and third modes of transcending (e.g., the world and Transcendence-Itself as the "physical" and "mental" poles of "prehension") within which there arises the concrete "occasion" of experience or, for Jaspers, the nascent "becoming" of possible Existenz. [4]

Furthermore, Jaspers' method of "transcending-thinking" distinguishes between two fundamentally different kinds of questions. The first has to do with the extrinsic question of "world" orientation and the limits of empirical "cogency" which tends to dominate "consciousness-at-large"; [5] and the second is the intrinsic question of the nature and the meaning of self both in terms of the relation of self to world, self to self, and self to Transcendence. The latter question is not resolved by a universally valid "stock of knowledge" but is dependent upon a "posture of consciousness," i.e., a "transcending-consciousness." [6] Thus Jaspers always demarcates between what can be called "mere cognition" or the ability whereby one is able to quantify and objectify the manifold of sense experience and "thinking" which is reflexively transcendental. This second kind of thinking – "transcending-thinking" – is, as Jaspers suggests, thinking aware of the fact that it is "rooted in freedom," [7] for it does not aim at any particular object but is both concerned with and

---

[4] Apart from this similarity, this is about as far as the analogy between Whitehead and Jaspers can be pressed, for in Whitehead's "reformed subjectivist principle" we have a theory of experience which applies to both organic and inorganic phenomena. Jaspers' language of Existenz maps out a far less pretentious terrain of inquiry and is, therefore (as Jaspers understands it), more in harmony with the spirit of "critical" philosophy. Although we have never found a reference to Whitehead in the writings of Jaspers, he probably would not exclude Whitehead when he says, "Every claim to a cosmology is doomed to be a mythical cosmology." *Way to Wisdom*, trans. Manheim (New Haven: Yale University Press, 1951), p. 76. Of course, this is not to imply that Jaspers' own metaphysic is beyond reproach, but it is certainly not a cellular approach to the nature of reality which, for Jaspers, would falsify the metaphysical project through "objectifying thinking" and reductionism however "metaphorical" in nature.

[5] *Phil.*, I, p. 84.
[6] *Ibid.*, p. 76.
[7] *Ibid.*, p. 78.

compelled by an awareness of the limits and boundaries of knowing. In Husserlian terms, it could be stated that "mere cognition" as characteristic of "consciousness-at-large" is thinking from the "natural standpoint," i.e., thinking that takes itself and its veridicy for granted and is concerned basically with the usefulness and functional application of knowing some "thing." In transcending-thinking, on the other hand, we are dealing with knowing which not only knows what it knows, but how it knows what it knows and even more so what it cannot know. For Jaspers knowledge that is aware of its foundations and the intrinsic role of the constituting subject in the act of knowing is existentially *and* epistemologically reflexive, that is, it is critical in both the Kierkegaardian and Kantian sense.

Yet neither the thinking of limit nor the existentially reflexive character of cognition is finally decisive for Jaspers. Speaking in relation to the ultimate level of transcending in the ciphers of speculative metaphysics, Jaspers advances his "theorem of consciousness," which bears similarity to the Husserlian understanding of *Wesensschau*, asserting that " . . . whatever has for us the character of being must be immanent to consciousness either as object or experience." [8] The decisive difference between Jaspers and Husserl, however, is the latter's belief that in pure or "eidetic" phenomenology, " . . . all thoughts *partially mystical in nature* and clinging chiefly to the concepts of *Eidos* and Essence are *rigorously excluded.*" [9] As we shall see, the logical veracity of Jaspers' philosophy of Existenz squarely rests on his ability to thematize clearly the ramifications of this theorem even though, as he says qualifiedly, its only exception is "the objectless certainty of a free, unconditioned self." [10] Thus, even though we should not be under the illusion that transcending-thinking will result in a new ontology of Being, Jaspers very definitely implies that a conceptual elucidation of the boundaries and limits of thinking can contribute to a heightened understanding of reality, for "Philosophical meaning comes from the boundary alone." [11] Throughout Jaspers' discourse on *Grenzen*, he accepts and avows a Kantian understanding of the subject-object structure of experience as underlying the consciousness of "boundary" and does not claim to go beyond it – at least not in the ordinary sense. But in deference to his mentor and against neo-Kantian interpretation (as we will see in Part II), Jaspers believes that the

---

[8] *Ibid.*, p. 87.
[9] Cf., *Ideen*, 1.3.
[10] *Phil*, I, p. 87.
[11] *Ibid.*, p. 81. The concept of "boundary" will be expanded descriptively in Part I and historically in Part II.

subject-object structure of experience is not the end but the "beginning" of true metaphysics and furthermore, that there is a reality or ground beyond the limits of cognition which is both the foundation and goal of transcending-thinking. Whether or not this is the case and whether such a claim can be delivered through the cipher language of Existenz will be a problem for consideration throughout this investigation.

It must also be emphasized that Jaspers insists repeatedly that true philosophizing is always rooted in *Lebenspraxis*, i.e., that the kind of metaphysics being proposed is not a new esoteric gnosticism but a *practognosis* grounded fully *in-der-Welt-sein*. However the kind of *Lebenspraxis* resulting from *transzendierenden Denken* is neither common sense nor a universally valid normative ethic. Its product is insight concerning the lived dynamics of freedom and historicity in the becoming of possible Existenz. What one might term a "transcending-transformation" of the consciousness of self-Being is not the result of a leap out of the world or away from the world but always within and through the world. It is, therefore, the qualified immanence of Jaspers' notion of Transcendence which distinguishes the conversion of consciousness to which he refers from that which is usually claimed as the source of so-called "religious" conversions. At the same time we must assert that religious conversion is by no means the univocal and simple-minded phenomenon which many – including Jaspers – sometimes regard it. No one has made this point more clearly than the brilliant Jesuit theologian, Bernard Lonergan. The degree to which Jaspers' "philosophical faith" is finally "free" from the soteriological problematics of religion and especially Christian theism is highly questionable as we will see in Part III.

Finally, and before turning to an analysis of Jaspers' formal modes of transcending, it should also be mentioned that the manner in which Being or Transcendence appears for Existenz is always something intrinsic to the process of transcending-thinking and not something which simply happens at the end of the process. If this were not the case, Jaspers would fit neatly into the tradition of gnosticism. Jaspers' philosophy of Existenz, however, is developed within the living matrix of the subject-object relation that vitiates the choice between science and metaphysics, immanence and Transcendence, phenomena and noumena. The philosophical task is rather that of elucidating the boundary between these two frequently objectified and hypostatized foci of experience, for to be in the realm of phenomena or appearance " ... is a way of becoming conscious, not of the *Ding-an-sich* beyond me, but of my own Existenz."[12]

---

[12] *Ibid.*, p. 61.

Apart from what Jaspers believes to be the synthetic but non-objectifying language of Existenz, all discourse concerning the relationship between existence and essence, appearance and reality, is faced with incompassability whereby one is forced to opt for a reduction of reality either to subjectivity or objectivity. However, grounded in the *fondement* of Existenz, Jaspers believes that Being or Transcendence can be grasped as "possibility" – a kind of "eschatological prolepsis" to use the phrase of Pannenberg (albeit minus its Christological referentiality) – which at once enables one to recognize the disjunctive character of human experience, affirming it through freedom, and thereby in some sense *overcoming* it. Of course, there are those who would maintain that this possibility is so ambiguous that it is like unto no possibility at all, and Jaspers would agree that for those in whom the question of certainty is compelled by objectifying thinking, this is inevitable. Even from the standpoint of Existenz and transcending in the cipher- language of speculative metaphysics, Transcendence is inherently evasive, for "indirectness is its essence . . . inconclusiveness its touchstone . . . For the real will to know originates in Existenz which, in itself, is unknowable." [13] In spite of, and in many ways because of, the disjunction present to human experience, Transcendence presents itself to experience; that is, through an analysis of that thinking which transcends, Transcendence is known not because of the imposition of an Otherness upon experience but because of the Otherness that is fundamental to experience-itself.

As we shall see, it is the indirect, metaphorical character of Transcendence in the philosophy of Jaspers which is both the basis of its attractiveness and that which causes the initial reader to look askance. As a "boundary philosophizing" whose mystical aim is the "fully suspended consciousness" whereby Transcendence can appear in its specificity, the reader is forced to struggle with the continuous temptation of trying to fixate and localize the conceptuality of Jaspers as though by this tactic one can finally and decisively lay hold of Transcendence-Itself. Again, and in connection with the cosmological residue of Transcendence to which we alluded in the introduction, this is precisely what cannot be done. Jaspers' intention is not the development of another ontology of Transcendence but an existentially descriptive and "lived" metaphysics of Transcendence. While the transcendental or critical turn of philosophical method demonstrates the impossibility of an ontology of Tran-

---

[13] *Ibid.*, p. 67.

scendence, it is just this impossibility which has liberated philosophy for what Jaspers believes to be the authentic possibility of a metaphysic of Transcendence. Playing on the Platonic metaphors of *chorismos* and *methexis* (with which we will be dealing further in Part II), one might say that the separation of the knowing subject from a naively extrinsic understanding of Transcendence provides the occasion for a conversion in one's way of thinking whereupon one's experience of Transcendence itself invalidates the initial question one has posed about Transcendence. What Jaspers delineates in his modalities of transcending-thinking is nothing less than the orchestration of the manner in which this transition from an objectifying-alienated-consciousness to the participating-transcending-consciousness takes place. To an analysis of these modalities we now turn.

CHAPTER ONE

TRANSCENDING IN WORLD-ORIENTATION

Jaspers' description of the nature and meaning of *Weltorientierung* occupies the entire first volume of *Philosophie*. In this chapter we will focus on three formal aspects of this analysis that are essential to obtaining an understanding of his overall method of "transcending-thinking." The first has to do with the phenomenon of "disjunction" (*die Trennung*) or being-in-the-world as an "indeterminate totality;" the second concerns the possibility of a "scientific world-view" in the light of this experience; and the third is a consideration of the "reversal" (*die Umkehrung*) in consciousness caused by a recognition of the limits of scientific inquiry and the conversion it can effect in the subject as the occasion for a movement into the language of interiority.

THE PHENOMENON OF DISJUNCTION

We have already mentioned that transcending or true philosophizing for Jaspers begins in a specific situation and that situation is the givenness of being-in-a-world. As a given, my being-in-a-world is a fact, a precondition for any questions raised concerning its meaning. However, with the event of the question and the reflection intrinsic to the genesis of questioning my being-in-a-world becomes problematic, for my orientation is now towards that which is both "apart" from me and towards that which "encompasses" me.[1] Thus, simultaneous with my first question concerning the nature of my relationship to the world is the experience of "disjunction" (*die Trennung*)[2] and apart from the "disjointness of being" (*der*

---

[1] *Philosophy of Existence*, trans. Richard Grabau (Philadelphia: University of Pennsylvania Press, 1971), p. 20ff.

[2] *Psychologie der Weltanschauungen* (Berlin: Springer Verlag, 1931), pp. 151 - 153. (Hereinafter cited as *Psych. der Welt.*) The phenomenon of "disjunction" plays an essential role throughout the philosophy of Jaspers, for he believes that the intuitive apprehension of disjointness is not only a primal philosophical experience initially giving rise to reflection but that it is characteristic of the very act of thinking itself. Because of this "disjointness"

Zerrissenheit des Seins) the question concerning the possibility of world would not arise. Suddenly aware of the fact that I am not only in a world and that I am very much a part of the world, I also begin to experience the world which stands over against me as the "not I"[3] and the task of making this "not I" my own as a known unity. The experience of disjointness for Jaspers is precisely the opposite of the conclusion of Shakespeare's tragic figure Macbeth, who says: "But let the frame of things disjoint, both the worlds suffer, ere we will eat our meal in fear and sleep in the affliction of more terrible dreams that shake us nightly." In Jaspers, one's experience of the disjunction between self and world generates the notion that the world as Whole or Unity is something far more than that which is cognizable as mere object, or the controlled management of an environment of objects, as in the case of Macbeth. What we call world begins to form as a limitless something with "infinite permutations of possibility."[4] This awareness of world, which both does and does not have to do with me, drives me beyond the particularity of my givenness-in-a-world to a more comprehensive standpoint whereby I may develop a unified world orientation.

The framework of this initial mode of transcending, however, is uncritical because my intention is formed from basically a materialistic and objectifying point of view. I am, according to Jaspers, captive to the misconception that the world may become a unity through quantitative analyses by simply localizing the world as an object. This objectifying misconception, however, can have a positive function, for the full impact and meaning of disjunction will not become evident until I have pushed my naive scientific realism to the extremities of possibility. The result of this attitude of extensive-extendedness – what Jaspers calls "objectivation" (*vergegenständlichen*) – is the discovery that no matter how far-reaching the parameters of my world orientation, I am still bounded, for "the world encompasses me no matter how much I attempt to encompass it."[5] Thus I am faced with the first limit of attempting to unify my world on the basis of empirical world-orientation alone. Just as

---

both "within" and "without," there can be no final system of transcending nor any final ontological statement concerning any one or all of its modalities, *viz.* world, self or God, the essential "presence" of which (especially the last) appears to me only in "ciphers." However, disjunction does provide the primary clue to a "systematics" of transcending and to the "form of its origin" which is the question of the Being implicit in the "moving center of Existenz." Transcending is therefore the fundamental operation of Existenz with, as Jaspers says, "the way of disjointness itself as its method." Cf., *Phil.*, I, pp. 280-284.

[3] *Phil.*, I, p. 99.
[4] *Ibid.*, p. 129.
[5] *Ibid.*, p. 116.

Socrates and Plato were driven to an *Urgrund* other than monistic-materialism in the attempt to account for the meaning of world, the transcending individual in Jaspers' scheme is driven to the necessity of a conversion in understanding whereby this *aporia* can be overcome and a more conclusive world-orientation may take place at another level.

Given the limits of Jaspers' understanding of world-orientation, is a scientific worldview possible at all?

JASPERS AND THE POSSIBILITY OF A SCIENTIFIC WOLRD-VIEW

Jaspers' attitude towards the possibility of a scientific world-view is problematic in several respects.[6] While it is true that he clearly demarcates the respective domains of science and philosophy as well as that of philosophy and religion, it is a demarcation which can be extremely deceptive, if it is construed to mean that these realms are wholly unrelated. As a trained scientist and a "religious" philosopher, Jaspers' apparent compartment theory of science and religion is developed out of a respect for the legitimate province of each and not out of any sense of hostility.[7] Moreover, it is precisely Jaspers' sense of the limits of both science and religion that informs his unique boundary conception of philosophy; a positioning which he derives from what he perceives to be the nature of human experience itself and not on the basis of some contrived division of labor. Hence, for Jaspers, the correspondence of science and *Weltorientierung*, philosophy and *Existenzerhellung* and religion and *Metaphysik* as the three basic modalities or "moments" of human consciousness and experience, with the concrescence of the first and the last taking place in the integrative modality of Existenz.

As we have already mentioned, Jaspers believes that both primitive and pseudo-science are the result of the "myth of the objectifying consciousness," i.e., the attempts to "conquer existence independently of the knowing subject" and develop "a systematic whole in which everything is connected with everything else."[8] The goal of the pseudo-scientific attempt at objectivity is a "public cogency" based on the belief that there

---

[6] Primary among these difficulties, it seems to us, is Jaspers' understanding of "objectivity", about which we will say more in Part III.

[7] Cf., Jean Piaget, *Insights and Illusions of Philosophy* (New York: World Publishing Co., 1971), pp. 209-213, for a misreading of this demarcation as simply a device whereby "wisdom" philosophy is "removed" from the province of what Piaget considers to be scientific "genetic" epistemology.

[8] *Phil.*, I, p. 120.

can be a "universally valid stock of knowledge" through which the observations and hypotheses of experience can be tested and scrutinized "universally." [9] In this domain of "consciousness-in-general" (*Bewusstsein-überhaupt*), one can either make a transition to authentic philosophizing or fall into various forms of reductionism.

No one, least of all Jaspers, would deny the genius of science and its achievement. [10] Nevertheless, what evades the scientific method – particularly when it extends itself as a *Weltanschauung* – is the sense of world as unity. The success of science rests squarely on its self-disciplined ability to suspend or bracket questions pertaining to an all-encompassing world-view, i.e., to remain "trans-subjective" as C.S. Peirce suggested. [11] To the extent science forgets this and absolutizes a particular claim to validity, science falsifies its own enterprise. The result is "scientific positivism" which, Jaspers says, " . . . equates being with what the natural sciences can know . . . being and objective being become one and the subject-object split dissolves into a principle of uniform objective being." [12] Contrasting two forms of positivism Jaspers says further that whereas the empirical positivist levels everything in the name of the object, the idealist schematizes everything in the name of the subject. However, it is not merely a matter of synthesizing these disparate points of view through "tacit respect for the mere existence and success of various syntheses as such," for in such cases, "metaphysical reveries will serve as a screen to keep the horror of the boundary situation gently out of sight." [13] Acceptance of the positivist conclusion, for Jaspers, nullifies altogether the authentic basis of scientific insight, namely the transcending quest for an experience of world not as a mere object, but as an intelligible unity. Authentic science arises both out of the quest for unity and the experience of being bounded, i.e., out of a dialectical realization which makes it clear, first, "that cognition is not exhausted with mere cognition of the world," and secondly, that this quest "originates from a source not subject to scientific cognition." [14] Thus the mere fact that a unified and therefore universally valid *Weltanschauung* is not cognizable to an objectifying scientific inquiry does not mean that it is non-existent, for without the idea of unity, i.e., the intention of "intelligibility," the scientific question would not have emerged to begin with.

[9] *Way to Wisdom*, trans. Ralph Manheim (New Haven: Yale, 1954), p. 147ff.
[10] Cf., *Chiffren der Transzendenz* (München: R. Piper, 1970), 7-11.
[11] *Charles S. Peirce: Selected Writings*, ed. Philip P. Wiener (New York: Dover Publications, Inc., 1958), p. 91ff.
[12] *Phil.*, I, p. 222.
[13] *Ibid.*, pp. 235-244.
[14] *Ibid.*, p. 120.

Thus the quest for a comprehensive worldview is, for Jaspers, an inevitable human instinct; as natural as the desire of any animal to be at home in its environment. But what is fundamentally different in the case of man is that "being-at-home-in-world" is "being-at-home-in-a-Unity" which is not possible on the basis of *Weltorientierung* alone, for the question of world then has to do more fundamentally with the origin of the question of world itself. Although Jaspers does not propose a traditional ontology or a dogmatic metaphysic as the means of elucidating the question, the modalities of *Existenzerhellung* and *spekulative Metaphysik* are the basic movements in that direction. In anticipation of these two essential modalities of transcending-thinking it is necessary to focus more extensively on what Jaspers has to say concerning the nature of limit, for through the knowledge of limit one not only discovers something essential concerning knowledge, but a preliminary clue concerning the boundary character of the experience of transcendence.

BOUNDARY EXPERIENCE

As in the case of the theologian Paul Tillich, "boundary" awareness is a fundamental feature of the Jaspersian philosophical perspective. Frequently characterized by Jaspers as a "situation," boundary awareness has to do with the subject becoming fundamentally conscious of the limitations of knowledge and the various designs and projects of cognition. In relation to what we have previously described as an epistemological "limit," the existential boundary situation has to do with an ineffable dimension of experience in which that which is characterized as "outer" and "inner" coincide and where the language of both objectivity and subjectivity is inadequate for communicating the *depth* of experience. As a thematic awareness, the language of boundary has roots dating to Anaximander and Socrates with full doctrinal development in the scholastic differentiation between the "known" and the "known Unknown." For Jaspers, it is in the initial mode of transcending in world-orientation that this boundary awareness first appears.

To recapitulate, in the process of objectifying the world which is all around me and within which I am as a seeker after world, the transcending subject becomes increasingly aware of the endlessness and unresolvability of objectifying thinking. Quantitative endlessness, initially intriguing, becomes increasingly oppressive as the unity of world escapes me. As a boundary in the face of the limits of objectifying thinking, the indeterminacy of this way of experience suggests that we must "have our being from another source, for in the world, we comprehend ourselves from beyond the world." [15] In the startling discovery that the nature of nature is not self-evident, Jaspers discerns at least four interrelated yet distinct levels of world-experience. First there is the level of empirical cognizability, viz., "matter... dead matter... only quantitatively comprehensible;" secondly, the visualization of specific forms of life but life "as an ever-changing entirety that is born, preserves itself and dies;" thirdly, the awakening of the soul in "inwardness as consciously experiencing life;" and finally, the existential appropriation of reality through the discovery that the mind has "self-conscious objective intentionality or purposiveness." [16] While each of these levels of experience presupposes the other in transcending-thinking, their relation is not smoothly continuous but discontinuous as if by a "jerk" backward and a "leap" forward the transcending subject is cognitively operative at an altogether different level of understanding. Statistical measurements can be applied to these movements of apprehension but cannot account for the seeming "irrational simplicity" of the experience. [17] Through statistical inquiries the inquirer is again faced with "endless permutations of possibility" and not unity. [18] As the object of quantification, Jaspers states further, "Nature does not answer ... it is mindless .... Nature leads me to the foundations of existence which in world orientation cannot even be meaningfully questioned anymore, but whose factuality makes them springboards for Existenz and chances to soar in transcending." [19] As the limit whereby mere quantification of data fails, I am aware that my quest for a *fondement* within the world as object has also failed. Unity remains an idea which cannot be grasped as object and has, as in the mysticism of Cusanus, the metaphorical character of an objective *wall* or barrier jerking or jarring the subject into the position of doubt and despair.

Although this leads Jaspers to conclude that traditional ontology or a categorical explanation of the world is impossible, boundary metaphysics remains very much at the heart of all true philosophy and "true

---

[15] *Ibid.*, p. 134. Cf. also *Reason and Existenz*, trans. William Earle (New York: Noonday Press, 1955), pp. 51-76.
[16] *Phil.*, I, pp. 189-196.
[17] "Dieser Ruck, der nicht durch ein rationales Nachedenken, sondern durch ein ursprüngliches Bewusstsein des Selbst auftritt ... das scheint mir das ursprünglich Menschliche zu sein, ganz Einfache." *Chiffren der Transzendenz*, p. 49.
[18] *Phil.*, I, p. 129.
[19] *Ibid.*, p. 206.

science." One might say, as Jaspers reminds us, that the statements "metaphysics has no place in science" and "metaphysics makes for meaningful science" are equally true. In a metaphysic of boundary situations, we are no longer speaking of dogmatic explanations but the *Grundoperation* of possible Existenz, that is, a self-positioning of the subject in relation to the question about the reality of world.[20] Such an attitude vis-à-vis the task and nature of metaphysics is utterly different from the skeptic's resignation that "no answer is the answer" which, for Jaspers, represents a banalization of the spirit and the destruction of true philosophizing. The critical and constructive task is rather, as he put it, "To regain what has been lost in the popularization of empiricism, viz., a synthesis of empirical science with transcending philosophy . . . a synthesis not accomplished by a combination with scientific results but by philosophizing in science."[21]

Thus the boundary demarcation which Jaspers establishes between science and philosophy through this initial mode of transcending and its limit is not at all intended to be dualistic. The boundary situation is rather consequent upon an awareness of the limit intrinsic to all objectifying disciplines and more immediately as cognizable within the very nature of experience itself. Recognizing this serves to remove the distance between natural science (*Naturwissenschaften*) and human science (*Geisteswissenschaften*) and the claim of the former that its removal from the relativities of history affords it a certain changelessness and universality in contrast to the latter. To the contrary, a participation in the boundary situation of the consciousness of limit means that all true cogency must ground itself in a sense of historicity, for "true intellectual science is the historic motion of the unclosed mind aware of its historicity."[22] Jaspers' position, as in the case of Bultmann, is very close to that of Collingwood: "The thesis which I maintain is that the science of human nature was a false attempt – falsified by the analogy of natural science – to understand the mind itself, and that, whereas the right way of investigating nature is by the methods merely scientific, the right way of investigating mind is by the methods of history." In short, "The science of mind is the science of history."[23]

[20] *Von der Wahrheit* (München: R. Piper, 1947), p. 156ff.

[21] *Phil.*, I, p. 166. This attitude, of course, is most definitively shared and developed by Edmund Husserl. Cf., *Phenomenology and the Crisis of Philosophy*, trans. Quentin Lauer (New York: Harper and Row, 1965), esp. pp. 149-192, and *The Crisis of European Sciences and Transcendental Phenomenology*, trans. David Carr (Evanston: Northwestern University Press, 1970).

[22] *Phil.*, I, p. 216.

[23] *The Idea of History* (London: Oxford, 1946), p. 209f.

In summary we can say that the result of Jaspers' initial formal mode of transcending in world-orientation consists first, in the awareness that the empirical order in and of itself does not yield an answer to the quest for the world as a Whole or Unity, and secondly, that this failure and its jolting effect on consciousness points the subject in the direction of a deeper possibility as the subject, thrown back upon himself, is forced to take cognizance of the manner in which his own subjectivity is intrinsic to the process of knowing. From this second formal mode of transcending, namely *Existenzerhellung*, emerges the possibility of an altogether different and authentic *Weltanschauung*; authentic not because it can lay claim to universality in the sense of being trans-subjective *nor* simply because it is subjective. For Jaspers its claim to authenticity rather lies in the fact that true philosophizing originates in the "freedom of Existenz;"[24] not a freedom which is iconoclastic and relativistic, but existential freedom which points beyond itself through an awareness that "before Transcendence, everything is nothing."[25]

To a clarification of this claim and a detailed consideration of the very central and synthetically integrative term Existenz, we now turn.

---

[24] *Chiffren der Transzendenz*, pp. 7-20.
[25] *Phil.*, I, p. 260.

CHAPTER TWO

TRANSCENDING AND EXISTENZ

Just as Socrates raised the question of self in response to the plethora of inconclusive materialist worldviews which preceded him, so also Jaspers' second formal mode of transcending, *Existenzerhellung*, introduces the "subject" and the subject's role in the development of world. As we have seen, the initial mode of transcending in "world-orientation" is extrinsic movement-towards-a-world sustained by a naive empirical realism. Enchanted by the quantitative endlessness of the material order, the transcending subject, according to Jaspers, is ultimately overwhelmed by the inconclusive and oppressive plurality of the external world – with the multifariousness of "things" – and no abiding unity. The subject's response to this debilitating state of affairs is characterized by Jaspers, as we have seen, as a kind of "recoil" or "reversal" whereby the subject is thrown back upon himself as subject and away from the world as object. While this Socratic moment can be the prelude to either subjectivism or metaphysical dualism, it can also function as the constructive conversion to a more intrinsic modality of world-Being and to a heightened level of cognitive transcending. The question concomitant with this conversion is simply, "What is there other than mundane being?" [1] – in short, the arrival of the meta-question induced by what might be termed an experience of the "limitedness of limitlessness."

In this section we will describe three essential features of Jaspers' "elucidation of Existenz" but qualify this description from the outset by stating that it is impossible to lay hold of Existenz *qua* Existenz. As in the case of *Weltorientierung, Existenzerhellung* is neither an ontology of existence nor a psychology of selfhood. It is rather the phenomenological description of the experience of transcending within and through the categories of subjectivity. Existenz, then, can only be addressed in the form of an appeal (*appellieren*) and never directly which also holds for world,

---

[1] *Phil.*, II, p. 3.

as we have seen, and will hold for Transcendence as well. This is no "bottomless relativism," Jaspers insists, for to make such a charge presupposes that there is some *thing* underlying all of our reflections which can be possessed as an *object*. Moreover, the destructive feature of this objectifying intention is an elimination of the spirit of *love* which is coterminous with the task of existential communication. While this is similar to Heideggerian *Sorge*, Jaspers insists on an "Otherness" in his elucidation of Existenz which, he believes, avoids an isomorphic reduction of meaning to subjectivity. Because of this Otherness present to Existenz, it, as in the case of Transcendence, can only be approached through the language of "ciphers" even though these ciphers can be highly conceptual as we shall see.[2] One can understand the modality of Existenzerhellung, then, only by entering into its problematic, that is, by participating in the intrinsic qualities of the question of Being. Such participation leads to a heightened sense of freedom and historicity which, in the Jaspersian scheme, is essential if there is to be authentic transcending in the ciphers of speculative metaphysics.

QUALIFIED NEGATIVITY AND BOUNDARY SITUATION

Jaspers elucidates the nature of Existenz by what he terms "qualified negativity"[3] and about which something must be said before dealing with the three central features of Existenz.

At the beginning of the second volume of *Philosophie*, Jaspers states, "As Existenz revolts from the real act of breaking through mundane existence, existential elucidation is the *thinking ascertainment* of that act."[4] By "thinking ascertainment" Jaspers means the implementation of a "qualified negativity" which is able to discern at once the possibilities and the limitations of the existential act of transcending. Now this understanding of *Negativität* is considerably different from the way in which negativity is understood by some theologians for whom the divine and the human, the sacred and secular constitute a fundamental dialectical opposition which cannot be outstripped except by supernatural *fait*.[5]

---

[2] *Ibid.*, pp. 373, 376.
[3] *Ibid.*, p. 10.
[4] *Ibid.*, p. 9.
[5] The exact shape of Protestant theological thinking on this matter especially is by no means an easy thing to pinpoint. However, after the nature-grace relation of scholastic thinking was transposed into the moral and soteriological language of law and Gospel, many Lutherans – especially during the period of Orthodoxy in the late 16th and 17th

In Jaspers, the function of negativity as "thinking ascertainment" is never the nullification of one dimension of experience by another, nor is it construed as an antithetical relationship subsumed and transcended by a higher form of objectivity in the Hegelian sense. The task for Jaspers is rather one of developing a language which can effectively mediate the dialectical opposition of subject and object – elucidating the "lived boundary" between the two, as it were – but not a conceptuality which claims to resolve schematically an opposition Jaspers believes to be fundamental.[6] To this end, Jaspers designs the evanescent language of *Existenzphilosophie*; a language uniquely suited for this mediatorial-evocative function because of its diaphanous character as a "language of personal communication," in other words, a language that can in terms of existential meaning overcome the subject-object dichotomy while remaining formally within it. The language of *mögliche Existenz*, then, is an open-ended and historically self-conscious language which understands that "there is no totality of the I am; the self is always more than I can know."[7]

Thus qualified negativity is an essential aspect of Jaspers' modality of *Existenzerhellung* and is a productive and not a destructive negativity. Its movement provides the basis for "transcending-thinking" as a dialectic which elucidates horizons of transcending that are more and more encompassing and less and less constrictive, but it does not, as negativity, make its claim in the absolute sense as Hegel's *Aufhebung*. Jaspers is convinced that ultimate metaphysical illumination is derived from this dynamic conceptual-existential center and that it is an illumination best understood on the basis of a transcending "ascertainment" of thinking itself; i.e., it is a consciously intellective process and not merely the result

centuries – have regarded this relationship to be an absolute ontological dialectic of opposition. Cf., for example, Gerhard Forde, *The Law-Gospel Debate* (Minneapolis; Augsburg, 1969), esp. p. 150ff., Werner Elert, *The Structure of Lutheranism* (Saint Louis; Concordia, 1962). Although Jaspers does not use such categories, his position is considerably closer to the Thomistic belief that "Grace does not destroy nature but fulfills it."

[6] Cf., *Phil.*, I, pp. 226-249 for an analysis of "faulty" resolutions of "qualified" and hence "creative" dialectical tension in absolute idealism and scientific positivism. From a sociological standpoint, Jaspers' understanding of qualified dialectical negativity bears similarity to Ernst Troeltsch's criticism of previous theological usage when he castigates the "illegitimate simplifying conceptuality" of both Hegelians and Ritschlians for whom it was not a question of the autonomy of "religion over metaphysics" as Goethe expressed it but the "supremacy of supernatural Christianity over against the entire non-Christian world." Cf., Wilhelm Pauck, *Harnack and Troeltsch* (New York: Oxford, 1968), pp. 103-106. Cf., also *Psych. der Welt.*, pp. 229-232.

[7] *Phil.*, II, p. 33. Cf., also Arthur Vogel, *Body Theology* (New York: Harper, 1973), and an analysis of the "embodied person" as an "inexhaustible" source of meaning not to be "formalized and contained in a totality," esp. chapter one, pp. 13-29.

of an appeal to the undifferentiated abyss of feeling.

Through this development of qualified negativity, we can better understand what Jaspers means by the existential and epistemological boundary situation. By boundary situation, Jaspers means those events and experiences which are impossible to consider or evaluate apart from the "lived" situation, viz., experiences such as death, freedom, struggle, guilt and the tragic – none of which lend their meanings to objectifying thinking.[8] From this lived boundary perspective, the boundary situation is that "beyond" which I cannot see. They are situations which ontologically delimit and particularize the transcending individual, on the one hand, and simultaneously provide the clues or "ciphers" to a more encompassing metaphysical reality, on the other. Using the distinction of Dilthey, such situations can only be understood through active participation and never explained. Most immediately boundary experiences reveal the "dubiousness and historicity of all existence,"[9] i.e., the disjunctive realization that all solutions to the problematic of human self-experience are finite and issue forth in new positions and counterpositions. The paralogisms and antinomies of Kantian epistemology are logically cogent for Jaspers *precisely* because they are rooted antecedently in the experience of boundary situations.

Because of the duplicity of boundary situations one is faced with the tempting but existentially destructive possibility of simply ignoring their presence, by being "noncommittal," as Heidegger puts it, or, as Jaspers says, "by living expansively rather than intensively."[10] Theologically the boundary situation presents the subject with what Bultmann terms a "crisis of decision" as to whether or not one will risk the leap of faith "in spite of the nature of our experience."[11] Boundary situations, in sum, represent the occasions for either conversion to a heightened modality of transcending-thinking or resignation to *apathia* in the face of the world one presumes to be out there "simply by taking a look" – the naive realism that is based, as Bernard Lonergan puts it, on the "principle of the empty head."[12] The potential conversion of consciousness present to the boundary situation, then, can never be regarded as automatic, for there is always the possibility of a reversal in which the subject opts for the secur-

---

[8] *Phil.*, II, p. 178.
[9] *Ibid.*, p. 210.
[10] *Ibid.*, p. 220. Cf. also *Nietzsche: An Introduction to an Understanding of His Philosophical Activity*, trans. C. Wallraff and F. Schmitz (Tucson: Arizona University Press, 1965), p. 292ff.
[11] Rudolf Bultmann, *Jesus Christ and Mythology* (New York: Scribners, 1958), p. 84.
[12] Bernard Lonergan, *Method in Theology* (New York: Herder, 1972), p. 204ff.

ity of abstractions – whether as the world of objects or the world of ideas – rather than plummeting into the abyss where objectifying thinking fails utterly. And an abyss it is indeed, very much as in the case of Sartre's Antoine Roquentin when he says, "I am illuminated within by a diminishing light." [13]

As in the case of so many other existentialist thinkers, death, for Jaspers, is the ultimate boundary situation. One is acquainted with the reality and presence of death; one knows that it is coming for oneself and that one cannot see beyond it. Yet, as Jaspers reminds us, it is the known-Unknown for we do not really experience our death at all – it rather *happens* as the ultimate involuntary with which (barring suicide), I have almost nothing to do. [14] The mere fact that death happens, however, is not what is metaphysically significant for Jaspers but rather the astonishing fact that in death even "appearance disappears." [15] Through one's encounter with death, the utterly phenomenal character of reality reveals itself to me in its devastating forcefulness, for in death even one's speculation concerning the reality of the phenomenal is no more and beyond this boundary is the bleak promise of nothingness-itself. As an essential feature of existential or transcending-thinking however, the event of death can have the salutary effect of "waking Existenz" in a "breakthrough to communication" [16] through which one is not only awakened to the reality of the phenomenal limitations of existential transcending but awakened to the cipher of Transcendence-Itself.

This existential awakening, then, is defined and understood by way of "qualified negativity" which, within the overall problematic of transcending-thinking, not only indicates the boundary of human experience but also points beyond it. Were this negativity total, effecting the reduction of Existenz to a temporally constituted Dasein as in Heidegger, or to the "prison of subjectivity" in Sartre, any further talk concerning the reality of Transcendence beyond the mere act of transcending would be impossible. Nor, to Jaspers' understanding, could there be productive discourse concerning the problems of freedom and historicity – to say nothing of the cipher of "Absolute Consciousness" – for the constraints of the purely phenomenal and of subjectivity-in-itself do not provide the kind of dialectic Jaspers believes necessary for a dynamic and ultimately

---

[13] Jean-Paul Sartre, *Nausea*, trans. Lloyd Alexander (New York: New Directions, French edition, 1938), pp. 24-25.
[14] *Phil.*, II, p. 197. Cf., also Martin Heidegger, *Being and Time*, p. 279ff.
[15] *Ibid.*, p. 193.
[16] *Ibid.*, p. 198.

metaphysical understanding of Existenz. It is Jaspers suggestion of an "Other" that is *more* than world or self – either viewed separately or as a composite – that makes his position different than that of either Sartre or Heidegger. For Jaspers the questions of Being and Existenz – to say nothing of Transcendence – are unresolvable at the level of "dasein analysis alone," and *mögliche Existenz* intends "deliverance out of the swamp of mere existence in which we are all stuck." [17]

Given the centrality of Jaspers' "qualified negativity" and its relation to understanding "boundary situations," we now turn to a consideration of freedom, historicity, and "Absolute Consciousness" in the becoming of possible self-Being.

FREEDOM, HISTORICITY AND ABSOLUTE CONSCIOUSNESS

As we stated at the beginning of this chapter, Jaspers believes that freedom, historicity and the cipher of Absolute Consciousness are three utterly central – albeit problematic – features of possible Existenz. Although all are interrelated, they can be understood, for formal purposes, as the ascending moments in the quest for the knowledge of Transcendence-Itself, i.e., as sub-species of the general modality of *Existenzerhellung* requiring elucidation en route to *spekulative Metaphysik*.

With reference to the first, Jaspers differentiates freedom and will for the purpose of showing that volition considered simply as a faculty easily runs the risk of being mechanized by identifying the will with that which is willed, forgetting that "the Being of the will lies in the willing itself." [18] Willing, for Jaspers, is possible only because of the "freedom" of the subject "to will." As an act, the will is related both intentionally and referentially to that which is other than the act of willing. Reflecting on the manner in which the problem of will has been treated in the past, Jaspers says that volition can too easily be "rationalized" and "authoritarianized" whereby the external rule of "law and order" shelters the individual from the pathos of decision in freedom. On the other hand, the will can be "eroticized" whereby it is completely captive and subservient to objec-

---

[17] *Chiffren der Transzendenz*, p. 57.
[18] *Phil.*, II, p. 144.

tivized forms of passion. [19] Or, in what is perhaps the most debilitating possibility, one might say, following Heidegger, that the will of "willing" can be so "covered up" by existential dullness and uncritical habituation to "everydayness" (*Alltäglichkeit*) that the question of "will" does not even arise. In this case Existenz as a transcending possibility is lost, and all that remains is mere existence or Dasein.

It is in these contexts of possibility that Jaspers suggests "volition is the presence of Existenz in the moment," [20] that is, the free moment in and through which decision and therefore Transcendence may take place. Thus "freedom" is far more profound and far-reaching anthropologically and metaphysically for Jaspers than the will considered in isolation as merely a problem for ethics. As the ground of possible Existenz, freedom *is* possibility. Thus the will may be inoperative in a specific moment or context of existential fallibility but not the reality of freedom which underlies it, for freedom-Itself provides the basis of its own denial. In this respect Jaspers' understanding of the will and freedom is very close to that of Sartre who says, "the only being which can be called free is the being which nihilates its being." [21] If we forget this, then, as Jaspers says, "We slip through the net of Being." [22] With the fragmentation of active transcending, Transcendence-Itself is no longer a possibility for communication but rather absurd and nonsensical as the object of detached speculation which it can never be. However, since freedom is coterminous with the act of transcending, it exists as neither object nor subjective idea but is the awesome reality which underlies all speculation concerning its nature from the outset – whether that speculation be ignorant or informed. Thus in relation to the cipher of freedom, one is faced with two alternatives: either "being afraid of freedom" or "being afraid in freedom." [23] In either case, freedom is a given. What one does with it, however, determines the shape of one's historicity. In other words, the manner in which transcending in relation to Transcendence is grounded in the "life-practice" (*Lebenspraxis*) of the specific individual determines the dialectical quality of freedom and will.

In relation to historicity, then, "Existenz has its time, not time pure

---

[19] *Ibid.*, pp. 141-142.

[20] *Ibid.*, p. 142. Cf., also Martin Heidegger, *Being and Time*, esp. pp. 149-224. In Part II we will see how Jaspers reacts to what he believes to be impoverished interpretations of Kantanian voluntarism where will is not understood within the larger "Encompassing" framework of *Vernunft* but only as a so-called "practical" matter.

[21] Jean-Paul Sartre, *The Philosophy of Existentialism* (New York: Philosophical Library, 1965), p. 72.

[22] *Phil.*, II, p. 161. In other words, "I am self-objectified."

[23] *Philosophy of Existence*, p. 25ff.

and simple," [24] for apart from the living, transcending subject, things merely "happen," whereas within the world of the self things happen by virtue of a "personal" act. I am involved in both that which I do and that which I do not do. The shape and quality of this involvement determines the nature of my historicity – the specificity of my self-Being. In fact, for Jaspers this is the only way in which Being is known at all, for "Being understood as something detached as Absolute Being, whether that of Transcendence or self-Being, is inaccessible to me." [25] In the mere occurrence of extra-existential events, no Transcendence or Being is present, but in the act of transcending-Existenz, the "unconditional" character of Being is present as lived, for that which I do or fail to do can never be undone or repeated. Thus, historicity for Jaspers, as for most philosophers of existence, is radically differentiated from historicality or historism since the latter terms have to do with the impersonal and deterministic aspect of temporal existence and not with "laying hold of the time," as it were. In Jaspers' understanding of historicity, one might say that the Greek understanding of *chronos* is intersected with what can be metaphorically characterized as the vertically unconditional nature of *kairos*, i.e., the "awakening" of the subject to the *ephapax* character of one's actions, whereas in the undifferentiated consciousness, repetition seems to be the order of the day. Both temporal foci are in a sense real insofar as they are descriptions of the ordering of human experience, but without the eventfulness of *Kairos* there can be no history. *Kairos*, then, is but a way of describing the unconditional nature of time which has its source in the self as living Existenz. [26]

In Existenz understood as historicity there is, therefore, an active albeit paradoxical coalescence of the intrinsic and extrinsic dimensions of human experience which Jaspers describes as follows: "The paradox of the existential sense of historicity – that fleeting time included Being – does not mean that there is an eternity somewhere else aside from its temporal appearance. It does mean that Being *is not* simply in existence but appears in existence as the outcome of decision in such a way as to make the outcome eternal." [27] One must also say that in Jaspers' model,

---

[24] *Phil.*, II, p. 17; i.e., Existenz is more than mere "time-consciousness."

[25] Cf., *Way to Wisdom*, "The Unconditional Imperative," pp. 52-62, and also *Myth and Christianity* where Jaspers says, "By historicity I mean the existential possibility of achieving and experiencing the actual unity of time and eternity in the moment. This possibility is grasped out of existential freedom," p. 99.

[26] *Way to Wisdom*, p. 55.

[27] *Phil.*, II, p. 113. Note: as in the case of the "inaccessibility" of non-existential Being, Jaspers does not say that "Eternity" is non-existent, for through the "cipher-script" of possible Existenz Kantian noumena are redefined as we shall see in the next chapter and in Part II.

whether or not the individual is aware of the fact that there is an eternal consequence for every act makes no difference *even though* there be no such thing as an hypostatized "eternity." What does make a difference is that once one has transcended to a consciousness of the cipher of historicity, once an awareness of the unconditional nature of experience impinges upon my awareness of self-Being, one cannot simply return to the way things were previously. Temporal and therefore existential innocence has been lost. One can, as Kierkegaard mused, continue rather indefinitely in the quest for an aesthetic reduplication of previous pleasant experiences, but only with the price of tragic inauthenticity. [28] On the other hand, and in Jaspers' model, one can begin an authentic movement towards historicity which takes the "unconditional" as its clue, namely, transcending towards the Transcendence of Absolute Consciousness. And for Jaspers this transcending towards Absolute Consciousness or the totally "comprehensive" standpoint is the preliminary motion towards his final modality of transcending-thinking, namely speculative metaphysics. But before one can fully enter this modality there must be recoil even more dramatic than was characterized in *Weltorientierung*. Through this recoil or reversal, Existenz is suddenly cognizant of the fact that the cosmological and psychological resources of both world and self have suddenly vanished. Analogous to the Kierkegaardian model [29] of transcendental relation, the inconclusive correlation of self to world and self to self generates the God-question which Jaspers defines in a preliminary way as Absolute Consciousness.

"Absolute Consciousness" for Jaspers is neither a thing nor a level of consciousness but an awareness of "cipher" corresponding to the ultimate cipher of rationality (*Vernünftigkeit*) as that encompassing power underlying reason, just as temporality underlies the historicity of possible Existenz. And when one begins to explain what Jaspers means by reason, as we shall see, one must be prepared to deal with all the mystifying permutations this term has known in the development of German idealism. Through the language of Existenz, however, Jasper tries to avoid the ontological pretentiousness of absolute idealism and still preserve what he perceives to be its essential insight. Therefore, when he says "Absolute consciousness is that boundary . . . which encompasses, persuades and transforms all existence that has experienced it," and that it is the "con-

---

[28] Cf., *Either/Or*, Vol. I, trans. David Swenson (New York: Doubleday, 1959), p. 229ff.
[29] Cf., the prologue to *Sickness unto Death*, trans. Walter Lowrie (New York: Doubleday, 1957).

stant, substantial undertone of reality as such," [30] it is the experientially eidetic and not the noetic as an ontological superstructure which is decisive for Jaspers. Hence the ultimately real is neither "consciousness-in-general," the "unconscious" nor "absolute mind" but rather the cipherous reality of Transcendence as the ultimately coherent reality underlying all our ideas concerning reason but which is apprehended only as possible Existenz. All individual acts of reflection derive their possibility from this underlying, enabling horizon of Absolute Consciousness which, as a "presence," is a preliminary movement for knowledge concerning *das Umgreifende* which both "encompasses" and "comprehends" all things, very much as in Hegel.

Thus the awareness of a cipher called "Absolute Consciousness" – however central to the thinking of Jaspers and the overall project of transcending-thinking – is not its final moment. Concomitant with the awareness that Being is more than either objectivity or subjectivity is the "unsettling feature" of the "mystery," vertigo and "dizziness" engendered by the Idea of the Absolute; an awareness which, in fact, is the origin of true philosophizing. Jaspers describes this experience as that of "foundering" (*scheitern*) on consciousness-itself, i.e., on the more of conscious experience becoming Otherness as Transcendence-Itself. What is experientially decisive then, about transcending-thinking in its project of *Existenzerhellung*, is the discovery that there is something which speaks out of the self " . . . from a ground which encompasses me." [31] And this is the acid test of Jaspers' philosophizing, for, as he himself says, "either this voice is the moved and moving source of the truth of Being or it is sheer deception." [32]

One might respond to this wager by saying that Jaspers is using highly sophisticated and existentialized jargon for what has traditionally been

[30] *Phil.*, II, p. 223. In Part II, we will further develop Jaspers' relationship to philosophical idealism under the thesis that his "retrieval" of the reality of Transcendence is both existentially descriptive and historically dependent. We undertake this historical project, however, not as a means of "explanation" but for the purpose of conceptual clarification.

[31] *Ibid.*, p. 241; *Reason and Existenz*, p. 64f. This "constant, substantial undertone" of *absolutes Bewusstsein* is what Jaspers calls the "indefinable undercurrent" (*unbestimmbare Unterströmung*) underlying Kant's first critique and from which any "true" interpretation of Kant must take its bearings as we shall see in Part II. Needless to say, there are many who would regard this – however qualified – as sheer, unadulterated idealism and there is much in Jaspers to support such objections. However, such references can be very deceptive if they are not read in the overall spirit of *Existenzphilosophie* as something "lived" and not merely a collection of conceptual abstractions.

[32] *Phil.*, II, p. 226. One is reminded of a similar Pascalian wager by one called St. Paul, viz., "If Christ has not been raised from the dead . . . and for this life alone we have hoped . . . then we of all men are most to be pitied," (RSV, I Cor., 15:1, 19). Much of "this world as passing away" is present to Jaspers' understanding of the "phenomenal."

referred to as the voice of the conscience or soul. Indeed, this is partially the case. However, Jaspers insists that it is not at all this simple – at least not in the sense in which "soul" and conscience are frequently understood. The voice to which he refers is rather that primordial "source" which calls for the self-Being of Existenz out of the potentiality of freedom and which, in order to realize itself, demands "philosophical faith" and not explanation by either an appeal to substance or divine revelation.

In summary, Jaspers' first two formal modes of transcending-thinking represent an elucidation of Being from extrinsic and intrinsic orientations respectively. Having delineated phenomenologically the disjunctive-recoil that arises upon the consideration of the world as object and the self considered as object qua subject, he points in the direction of an ultimate ground that is antecedent to both object and subject; a ground that is both the basis of experiential disjunction and the unifying goal of a partial resolution of the meaning of Being in the encipherment of all experience. This all-encompassing ground is the absolute Being of Transcendence. Thus, to objectify and therefore absolutize either the object as object or the subject as object is to void Transcendence and therefore to deny possible Existenz. [33] What is significant about the discovery concerning the limits of objectivity and subjectivity is the realization that such limits do not mark the end of transcending-thinking but rather its true commencement. [34] In this belief, Jaspers shares in the radical reinterpretation of Kant that one finds in Heidegger and Ricoeur. Although the motion of Jaspers' philosophizing seems to suggest a kind of primordial retrieval of the meanings of Being, he is not, however, as archaic and romantic as Heidegger. Jaspers' "remembrance" of the "ancient name of Being" is, as we shall see, also combined with "foresight" and a certain eschatological dimension that is closely tied to his ethics. [35] However, Transcendence, for Jaspers, is so closely tied to the theistic metaphysics of the mystics (and Cusanus in particular, as we will see in Part II) that it ultimately admits no distinctions concerning the past and the future. It is the All-Encompassing and, as such, it is very difficult for Jaspers to final-

---

[33] This cannot be overly emphasized, for even though "possible Existenz" is the primary feature of *Existenzerhellung*, it is the *fondement* of every modality of transcending. Thus whether world, self or God, is the point of relation, my perspective is always that of "possible" Existenz and not analytical neutrality, for "Only Existenz asks the question of Transcendence and only Existenz understands the answer." Cf., *Phil.*, II, pp. 361-364; III, p. 14.

[34] It is truly a "beginning" in the sense that for the first time the subject is aware of the "meaning" of what he does "not know." We will develop this further in Part II, in relation to Cusanus and the notion of *docta ignorantia*.

[35] *Phil.*, III, pp. 184-186.

ly avoid a kind of monism. Indeed, the eschatological dimension of Jaspers' thought is its Achilles' heel as Paul Ricoeur has seen. We will discuss this further in Part III.

For now, we turn to a descriptive analysis of Jaspers' third formal modality of transcending in speculative metaphysics.

CHAPTER THREE

TRANSCENDING IN SPECULATIVE METAPHYSICS

In the previous two sections we delineated world and self as the extrinsic and intrinsic modalities of transcending-thinking. In each of these moments we noted the decisive role of "disjunction" and "recoil" whereby the subject is driven to a more comprehensive mode of philosophical integration. These processes have both a positive and a negative aspect. They are positive insofar as the transcending-subject is driven to question the coherence of mere outwardness or mere inwardness as autonomous regions of experience capable of answering the question of Being. But they are also potentially negative if, in either region, the transcending subject grows weary of the task of integration, resigning himself to *apathia* in the face of an insurmountable dualism, or if one absolutizes either object or subject as the key to Being. In the former case, the subject becomes oblivious to the call of Being, and in the latter case reaps the consequences of reductionism where, as in the case of the logical positivist, metaphysical and religious questions are consigned to mere value and relativity, or, in the case of the subjectivist, when everything becomes a matter of the intensity of emotion and "feeling" and questions of structure and logic are not even entertained. In either case, the dialectical nature of reality is lost, and freedom (which provides the basis for transcending) is nullified. It is only when the dialectic of subject and object, self and world remain in tension that freedom is able to grasp the mystery of its *presence* both as ground and possibility. When this takes place, then the objectifying or quantitative more of experience has the potentiality of becoming the Otherness of Transcendence. For Jaspers, this is the constructive and really decisive moment of transcending-thinking as experience is now transcendentally reflective and not just transcendentally functional. In short, *cognition* has become *thinking*, awareness of Dasein and commonsense world-orientation have moved beyond mere consciousness-in-general: the question of world has become the question of possible self-Being and the Idea of Absolute Consciousness has engendered the question and goal of the comprehensive standpoint of Transcendence-Itself. Thus the initial failing or "foundering" of transcending-thinking over against its object appearing as limit provides not the end of thinking but is rather the occasion for a conversion to a more encompassing horizon of transcending. [1]

Before entering into a discussion of Jaspers' third modality of transcending-thinking, we must offer a few preliminary remarks as to the nature of Jaspers' understanding of metaphysics in general.

JASPERS AND METAPHYSICS

Just as the words *Dasein, Existenz* and *Transzendenz* have a unique Jaspersian nuance, so also the term *Metaphysik* assumes distinctive meaning in Jaspers' philosophical lexicon. Most productive during the period dominated by scientific positivism on the one hand and brooding existentialistic nihilism on the other, Jaspers came unabashedly to the defense of metaphysics very early in his philosophical career when it was extremely unpopular to do so. Jaspers insists that it is not metaphysics that is precluded by the rise of modern critical philosophy but rather categorial ontology and, in fact, dogmatism of any kind, whether scientific, nihilistic or religious. Much in the manner of Josiah Royce, Jaspers believes that metaphysics has to do primarily with the *spirit* of philosophizing; in other words, with the essential task of being human. Far from being a sterile and fleshless preoccupation with concepts and ideas removed from the stream of life, metaphysics deals with that which is most immediate to experience and apart from which experience is meaningless. In short, metaphysics – as true philosophizing – has to do with questions about Transcendence. Thus it was the nullification of the authentic spirit of metaphysics by the pseudo-scientific philosophy of the late 19th and early 20th century that compelled Jaspers to challenge philosophy at its very roots and to begin what he perceived to be a "retrieval" of *philosophia perennis*. As Jaspers puts it, "this realization overcame me that ...

---

[1] The positive and really "eschatological" nature of Jaspers' position cannot be overemphasized, for it stands directly opposed to the existentialism of nihilistic heroism, particularly Sartre where the pure "transcendental" purification of consciousness is valued only as a self-constituting "emptiness" which in turn provides for a sense of "unimpeded spontaneity." Cf., *Philosophy of Existentialism*, ed. Wade Baskin (New York: Philosophical Library, 1965), esp. pp. 31-73; *The Transcendence of the Ego*, trans. Forrest Williams (New York: Noonday, 1957), pp. 103-106. Jaspers, by contrast, stands much closer to the Socratic and indeed the New Testament motif of "dying," e.g., "To philosophize is to learn how to die," *Way to Wisdom*, p. 53. Cf., also Jaspers' "Article of Faith" in *Origin and Goal of History*, trans. Michael Bullock (New Haven: Yale, 1959), p. xv ff.

there was no true philosophy at the universities. I thought that facing such a vacuum even he, who was too weak to create his own philosophy, had the right to hold forth about philosophy, to declare what it once was and what it could be. Only then, approaching my fortieth birthday, did I make philosophy my life's work." [2]

Grounding his work in the famous questions of Kant, viz., "What can I know, what must I do, and for what may I hope?" Jaspers states that such inquiries are complemented necessarily by the question of God: that *deum et animam scire cupio* characterizes "true philosophizing" whatever the age or epoch. [3] Such foundational questions are nothing less than the relationship between transcending and Transcendence. Therefore *great philosophy* is essentially and not accidentally related to religion and vice versa, for without the "spirit of metaphysics" which transcending-thinking presupposes, the Judaeo-Christian mandate that "*Du sollst Dir kein Bildnis und Gleichnis machen*" is incomprehensible; an insight which Jaspers like Kant considers to be "*Das tiefste Wort in der Bibel.*" [4] Far from domesticating the Absolute, true metaphysics stands in awe before and is motivated by its presence. Far from being the claim to absolute knowledge, whether in the form of some kind of empirical reduction or a dogmatic disclosure of the reality behind the appearance of things, authentic metaphysics acknowledges fully the impossibility of such claims. Nor, by the same token, does Jaspers believe that his own form of metaphysical transcending in ciphers can completely avoid the objectifying nature of language. On the contrary, metaphysics is fully operative on the basis of limiting principles cognizant of an objectivity which is directly proportional to an awareness of the limits of objectivity. Thus any and all attempts to schematize the nature of Being or Transcendence-Itself not only fail but nullify the task of authentic metaphysical transcending. Again, failing or "foundering" has a double-sided meaning, for

---

[2] "On My Philosophy," *Existentialism from Dostoevsky to Sartre*, ed. Walter Kaufman (New York: Meridian, 1956), p. 133.
[3] Cf., *The Perennial Scope of Philosophy*, trans. Ralph Manheim (New York: Philosophical Library, 1949), *passim.*
[4] *Chiffren der Transzendenz*, p. 44. Jaspers' notion of the proper role of metaphysics bears a remarkable similarity to the Lutheran understanding of the *deus absconditus* (albeit less its resolution in the *deus revelatus*), for it is a metaphysics which "keeps the Godhead flatly concealed. Only indirectly – and always at a distance – does God reveal himself .... Transcendence becomes visible in its traces, not in itself and always ambiguously. It does not become extant in the world. But to Existenz it may mean the perfect peace of Being, a superabundant Being that has nothing indefinite about it anymore." *Phil.*, III, P. 60. The theological implications of Jaspers' "foundering metaphysics" will be further explored in Part III.

while pseudo-scientific philosophy fails in the very claim to success, authentic metaphysics succeeds *in* failing; that is, true metaphysical philosophizing realizes the qualified nature of all symbolizations of Being and by maintaining strenuously this qualification the subject-object structure of human experience remains intact. One can neither resolve this necessary tension through the development of an absolute logic of Transcendence (as in the case of Hegel), nor can one pass to some gnostic ground-of-Being beyond worldly experience as in the case of the claims of some mystics. Being or Transcendence-Itself, for Jaspers, rather speaks *through* the language of human experience and not around it or in spite of it. For Jaspers there is simply no privileged metaphysical or ontological standpoint other than experience-itself. Therefore, if there is to be a case for the reality of Transcendence, it must be shown through and within human experience, even though what is called experience is frequently misunderstood. [5]

Thus when Jaspers asserts that there is a simultaneous "alternation of Being and Non-Being" [6] in metaphysical transcending, the paradoxical character of his language conforms to a belief that while Transcendence-Itself is meta-ontological it is not meta-experiential. What seems to be ultimately real from our sense of material objectivity is less than real for our subjectivity, and conversely what seems to be ultimately real for subjectivity is transient and evanescent when measured by the standards of scientific objectivity. Sounding very Buddhistic, Jaspers can say that every objectifying attempt to solve or fixate the experience of Transcendence is doomed to "logical collapse, for the truer our grasp of Transcendent Being, the more decisively will its supports be destroyed." [7] Thus the paradoxical "cipher" is not merely an attempt to claim "more" for experience than is really there, nor is it meant to confound and mystify it. It is rather to indicate that no matter what language is chosen for elucidating the experience of Transcendence, the experience remains even when language fails, as it must. Because experience similarly is not a thing but rather co-extensive with what Jaspers calls the "moving center of Exi-

---

[5] Cf., *Truth and Symbol*, trans. Jean Wilde (New Haven: College and University Press, 1959), pp. 33-35. While much is claimed in the name of experience, Jaspers' attitude is highly historical as when he says, "It is only within the world that we can live above and beyond the world . . . There is no way around the world, no way around history, only a way through history." *The Origin and Goal of History*, p. 275. It is a similar sense of historicity which leads Karl Rahner to say, "Divine things are no longer considered as the subject of science but as the principle of the subject." *Spirit in the World* (New York: Herder, 1968), p. 389.

[6] *Phil.*, III, p. 17.

[7] *Ibid.*, p. 16.

stenz," metaphysics as well is essentially "movement" and "play." Because this movement is coterminous with "being historical" Jaspers can say, " . . . we can only grasp Transcendence-Itself historically; we can never consider it as being historic." The question *what*, of course, must always be approached with the utmost caution when dealing with Jaspers, for neither the act of transcending nor the Being of Transcendence lends itself to the spectator attitude. Jaspers' entire project is one of *communication*; as he states, "The will to communicate out of Existenz and reason" cannot be judged as true or false in the manner that one judges the truth or falsity of impersonal propositions for the awareness of Transcendence requires the personal investment of the subject. "Either the question asks something that is for us perfectly empty or it becomes an unquestionable certitude which dispenses with communication and, falsely expressed, only destroys itself. That is, it would paralyze the working of an unconditioned will-to-communicate by a specious knowledge about perfect communication . . . One can only speak out of this experience and not of it."[8] As in the case of an examination of mysticism, one cannot ultimately test the "object" of the experience of any given mystic but only the method of "elucidating" that experience and what it means for reality as "lived." This is all we can hope to do in relation to Jaspers' *Existenzphilosophie* as well.

Here we are faced by a series of difficult questions. If, as Jaspers suggests, Transcendence is present to the ciphers of speculative metaphysics, what then *is* a cipher and how do ciphers differ from signs and symbols? How are ciphers known to *be* ciphers and what is ultimately known through them? All of these questions are central, particularly the last, for Jaspers is convinced that something speaks *through* ciphers and not only speaks but confronts Existenz with both its origin and goal. Is there any precedent for Jaspers' peculiar and highly provocative understanding of symbolism, and how does this understanding function in relation to specific religious symbols, particularly the symbol of Transcendence-Itself or God? In the remainder of this chapter we will begin to deal with some of these questions, further explore their origin in Part II and move towards a critique in Part III, focusing specifically on transcending-thinking as a hermeneutic of symbol.

[8] *Reason and Existenz*, pp. 105-106.

THE CIPHER AND TRANSCENDENCE

Although the terms symbol and cipher appear interchangeably in translation of the works of Jaspers, the term *cipher* is uniquely Jaspersian and should be distinguished from sign and symbol for the following reasons.

First, both sign and symbol have a tendency towards empirical and aesthetic neutrality. Dogmatic theology usually interprets the English word *sign* in the Johannine sense of symbol; in other words as not only an "indicator" but a "participant" in the reality "signified". While the *presence* of the signified presupposes faith, its validity does not depend on existential involvement. For example, in various New Testament Christological formulae the fact that "the Word became flesh" (John 1:14) or that the "fullness" (*pleroma*) of the Divine or Transcendence-Itself is present to the Christ (Colossians 1:19) or in the consubstantial imagery of the Chalcedonian formulations (*homōousias*), one encounters symbolism which, while the product of faith, nevertheless refers to quasi-empirical and historical realities asserted to be the case independently of faith. For Jaspers a great amount of religious symbolism is *deutbar* symbolism, that is "explainable" symbolism based both upon historic occurrence removed from the horizon of my present experience and furthermore upon quasi-ontological interpretations of these historical events. While the church has always emphasized the centrality of the act of faith in relation to both the experience and the interpretation of these symbols, it has equally been wary of fideism or the reduction of external referents to the validation of mere subjectivity. Hence the theological distinction that while the doctrinal interpretation of symbols of faith may change and develop, their dogmatic objectivity and truth remains "fixed." [9]

In Jaspers, by contrast, the symbol is capable of becoming a metaphysical cipher only through the participation of the individual, experiential subject. Thus there can be no dogmatic hierarchy of symbols nor can there be a dogmatic hierarchy of the proper interpretations of symbols. Value is not attributed to a particular symbol on the basis of an extrinsic relationship between the sign and that which is signified (that is, "experience" plus historic-ontological explanation *ab extra*), but only on the basis of the intrinsic participation of Existenz in relation to symbol becoming cipher. From the standpoint of the symbolism of Christian sacramentology, Jaspers would extend the Protestant delimitation of *ex*

---

[9] Cf. Bernard Lonergan, *Method in Theology* (New York: Herder, 1972), pp. 320-329.

opere operato (namely that faith is very immediately bound up with the reality of presence not as the effective agent of that presence but as appropriating that which, *sola gratia*, is present) to a position which says that it is precisely the experiential dimension of faith (*Glaube als Existenz*) which realizes that the Transcendence-Itself is never present as being identical with any particular symbol. While Jaspers rarely goes into questions of Christology, it is plain that if he did he would be basically docetic. Nonetheless, and apart from Christological considerations, Jaspers' Plotinian attitude towards Transcendence-Itself does have a very definite bearing on the overall shape of his metaphysic. Here then is the essential difference between *deutbar* and *schaubar* symbolism in Jaspers, for while the symbolism of the church has always emphasized the experiential, i.e., "spirit filled faith," it inevitably supplements experience with *explanation* and, in Jaspers' terms, becomes *eindeutig*. Owing the institutional horizon of most theology, of course, religious symbolism supplemented by some kind of historical verification and explanation is inevitable. And this is why, Jaspers laments that "discussion with, theologians always dries up at crucial points; they fall silent, state an incomprehensible proposition, speak of something else, make some categoric statement, engage in amiable talk, without really taking cognizance of what one has said – and in the last analysis, they are not really interested." [10] However, irrespective of problems of authority, etc., there is a very real question concerning the degree to which Jaspers qua philosopher maintains a kind of aesthetic neutrality especially vis-à-vis the mediational role of a community. We will address this further in Part III.

It is in the context of an empirical-historical explanation of symbol that we also perceive a fundamental difference between the Anglo-American understanding of empiric and Jaspers' understanding and use of *empirisch*. Even though both regard the empirical as that which is grounded in "experience" (*auf Erfahrung gegründet*), Anglo-American usage has tended towards an understanding of empirical objectivity as facticity in which the experiential role of the subject is less than central. In other words, the objectivity of the empirical fact is formulated on the basis of a one-to-one correlation between subject and object without any protracted consideration as to *how* one comes both to know and understand that which is asserted to be empirically real, objective and true. In Jaspers, by contrast and true to Kant, *schaubar* symbolism is informed by a transcendental consideration of the manner in which the subject

---

[10] *The Perennial Scope of Philosophy*, p. 77.

always participates in and influences the shape of that which is known. Thus the *empirisch* is an essential dimension of *Anschauung*. The *Schaubar* or "intuited" symbol, therefore, can never assume a one-to-one correspondence between the sign and the signified either in ordinary language or in the far more evasive language of religious and metaphysical symbolism where Transcendence-Itself is believed to be in some way present to the symbol. [11] All explanations which attempt to verify that which is present either historically or ontologically not only fail, but, for Jaspers, destroy any possibility of symbols becoming ciphers. In short, symbolism explained subsumes the experiential act as transcending-thinking under correct interpretation. This, for Jaspers, is the basic shortcoming of theology which "never gets any further than an intellectual conception of the language of ciphers." [12]

On the other hand, that which determines the veracity of a particular cipher is what Jaspers describes phenomenologically as a sense of "hovering" (*schweben*) whereby both subject and object are "suspended in mysterious indefiniteness." [13] Transcendence-Itself is present only to the degree particular ciphers are capable of manifesting this hovering sensation in experience and is best illustrated by those ciphers which disappear even as they are being experienced. Yet within the foundering of human sensibility in the face of Transcendence-Itself, something remains even though "ambiguously." [14] In sum, one might say that stabilizing interpretations of metaphysical symbols void Transcendence through the Jaspersian version of Whitehead's "fallacy of misplaced concreteness." The essence of Jaspers' position on the difference between symbol and cipher and the primary area of his interest is precisely that boundary situation separating a metaphorical aestheticism on the one hand and a theological dogmatism on the other. [15]

One is tempted to conclude that the essential ambiguity of both ciphers and that which they present implies that neither have anything to

---

[11] While Wittgenstein's "model theory" of language would differ insofar as ordinary usage is able to correspond to reality, he is very close to Jaspers insofar as *Sprachkritik* aims at discerning the "limits" of language as preparation for that "which cannot be said," i.e., the discovery that "The sense of the world must lie outside the world" and that all ethical, religious, aesthetic statements are only capable of "indirect" communication through the "poetic." *Tractatus Logico-Philosophicus*, 6.421, 6.432. Wittgenstein therefore stands as a notable exception to what I have characterized as the Anglo-American tradition.
[12] *Truth and Symbol*, p. 75. Cf., also *Phil.*, III, p. 144ff., and *Chiffren der Transzendenz*, pp. 59-83.
[13] *Phil.*, III, pp. 119, 192-194; *Psych. der Welt*, p. 52ff.
[14] *Ibid.*, p. 193.
[15] *Truth and Symbol*, p. 27ff.

do with the concrete and the historical; that both the cipher and Transcendence as well are but the reified neologisms of an idealist metaphysic reconstituted in existentialist jargon. This, however, is not at all the case as Jaspers insists that "there is nothing which cannot be a cipher." [16] In other words, everything within the horizon of possible experience can undergo the transformation from symbol to cipher. Moreover, it is not only natural experience but experience become historical as possible Existenz which makes the decisive difference. [17] Although the transcending experience of ciphers can be formally differentiated, it cannot be materially or empirically localized except at the expense of detaching it from the historicity of particular experience whereupon it is voided through objectification. While schematic differentiations can be made, this must be done only within the constraints of a larger awareness that the experience of Transcendence itself points to an antecedent ground where formal and material differentiations are not only confusing but counterproductive for authentic philosophizing. In other words, it is precisely the disjunction implicit to ordinary experience that Transcendence overcomes. On the other hand, one must also state that there is an implicit value judgement by Jaspers as to which of the three formal levels of transcending-thinking produces the most germinal ciphers of Transcendence. Ciphers of the external world – while essential – are the least productive metaphysically since they are the most prone to objectivation. It is at the level of *Existenzerhellung* and the transition to concentrated analysis of the experiential reflexivity of thinking-itself that a conversion to transcending in the ciphers of speculative metaphysics fully takes place whereupon consciousness-itself becomes its own primary myth. Thus with reference to the question of the "material worldliness" of ciphers, one is left with the paradoxical conclusion that while ciphers are not cognizable apart from being-in-a-world, they are never wholly identifiable with the world but rather subsist, like some Platonic agency of mediation, as "hovering" realities midway between Being and non-Being. [18] Their stated purpose is always that of engendering a heightened consciousness whereby I come to know that All-Encompassing-Tran-

---

[16] *Chiffren der Transzendenz*, pp. 34-58; *Phil.*, III, p. 114.
[17] Cf., *Origin and Goal of History*, pp. 262, 272ff. One cannot over-emphasize that for Jaspers the reality question is almost completely equated with experience and not just experience in the naive sense but experience "consciously heightened" through transcending-thinking.
[18] More will be stated concerning Jaspers' "rootage" in the Platonic tradition in Part II. Ultimately his existentialism is incomprehensible apart from it.

scendence which is both within me and from which I have the source and origin of possibility as that which is beyond me.

Even though Jaspers' discourse concerning ciphers has the tendency to sound abstract and idealistic, he always insists that the test of transcending-thinking – even in this third modality – is found in *Lebenspraxis*. However, by *Lebenspraxis* Jaspers does not suggest merely a practical or moral verification of transcending-thinking. Rather, once having "scaled the heights of Transcendence," so to speak, it is not a matter of simply returning to the world but of participating in the world-become-World or reality for the first time, that is, to a world transformed or, as Muriel Spark once put it picking up on the biblical motif, a "transfiguration of the commonplace." [19] As in the case of the mythical Daedalus, once the process of transcending has begun, the price of simply returning or turning back is existential death. Were Jaspers merely to give a passing nod to the so-called practical, the serious play of transcending in relation to Transcendence would not be transcending in historicity but a dispassionate fraud. As a metaphysical art authentic transcending becomes authentic only insofar as one's sense of world is opened to the unrestricted domain of Transcendence-Itself as the "All Encompassing" (*das Umgreifende*) of all possible transcending. [20] This is entirely different than the claim of Hegel's later writings in which everything has been "settled," so to speak, for in Jaspers the world has not been lost or surrendered to Absolute Logic any more than it has been relinquished to the natural sciences as having the only proper understanding of world. [21] All that is lost, according to Jaspers, are the precritical chains of Dasein's objectifying thinking now placed with the freedom of possible Existenz and its goal of Eternalization through the knowledge of Transcendence. [22]

Jaspers' notion of *Eternalization* as the ultimate end of transcending-thinking is not unlike the positions of both Augustine and Kierkegaard. But in spite of this proximity there is a substantial difference residing in the fact that for Jaspers the residue of Transcendence discernible as the ground of possible Existenz is found immanently in its "ruins," whereas Augustine's *cor inquietum* and Kierkegaardian *Angst* depend finally on

---

[19] Cf., *Phil.*, III, p. 146, "Worldless love is love of nothing; an unfounded bliss. I really love Transcendence only as my love transfigures the world."

[20] *Ibid.*, pp. 147-174, *Reason and Existenz*, pp. 69-74.

[21] *Von der Wahrheit*, pp. 158ff. Jaspers' position is not ontological but "periechontological," i.e., not what but *how* Being can be for us, as in the case of the Greek verb , to "surround" or "encircle" Being. We will speak more on this in Part III.

[22] *Phil.*, III, pp. 194ff.

an external source for the attainment of an "eternal consciousness." [23] For Jaspers, "What is revealed in foundering – the non-Being of all Being accessible to us – is the Being of Transcendence." [24] All that can be uttered in response to this interior but ineffable realization is "Being" and even then "it is as though we were saying nothing; breaks in the silence that cannot break." [25]

This difference, in fact, represents both the philosophically intriguing and the theologically troublesome feature of Jaspers' position, for on the one hand, transcending-thinking *founders* in the face of its own project, which is to say that in the face of Transcendence-Itself, transcending-thinking may be overcome only by a mystery of its own design. No one can deny the force of Jaspers' very careful existential-phenomenological description of this process as it is, to be sure, an investigation which takes *Deum et animam scire cupio* as its primary cue. On the other hand, however, everything seems to point in the direction of a Christian understanding of revelation as that "break" in transcending-thinking through which Transcendence appears. But this is the step or leap which Jaspers, in contradistinction to Augustine and Kierkegaard, is unwilling to make.

As in the case of Wittgenstein's *Sprachkritik*, which can similarily be looked upon as a form of transcending-thinking (that is, as the first and essential movement towards that "silence" before which, as he says, the "higher" things are "indifferent"), [26] the very discursiveness which has characterized transcending-thinking as a form of communication moves towards the end of communication altogether. Jaspers puts it this way: "All communication must be thought of as canceled in Transcendence, as a lack in temporal existence, then all conceivability in general is also canceled. For example, I think of the old proposition that God is the Truth. Then such a Truth has nothing to correspondend to since it is undivided and without opposition, whereas all other truths are modes of agreement. In fact, such an idea is empty and can only be felt existentially by me historically. Here where I cannot penetrate, truth can retain no

---

[23] *Philosophical Fragments*, pp. 71-73.
[24] *Phil.*, III, pp. 202-203.
[25] *Ibid.*, p. 205.
[26] *Tractatus Logico-Philosophicus, op. cit.*, 6.432. Though Wittgenstein does not speak of *Chiffren*, the movement of the *Tractatus* towards "Indirect" or poetic discourse as the only possible way of dealing with ethics, aesthetics and religion is in many ways similar to what Jaspers develops as transcending-thinking – even what Jaspers describes as foundering; for example, "My propositions serve as elucidations in the following way: anyone who understands me eventually recognizes them as nonsensical, when he uses them – as steps – to climb beyond them. (He must, so to speak, throw away the ladder after he has climbed up it.) He must transcend these propositions and then he will see the world aright." 6.54.

thinkable sense. The shipwrecking of all thinking about truth can shake one in his depth, but it cannot provide a tenable thought ... The ultimate thinking as in communication is silence. [27]

Thus Jaspers believes that Transcendence-Itself is "beyond exegesis,"[28] that it is a reality which grasps us even as we grasp it tentatively but decisively through the posture of "philosophical faith." [29] What Jaspers understands as Eternalization then, is substantially different from both the Hegelian *Aufhebung* and from the notion of salvation as deliverance through the assurance provided by historical revelation. One participates in Eternalization only insofar as one is willing to assume a faith which strips itself of all material and empirical supports and whose only content is known in founding before a limit which knows no limit except the limitlessness of the Encompassing. Whether and to what degree this kind of faith and its end of eternalization is critically defensible from either a philosophical or theological point of reference will be a continuing problem for consideration in both Parts II and III.

In summary, it must again be emphasized that while it is very tempting to stratify these three formal modalities of transcending as three distinct regions or levels of consciousness, this is not what we or Jaspers intend. While the modalities of world, self and speculative metaphysics in some sense reflect a growth of consciousness, they are more accurately understood as "moments" of heightened or intensified consciousness and never as modalities which can be completely isolated one from the other.

The salutary feature of any descriptive technique is the degree to which coherence is achieved without fragmentation. However, before we can advance a final judgement as to whether this particular method is efficacious for both metaphysics and theology, it is necessary first to scrutinize Jaspers' position in relationship to the overall problem of historical consciousness and then in relationship to what appear to be the historical roots of Jaspers' conceptuality. After we have delineated some of these connections and further illuminated transcending-thinking as

not only a retrieval of that Transcendence which is intrinsic to experience but also as a retrieval of the historic meaning of Transcendence, we will be in a position to test transcending-thinking as a hermeneutic of specific symbols, in this case, the symbol of Transcendence-Itself or God.

---

[27] *Reason and Existenz*, pp. 105-106.
[28] *Phil.*, III, P. 207ff.; *Nietzsche*, p. 292f.
[29] *Philosophical Faith and Revelation*, passim.

PART II

TRANSCENDING-THINKING AND PHILOSOPHICAL IDEALISM

PART II INTRODUCTION

In Part I we attempted to show how Jaspers develops a metaphysics of Transcendence through an existential-phenomenological description of experience as "transcending-thinking." Whereas many philosophers have tried to make the case for Transcendence through experientially analogical descriptions of Being (most notably Thomistic realists), such approaches, especially since Kant, have been hard pressed to escape the charge of cosmological extrinsicism and, since Feuerbach and Freud, the charge of projection theory. Jaspers' project by contrast is experientially intrinsic. Transcendence is not understood as an ontological Absolute providing the basis for the development of a metaphysic in a cosmological or scientific sense but as something which, as underlying the transcending "movement" of thinking within experience-itself, strives towards greater and greater levels of self-intelligibility and coherence. In short, transcending is experientially related to Transcendence, the act and Being of which, as its internal dialectical foci, account for the very possibility *of* experience.

But while it can thus be stated that Jaspers reaches deeply into the structures of experience and consciousness in order to recover Transcendence as both the origin and goal of *mögliche Existenz*, it can also be shown, we believe, that Jaspers reaches back into the history of Western philosophy in order to confirm his existential-phenomenological description of transcending-thinking. While Jaspers openly confesses his high regard for the history of philosophical thinking, and that genuine philosophizing cannot take place apart from an understanding of history, he is equally candid in indicating which of the philosophers in the Western tradition he considers to be *great*. Not surprisingly, the great philosophers avowed as representing all the basic requirements of *Existenzphilosophie* invariably fall into the grand tradition of idealism. Whatever the peculiarities of Jaspers' method of selection and regardless of how his interpretation stands in relation to the canons of exegetical propriety, it is clear that Jaspers' philosophy of Transcendence is much more intelligible when apprehended against the horizon of idealism than in isolation from it.

In making these preliminary remarks we are not suggesting that Jaspers simply repristinates the position of certain idealists. Nor is Jaspers a philosophical eclectic. We suggest rather that it is precisely in relation to the tradition that Jaspers emerges somewhere between Heidegger and Cassirer in terms of what he considers to be the fundamental nature and task of philosophy. Contrary to Husserl and the early Heidegger, Jaspers did not believe that Transcendence or Being could be retrieved at the level of "pure" phenomenological description. [1] Therefore Jaspers did not consider a bracketing of the history of ontology and metaphysics as the necessary prerequisite to the reconstruction of philosophical language. On the contrary, reading the history of western philosophy from the standpoint of possible Existenz, that is, out of a posture of transcending-thinking in which the subject plays an essential role, Jaspers believes that there is a "perennial scope of philosophy." [2] This perennial scope has to do with cognitive transcending in relation to Transcendence which is formally the same throughout the ages even though the material features of cognitive transcending may change. Jaspers' position, then, is closer to that of Ernst Cassirer even though he does not attempt, as does Cassirer, to fix the origin of symbolic (poetic) language in a strictly neo-Kantian theory of consciousness, i.e., as the *Urgrund* of all language. With Cassirer, however, and Dilthey as well, Jaspers shares the conviction that the primary task of the historiographer is always the recovery or re-presentation of the "spirit" out of which and through which great systems arise. The world's great religions, therefore, are not to be devalued as primitive but as the originating expression of the experience of Transcendence; the formative milieux of the history of metaphysics.

We will begin this inquiry, then, by developing Jaspers' attitude towards the history of thinking under the rubric, "Transcending-Thinking as Historical Consciousness." In the Jaspersian scheme this is utterly central, for there can be no development of transcending-thinking in its full metaphysical sense without the simultaneous development of historical consciousness. As we have seen in Part I, the second and third formal modalities of transcending-thinking involve temporal reflexivity, which

---

[1] The so-called "later" Heidegger's attitude concerning the "linguisticality" of Being, of course, comes much closer to the Jaspersian notion concerning the *Chifferwerden* of the "world" for possible Existenz, as we shall see.

[2] Cf., Jaspers' book by the same title, *The Perennial Scope of Philosophy, passim.*

means that any claims concerning the reality or unreality of Being or Transcendence will be utterly spurious apart from the fullest possible understanding of how what one says in the present is related to what has been thought and believed in the past. As in the case of Kierkegaard, Jaspers believes that any claim to a metaphysics of Transcendence must be grounded in an anthropology which shows that man is not accidentally but essentially historical. Without an interlocking of the temporal foci of past and future in the present, one will either be in bondage to the past or the victim of fanciful speculations concerning the shape of the future. Far from relativizing one's beliefs and convictions, historical consciousness provides the essential medium for transcending-thinking whereby the thinker as individual is bonded to the experience and vision of the past. This attitude towards historical consciousness bears a strong resemblance towards Hans Gadamer's later theory of *Horizontverschmelzung*, namely that it is the reality of Transcendence as meaning, whether concealed in the nature of language or otherwise, which enables the "fusion of horizons" *through* the mediational dynamics of traditions both personal and collective. [3]

Thus, what we are calling a historical retrieval of Transcendence is not merely a personalistic transposition of the history of idealism into existentialist jargon. Jaspers' existential relation to the history of philosophy is rather participatory in the sense that the history of thought, like any other dimension of Experience and Being, will remain closed to the subject unless it is understood existentially as something *pro me*. But by participatory, we do not mean psychologistic as though by thinking-into one might be able to discern why a particular philosopher said what he said when he said it. As a trained psychologist, Jaspers was as hostile towards psychologism as historicism. It is understanding and not explanation which for Jaspers, as in the case of Dilthey and Collingwood, leads to historical consciousness. Jaspers therefore presupposes, that both *Weltorientierung* and *Existenzerhellung* are fully operative en route to historical consciousness.

Of course it is impossible to focus on every philosopher who may have influenced Jaspers in one way or another. Therefore, lest our selection of Plato, Plotinus, Kant and Cusanus seem arbitrary, we offer additional rationale for these choices. As an existentialist Jaspers' immediate relation to Hegel, Kierkegaard and Nietzsche is well known and documented. Less obvious, but perhaps more significant, is the precise nature of

---

[3] Cf., *Wahrheit und Methode*, (Tübingen, 1960), pp. 355ff.

Jaspers' relationship to the thinkers we have named as principals for the following inquiry as they relate to the formal/structural features of his system. Under the rubrics of the source, the medium and the goal of Jaspers' philosophizing, we will develop the following historical analogies. First, since Jaspers is both German and Protestant, Plato and Plotinus represent an unavoidable and almost involuntary source of metaphysical and religious inspiration. Particularly in relation to its Socratic aspect, Plato's philosophy affords Jaspers the basic paradigm for transcending in relation to Transcendence-Itself. All that is lacking in the Platonist tradition for Jaspers is the epistemological refinement which, for Jaspers, emerges in the critical philosophy of Immanuel Kant. Through the development of transcendental method, Jaspers believes we have a way of logically clarifying the relationship between transcending and Transcendence which does not alter or nullify the metaphysical substance of Plato and Plotinus, but reaffirms their fundamental insight through the establishment of limiting principles that effectively recontextualize originating intentions. The goal of Jaspers' philosophizing, finally, is clearly spiritual and mystical, the basic features of which are paralleled amazingly by the works of the great Cardinal from the Mosel River in the German Rhineland, Nicholas of Cusa. Chronologically, of course, Cusanus antedates Kant by two hundred and fifty years. For our purposes, however, we have chosen to invert this sequence in order to conform to the principles of source, medium and goal. We might also suggest that with respect to the triadic organization of Jaspers' system, his intent is not unlike that expressed in Kant's question. "For what may I hope?" But since Jaspers' answer to that question is mystically speculative, one simply cannot avoid comparisons to Cusanus, for in Jaspers' view the mystical philosophical theology of Cusanus – albeit stripped of its medieval dogmatic and ecclesial features – is the historical paradigm of transcending-thinking and philosophical faith par excellence. [4] Moreover, for Jaspers Cusanus is the first medieval thinker to strip away decisively the extrinsic cosmological encrustations of Platonic metaphysics whereby speculation becomes wholly existential *and* transcendental. We will note, however, that the speculations of Cusanus have currency precisely because they are rooted firmly in concrete religious symbols, and this will lead us to question extensively (in Part III) the degree to which Jaspers can simply adapt or extract the formal principles of tran-

---

[4] Ernst Cassirer is attracted to Cusanus for similar reasons. Cf., *The Individual and the Cosmos in Renaissance Philosophy*, trans. Mario Domandi (New York: Barnes and Noble, 1963), pp. 7-72.

scending from the work of a thinker like Cusanus – discarding the contents from which the arise – and still maintain a critical hermeneutic of symbol.

The central question, of course, does not have to do with how Jaspers went about his historical retrieval of some of the lost resonances of Transcendence or even the location of those figures within the idealist tradition upon whom he is most dependent. The critical question is whether Jaspers is finally convincing in his overall project and whether the rationale underlying his selectivity really enhances transcending-thinking as a hermeneutic for the interpretation of ciphers of Transcendence. After delineating what we believe these historical influences are, we will be in a position to pose the hermeneutical question as *the* critical question regarding the veridicy of Jaspers' foundering metaphysics of Transcendence.

CHAPTER FOUR

TRANSCENDING IN HISTORICAL CONSCIOUSNESS

In Jaspers' historical work as in the formally philosophical, it is the principle of "transcending-thinking" as *hic et nunc* that compels the reader to interpretation and judgement. Jaspers states: "Genuine interpretation ... does not subsume but penetrates; it does not claim to know with finality but while always taking cognizance of what has just been apprehended, it proceeds by a method of questioning and answering. It thereby begins a process of assimilation, the conditions and limits of which it determines for itself ... False interpretation provides for the pleasurable illusion of a general survey by placing its object at a distance and viewing it *ab extra* as an exotic specimen; the true interpretation is a means to the possibility of self-involvement." [1]

While, of course, some kind of objective and methodical distanciation is necessary for the attainment of philosophical as well as scientific veracity (*Wahrhaftigkeit*), [2] this does not mean that objectivity must come at the price of bracketing out the "personal" or spiritual foundation of any truly creative work. To do so is to destroy the nascent origin of all transcending. If, for example, the texts of Anselm or Cusanus are evaluated from the standpoint of empirical objectivity alone, then practically everything they say dissolves into nonsense. [3] Great philosophy, therefore, does not represent merely a point of view accidentally related to the author, but a "mode of thinking" or a "transcending" that is intrinsic to

---

[1] *Nietzsche*, p. 6.
[2] *Chiffren der Transzendenz*, p. 107.
[3] Toulmin's reference to J.L. Austin's doubt that " ... the question whether a philosophical question was an important question was *itself* an important question," is characteristic of this attitude. *Wittgenstein's Vienna* (New York: Simon and Schuster, 1973), p. 259. One can deal with foundational questions at strictly the level of sophistry that has characterized so much recent philosophy, or, as in Jaspers, as questions of human significance and more than mere academic interest.

the work itself. A productive reading of the history of great philosophy, then, is not the detached spectator standpoint, but participation in the transcending struggle of the author.[4] Only this kind of participation can comprehend the life-questions which have always moved great philosophy.[5]

In philosophical interpretation as in the case of writing one's own philosophy, it is philosophizing and not dogma that is important for Jaspers, for the truths to be gleaned through a study of philosophy are not truths which can be schematically applied to impersonal problems but truths "apprehended in communication."[6] As one of the primary modalities for transcending-thinking, history is not a "thing" in the sense of some gigantic repository of information or data, but the recorded body of communication. Thus both the reading and the writing of philosophy is concomitant with transcending in the will to historical truth. Such a realization, Jaspers states, " . . . cuts the ground out from under the questioner; renders every determinate appearance dubious and, in widening the questioner's horizon to the utmost, detaches him from any and every specific logical ground."[7]

A transcending orientation to the task of philosophical interpretation, therefore, achieves historical consciousness *through* foundering; foundering here viewed as a kind of failure in which historical meaning has become my own. Authentic historical science, then, is entirely different from a so-called interpretation of facts. As Jaspers puts it, "On the one hand, genuine history can never become strictly scientific, while on the other, it cannot preserve its truthfulness without exact investigation. Exact investigation, however, applies to materials, presuppositions, and all the things that every human understanding alike recognizes and is forced to accept as factual and is precisely what it has always meant. In contradistinction to this, historical memory (*geschichtliche Erinnerung*), as it proceeds within the fully apprehended medium of this factual material, sees with the historical eyes of a being whose reach exceeds that of the understanding and that is capable of realizing itself through the very memory that it makes possible."[8] Historical contempo-

---

[4] *The Great Philosophers*, Vol. II, trans. Ralph Manheim (New York: Harcourt, Brace and World), p. 225. (Hereinafter cited as *Great Phil.*)
[5] *Ibid.*, p. 256.
[6] *Nietzsche*, p. 219.Cf., also *Von der Wahrheit*, pp. 26-28.
[7] *Ibid.*, p. 237. As we will see in Part III, Jaspers' differentiation between *historie* and *Geschichte* is more radical than Bultmann's.

raneity for Jaspers, as in the case of Kierkegaard, [9] is never achieved through a laboratory reduction of data to so-called "facts," but is the result of transcending through "communication." As in the case of interpersonal communication or dialogue, all historical investigation is fraught with risk; not only the risk of ascertaining what is or is not the case and standing by one's claim, but also the risk of being disabled by this very claim. Agreeing with Nietzsche, Jaspers believes that there is a "life destroying effect of historical science," namely that as a substitute for life, historical inquiry can "rob man of his instincts . . . as man develops a knowledge of greatness but no capacity for it." For this reason alone, it is incumbent upon the reader of philosophy to move beyond an interest in historical objectivity as a form of aestheticism to a full awareness of the existential demand that the past makes upon me. The quest for historic information as opposed to the development of historical consciousness, Jaspers claims, can also produce a sense of "nihilism" as the subject becomes aware that "the world as it is ought not to be and the world that ought to be is non-existent." [10] In contrast to this, the constructive or "transcending" orientation to history discovers that while the data of history is in some sense *extra nos* (as in the case of world-orientation), its meaning is communicated only by virtue of a fusion of the "attending" and "intending" dynamics of both author and reader. Therefore, as in the case of Jaspers' second formal mode of transcending, historical consciousness is possible only by becoming aware of the boundary situation intrinsic to both subject and object, reader and text, whereupon the sharp edges of supposed facts dissolve within the ambiguity and mystery of life itself. This, as we stated before, does not mean that historical interpretation is hopelessly ambiguous and always unreliable for, as Jaspers says, "Courageous truthfulness means risking ambiguity rather than willing it." [11] To put it simply, one can never presume to have communicated the meaning of history by merely representing its data accurately. Historical meaning, for Jaspers, has very much to do with understanding what Bernard Lonergan much later termed the "polymorphous structure of human consciousness," i.e., with understanding a multiple series of cognitive operations from which subjectivity is never

---

[9] Cf., *Philosophical Fragments*, p. 44ff. Jaspers' approach to history is very close to the *Erlebniskunst* of Dilthey.

[10] *Nietzsche*, p. 244. Jaspers, however, also notes the inconsistency in Nietzsche's conclusion that nihilism is the necessary outcome of historical consciousness for in the statement that "God is Dead," the "pathos" implicit in the assertion remains. In other words, unless all the "traces" of Transcendence are "vanquished," "surrogate forms of Transcendence" are bound to appear. *Ibid.*, pp. 430 ff. Cf., also *Psych. der Welt.*, pp. 285-303.

[11] *Nietzsche*, p. 9.

completely dislocated. [12] In relation to the task of historical interpretation this polymorphousness is doubly compounded, for one is immediately faced with the realization that it is even more difficult to retrieve what is hidden in a text than, for example, to apprehend what is present in a human gesture. [13] Yet in spite of these difficulties something remains – namely, a presence caught indirectly – the mysterious trace of Transcendence-Itself even though its essence, obscured by an intentionally objectifying naïveté, can never be grasped directly. Without this transcending orientation to the reading of history, one could not understand this indirectness because one would not know that the objectifying or direct question must falsify itself as preliminary to the answer which is always indirect.

Thus the Jaspersian attitude is far different from the suggestion that man is "condemned" to interpretations that always fall short of the truth as some existentialist thinkers would imply. In Jaspers' case the "boundary" which stands between the subject and his quest for historical objectivity is not the end but the beginning of a far more profound metaphysical reality, namely an awareness of *das Umgreifende* that underlies all authentic interpretations and communications. As Jaspers puts it, "All knowledge is an interpretation of Being provided by a living and cognizing subject. There is no truth that is not entertained in thought and believed, that is, that is not found within that Encompassing Being in which we all are." [14] Thus the self-apprehension so essential to a transcending orientation to the task of interpretation, then, not only lays bare the problem of historicity in all interpretation but also serves as the primary clue to the manner in which meaning is grounded in Being-Itself. In his commentary on Nietzsche, Jaspers states, "The limitlessness of the many historically developed exegeses is the basis of our own being which, as an authentic source, not surveying all exegeses and looking through them, is directed upon the text itself. At this point the truth is not experienced as just as another mode of interpretation to be tried out as part of a game, as it were, but is experienced as the truth of Existenz-

---

[12] This polymorphism of consciousness based upon an intentionality psychology casts an entirely different light on the phenomenon of pluralism as well as interpretation once, as Lonergan also states, the subject is understood as an "originating center of value." Plurality is therefore no longer something "out there" (as it tends to be in William James, for example) but primarily the problem of interiority. Likewise historical interpretation is no longer merely a problem of getting one's data straight or one's "faculties" functioning properly but of understanding the "heuristic structure" represented not only in the subject but also the text. In such a situation, neither "positivism" nor the "principle of the empty head" will suffice. *Method in Theology*, pp. 27f., 268f.

[13] Cf., Arthur Vogel, *op. cit.*, pp. 13ff.

[14] *Reason and Existenz*, p. 36.

Itself – the absolute truth which is present to Existenz when, in the *fullness of historical consciousness*, it reads the world as a cipher. Here special knowledge of the exegetical process and every special exegesis that is knowable *ab extra* is fused within the presence of Being-Itself. Then the truth is *my* truth, but at the same time, not *mine merely*, for while, in the first place, *it becomes historical* as that within which I find myself fused with Being, in the second place, it has become Being-Itself ... as the mode in which it becomes existential as myself." [15]

There can be, then, no "fullness of historical consciousness" apart from the risks of "self-apprehension" in and through the "act" of interpretation. It was precisely this existential dimension which Jaspers found missing in what he termed the "pseudo-scientific" philosophy of his colleagues at Heidelberg and particularly in the work of his sometime enemy Heinrich Rickert, whose philosophy he regarded as particularly devoid of human meaning. [16] One might say with respect to Lessing's comment concerning the "accidental truths of history," [17] that such truths inevitably remain culture bound and seemingly arbitrary whenever the expositor maintains the trans-subjective analycity of a positivist. Not only is such a self-positioning destructive of world-orientation in its initial stages (as we observe in the highly developed technology of our time), but it can easily lead to a completely schizophrenic relationship between fact and value. In the context of historical studies not only does spectator detachment lead to denial of possible self-Being in the reader, but it is utterly insensitive to the integrity of self-Being which may or may not be present in the author. However, given an orientation of 'transcending-thinking" in the interpreter who has grounded his method in something akin to what Jaspers calls *verstehende Psychologie* [18] and criti-

---

[15] *Nietzsche*, p. 291, (emphasis, Jaspers').

[16] Wilhelm Windelband, although not a colleague of Jaspers, was one of his teachers and regarded by Jaspers as being of the same delimited frame of mind as Rickert since both, according to Jaspers, suffered from the misconception that philosophy could become "scientific" in the same manner as the natural sciences by simply imitating its methods. Cf. Jaspers' "Philosophical Autobiography" in *The Philosophy of Karl Jaspers*, Schilpp edition (New York: Tudor Press, 1957), pp. 24, 34; and "On My Philosophy" in *Existentialism from Dostoevsky to Sartre*, ed. Walter Kaufmann (New York: Meridian, 1956), pp. 136-137.

[17] Cf., *Lessing's Theological Writings*, ed. Henry Chadwick, "Library of Modern Religious Thought" (Stanford, 1956), p. 51ff.

[18] Jaspers' notion of *verstehende Psychologie* is influenced by the early phenomenological movement, particularly by Dilthey and Husserl. As a psychology which understands rather than explains, it represents a decisive movement away from "categorical explanations to phenomenologically descriptive ones;" i.e., descriptions which attempt to respect the integrity of all experience, even the psychopathological, by attempting to deal with it from within and not merely affix a label from without. Jaspers' *Allgemeine Psychopathologie* first published in 1913 is the clinical result of this guiding principle and *Psychologie der Weltan-*

cal differentiation of the multiple operations which are always present to consciousness at any moment of experience, that which once appeared merely accidental and even superfluous may well become the most important aspect of a particular text.

Thus historical inquiry by the philosopher is not merely a matter of reconstructing the past nor the means of legitimating a particular theory about the past. Its purpose is rather that of existential communication with the great philosophers and thinkers of the past who were equally concerned about "being historical" through struggling with the fundamental questions about the nature of reality. Reading history as a cipher of transcendence, Jaspers says, "is the contemplative complement of the activity of present action." Moreover, this participation or communication is possible historically because of the transcendental (in this case specifically implying "trans-cultural") nature of fundamental philosophical questions. [19] The compossibility of subject and object in this historical communication is, therefore, not achieved simply on the basis of merely the historiographer's technical accuracy, nor, for that matter, is it achieved through the free, undisciplined play of the imagination. The most important dimension of a philosophical reading of history is the relationship of the data to possible Existenz or what Kierkegaard and Berdyaev simply call the reality of "Spirit." [20]

In sum, and again reminiscent of Kierkegaard's famous question, "Is an historical point of departure possible for eternal consciousness?" one does not, for Jaspers, merely transcend *in* historical consciousness. Transcending-thinking is, as it were, unthinkable *apart* from historical consciousness. [21] While subject-object differentiations are inevitable, it is

schauungen (1919) is its philosophical extension. The very title of this latter work, namely "worldviews" suggests that each perspective has its own uniqueness and non-reducible features.

[19] Jaspers has much in common with Heidegger in suggesting that Transcendence or meaning is intentional, i.e., in large measure determined by the shape or horizon of the question, Cf., *Vom Wesen des Grundes*, Pt. II.

[20] Cf., Kierkegaard, *The Sickness Unto Death* (New York: Doubleday, 1946), pp. 146-147; Berdyaev, *Spirit and Reality* (London: Centenary, 1939), pp. 7-32. Cf., also Jaspers' chapter "Der Geist zwischen Gegensätzen," *Psych. der Welt*, p. 345ff. It is interesting to note that in Jaspers' later works (in fact, beginning with *Philosophie* in 1932) the term "spirit" appears with decreasing frequency, perhaps in order to avoid both theological and Hegelian associations. Nonetheless, it is nothing short of the spiritual dimension of Being which leads to Jaspers' redefined notion of universal history. Cf., "On My Philosophy," *Existentialism from Dostoevsky to Sartre, op. cit.*, pp. 135ff.

[21] This, of course, is the leading principle behind Jaspers' *The Origin and Goal of History*: "We and the present in which we live are situated in the midst of history. The present becomes null and void if it loses itself within the narrow horizon of the day and degenerates into a *mere* present ... A present that has attained fulfillment (that is by being rooted in past and future) allows us to cast anchor in the eternal origin," p. vi.

precisely the historical frame of reference which shows that the subject-object structure of human experience is a functionally epistemic and not an ontological division. In historical communication – as in inter-subjective communication – the disjunctiveness of subject and object is personally overcome through the appropriation of meaning. Therefore, what sometimes in Jaspers seems to be an attitude towards history not dissimilar to that of Hegel is substantially qualified by always reading and interpreting history *aus möglicher Existenz*, that is, not on the basis of the presumption of an "absolute logic" but as a "cipher of Transcendence." [22] What is lost is not historical objectivity unless by that one means some kind of atomistic empirical objectivity which can be attained by simply bracketing out the question of self. What is lost for Jaspers are positivistic presuppositions based on a deficient anthropology that generate deceptive principles of interpretation. What is gained is the indispensable connection between *philo-sophia*, historiography and a consciousness of Transcendence which is not only rooted in the present but in the future and past as well. [23] As Jaspers suggests, "philosophical metaphysics" is precisely that "boundary area" which lies between a "knowledge of tradition" and "existential" phenomenology. [24]

In the following chapters we will begin to see how Jaspers' historical investigations have contributed to the formulation of his philosophy of Transcendence. On the basis of what we have already said it should be clear that the idealists who occupy the lion's share of Jaspers' inquiries do not enjoy this position of privilege because they are the advocates of a superior ontology or metaphysic but because "self-apprehension" has always been a fundamental feature of the idealist tradition, especially in the critical idealists. If one fails to grasp the degree to which self-apprehension is less than central to Jaspers' admiration of idealism, then one is very likely to regard Jaspers' notion of transcending-thinking as still another permutation in a long tradition of outlandish and insupportable claims concerning the nature of Truth-Itself. What Jaspers is saying is that any claim to the knowledge of Truth – whatever is affirmed and

---

[22] With reference to Hegel and also in connection with the previous footnote, Jaspers is quite candid in confessing that together with the writings of Kierkegaard and Nietzsche, Hegel's *Phänomenologie des Geistes* was the most formidable influence in his transition from descriptive psychology to existential philosophy. Cf., "Philosophical Autobiography," *The Philosophy of Karl Jaspers*; *Von der Wahrheit*, pp. 120ff.

[23] *Way to Wisdom*, pp. 96ff.; *Origin and Goal of History*, pp. 141ff.; *Man in the Modern Age*, trans. Eden and Cedar Paul (New York: Doubleday, 1951), pp. 4-15.

[24] Cf., *Phil.*, III, pp. 10ff.

whenever it is stated – is utterly impossible to assess apart from a full consideration of the subject making the claim. This does not mean that a particular claim is psychologized any more than it is historicized but rather, as we have tried to demonstrate in Part I, that one must be fully aware of the cognitive operations of the transcending subject in the communication of experience. In short, the critical method of interpretation must be informed by epistemologically critical anthropology. Again, Jaspers' principle of "qualified negativity" comes into play, for this kind of propaedeutic does not provide the reader of history with a priori knowledge of exactly the right questions but it does make him sensitive to the kinds of questions which cannot be asked, especially the question that intends to fix the meaning of historical expressions independently of both author and reader as an object in the text. The existentially critical attitude, then, does not relativize the content of history but frees it for my own experience and the experience of others. In the language of theology, the *extra nos* of the historical datum becomes *pro me* not as fact in the sense of empirical objectivity but as something essential to the horizon of my own Existenz and apart from which my self-Being would be diminished. As in the case of Bultmann and Heidegger, *Historie* becomes *Geschichte* in "comprehension." Whether one is in dialogue with another person in the past, present or future, "Truth," as Jaspers states, "has its origin in communication." [25] In such a manner it can be stated that transcending-thinking *is* historical consciousness or, at the very least, that apart from historical consciousness transcending-thinking is a fiction.

---

[25] *The Perennial Scope of Philosophy*, p. 46.

CHAPTER FIVE

JASPERS AND PLATONIC IDEALISM

The bond between Jaspers and Plato is deep and fascinating. Indeed, it is impossible to survey and adjudicate the significance of transcending-thinking as a primary motif in Jaspers' thought without a consideration of Plato who, together with Augustine and Kant, Jaspers regards as the "greatest" of the "great philosophers."[1] In this chapter I will attempt to clarify this relationship by exploring three conceptual features of "transcending-thinking" directly influenced by Plato and Platonism generally. First we will focus on Platonic *dialectic* in relation to Jaspers' *possible Existenz*; secondly, on Platonic *chorismos* and the Jaspersian *boundary situation*; and thirdly, on the eidetic *One* of Plato and Plotinus and Jaspers' *Transcendence-Itself* or the *Encompassing*.

---

[1] Two of the five or six projected volumes of *Die grossen Philosophen* were completed prior to Jaspers' death in 1968. From the very outset he makes it clear that this project was not to be a history of philosophy in the philologist's understanding of historiography but is rather to be an individual philosopher's "encounter" with other philosophers. In fact, Jaspers believes that this is the only way an authentic history of philosophy can be written. Comparing the art historian with the historian of philosophy he states quite candidly that the former "does not have to be an artist" in order to deal with the history of art, but he who deals with the "history of ideas must be a philosopher," *Great Phil.*, I, p. 5. Jaspers' candor is both fortunate and unfortunate; fortunate by way of clearly stating that in relation to the history of ideas there can be no such thing as trans-subjective neutrality, but also unfortunate in that while presuppositions are stated openly, one is frequently hard pressed to differentiate Jaspers from the philosopher in question. This, of course, as in Dilthey, is the danger in a *spiritual* or *existential* history of philosophy. Even though the contents of these volumes are arranged thematically rather than chronologically, one can hardly fail to notice what seem to be fairly arbitrary selections and groupings of philosophers under these various headings. For example, Aristotle and Aquinas are included in the projected final volume together with Hegel, Shankara and Chu Hsi under the heading "creative orderers . . . whose systems are the culmination of long developments," *Ibid.*, p. 7. For the student of Jaspers, it would have been highly advantageous to have access to this work, particularly with reference to Aristotle and Aquinas to whom Jaspers makes scant and frequently disparaging remarks in other parts of his works. Moreover, the fact that neither Aristotle nor Aquinas is considered "paradigmatic," "seminal thinker" or "original metaphysician" is highly disturbing, to say nothing of the fact that Jaspers saw fit to include only two British empiricists, viz., Hobbes and Hume, in his initial prospectus. In retrospect, of course, it is not too difficult to understand Jaspers' minimalist appreciation of Aristotle and Aquinas, for he was writing during a time in which neo-Thomist contemporaries, such as Gilson and Maritain, were proclaiming Aquinas as the original existentialist. It was only towards the end of Jaspers' career that an entirely different school of Thomistic philoso-

POSSIBLE EXISTENZ AND DIALECTIC

Plato, for Jaspers, represents the first decisive breakthrough or *axial* point in the history of philosophy, [2] for it was Plato who demonstrated that in authentic or "transcending" philosophizing there is a unity of "thinking and being." [3] Inspired by Socrates' movement into the problematic of interiority, Plato turned from the materialist orientation of pre-Socratic philosophy towards an investigation of the nature of thinking itself. As Jaspers puts it, Plato "won independance in thinking through thinking . . . through the knowledge of non-knowledge." [4] Fundamental knowledge or authentic philosophical insight therefore comes about as the result of a conversion to reflective or, more properly, "reflexive" thinking through which the subject begins to become aware of the thematic role of subjectivity in the constitution of meaning through that method known as "dialectic." Furthermore, that thinking which is here referred to as dialectical does not merely have to do with a subject-object or subject-subject relationship but, in a deeper sense, has to do with a dialectic present to thinking itself, viz., the primordial consciousness of an Other as primal source and out of which subject-object differentiations arise. [5] By Platonic dialectic then, Jaspers understands the first formal indication that there can be an *indirect* communication of Truth. [6] It is indirect because the truth of Being-Itself cannot be apprehended directly as some kind of entity cognizable through categorial formulae but rather as a *presence* elicited dialectically in all depth communication. "Dialectic," Jaspers states, "is the logic of communicable movement of thought. This movement of thought does not hold fast to its momentary content. As movement it is itself content. It is a thinking in the realm of the incommunicable which is manifested in philosophically

phers, namely transcendental Thomists under the effective but for most non-Catholics obscure tutelage of Fr. Joseph Marechal, began to emerge into prominence. It is now becoming clear that as mediated by people like Emerich Coreth, Otto Muck, Karl Rahner and especially Bernard Lonergan, both Aristotle and Aquinas provide a great deal by way of both complementing and correcting Jaspers' notion of "transcending-thinking" and providing a balance to the implicit idealism of Jaspers' system. It seems to this writer that the long-awaited rapprochement between critical idealists and critical realists may rest squarely on the problem of Transcendence. Indeed, both Heidegger and especially Jaspers' successor at Heidelberg, Hans-Georg Gadamer, have seen this and it is through Gadamer's representation of Aristotle that it is beginning to happen.

[2] *Origin and Goal of History*, p. 244.
[3] *Great Phil.*, I, pp. 169, 380.
[4] *Ibid.*, I., p. 161.
[5] Cf., *Reason and Existenz*, p. 19ff; *Per. Scope*, p. 61f.
[6] *Great Phil.*, I., p. 131.

communicable movement." [7]

The dialectical communication of Truth also effects "existential transformation." Far from being merely a language game, dialectic in its authentic usage always entails a form of self-transformation or *conversion*. It is in this sense that Jaspers regards Plato as the formal originator of existentialism: "In its rise to pure thought in the apperception of Being-Itself, dialectic transcends all provincial fixations without which it would become dogma ... Dialectic is the thought dynamic of the thinker who transforms himself in rising to higher knowledge." [8] It should be noted that this transformation is not the result of a solipsistic gnosticism but happens only in the matrix of "communication." Subject-object limitations are not transcended in an ontological sense but *existentially*. The existential manner in which Jaspers interprets both Plato and Plotinus means that this conversion is not a sudden and unequivocal result of being grounded in Being-Itself but the process of a gradual and disciplined heightening of consciousness, the philosophical analogue of salvation.

The structural similarities between Jaspers' formal modalities of transcending-thinking are even more pronounced in relation to the philosophy of Plotinus where Jaspers delineates the two basic "thought steps" of dialectical transcending consonant with his own method. The first step has to do with the movement from sense perception to thinking, and the second from thought to thinking in unity with the *Unthinkable* or Transcendence-Itself: "Both the sensuous and the spiritual world are immanent; both are within the range of man's perceiving and thinking. The first transcending step from the perceptible to the intelligible, to that which can only be thought, merely provides the starting point for the second step, thinkable as well. In the world of the thinkable Plotinus finds no rest, but goes on the search for its ground, its source. But this question cannot be answered by determinate thought. Anything we can think belongs to the intellectual world we are trying to transcend. Thinking, we take a step which is no longer thought, for as thought it cannot stand up against the proposition that the existence of the unthinkable is thinkable. *Thinking presses to the limit that it cannot transcend but in thinking this limit spurs us to pass beyond it ... to the One.*" [9] The formal

---

[7] *Ibid.*, p. 150.
[8] *Ibid.*, I., p. 145.
[9] *Ibid.*, Vol. II, pp. 48ff. Cf., also *Philosophy of Existenz*, pp. 20-21, where Jaspers specifically develops "transcending-thinking" in terms of "thought steps."

correspondence of Jaspers' modalities of transcending-thinking with the *movement* intrinsic to Plotinian dialectic is unmistakable. Consider the following passage from the *Enneads* where Plotinus talks about the "path of dialectic:" "There are two stages ... The first degree is the conversion from the lower life, the second – held by those that have already made their way to the sphere of the Intelligibles, have set as it were a footprint there but must still advance within the realm – lasts until they reach the extreme hold of the place, the Term attained when the topmost peak of the Intellectual realm is won ... But this highest degree must bide its time." [10]

Far from being a metaphysical formula based on a kind of heuristic magic, dialectic, for Jaspers, has to do with the personal movement of *faith* or *Quest*; that is, it is inconceivable and incomprehensible apart from an individual's struggle with the exigencies of possible Existenz. In fact, it is precisely Jaspers' interposition of Existenz as the mediating ground of dialectic which reinforces and recalls the profoundly human character of dialectic so frequently overlooked in both Plato and Plotinus. The possibility of dialectic, therefore, does not derive from a dualistic ontology which, in turn, renders such language "mythological." [11] Such conclusions are based on wholly extrinsic readings of the Platonic tradition. The truly dialectical rather has to do with an essential reflexivity present to Existenz as the mediating experiential ground between God and world, universal and particular. Jaspers, of course, does not accept the Plotinian system without qualifications. For example, Plotinus' statement that the "intellectual principle" is discernible simply by "withdrawing into one's self and taking a look ... letting each become godlike," Jaspers would find uncritical. Nevertheless, as we will see in Part III, there is a real sense in which Jaspers' understanding of dialectic as a basically "intuitive" reality is quite similar to Plotinus, namely, as "having to do with the operations of the soul, affirmation and denial, whether denial is of affirmation or something else, it knows both identity and difference. *These it grasps as immediately as sensation grasps its objects.*" [12]

In order to clarify this *mediating ground*, it is helpful to extend our analogy by dealing comparatively with the Platonic *chorismos-methexis*

---

[10] *Enneads*, I, 3, 1.
[11] It would appear that Gordon D. Kaufman has overlooked this in his article "Transcendence Without Mythology." Cf., *God the Problem* (Cambridge: Harvard, 1973), pp. 41-71.
[12] Cf. *Enneads*, I, 6, 5.

relationship and the Jaspersian *boundary situation*.

BOUNDARY SITUATION AND *CHORISMOS-METHEXIS*

Although Jaspers faithfully adheres to the subject-object structure of human experience, it is a dialectic which coalesces metaphorically in the *boundary situation*. On the one hand, the boundary situation represents a fundamental limit beyond which cogent or objectifying thinking cannot transgress, but on the other hand it is precisely the boundary situation which, in the very process of heightening and intensifying the disjunctiveness of the subject-object cleavage, points beyond itself in *ciphers*. In Plato, *chorismos* is a conceptual metaphor representing the conviction that there is a fundamental duplicity in experience – not only the fundamental difference between appearance and reality – but a condition intrinsic to the human mind itself. [13] In Plotinus, this *chorismos* is cosmologized through hypostases of emanations from the One progressively deficient in Being relative to their degree of separation. Because of the cosmogonic quality of Plotinus' imagery, one easily receives the impression that these transcending *thought-steps* quite literally represent a dualistic movement from the material to the spiritual or purely intellective realm of Being, and frequently with good reason. Jaspers, taking his cue from Plato, is cautious on this matter maintaining that as movement it is entirely transcendental: "The eristic speeches . . . which seem to crush the adversary by logic are possible only because of the contradiction in thinking itself." [14] Whatever the ontological status of *chorismos*, then, it is a disjunction present to thinking-itself which makes transcending-thinking a dialectical possibility, viz., a *limit* which engenders "a movement of thought kindled by oppositions." [15]

One might say that Jaspers tries to maintain something of a "boundary position" between Plato and Plotinus concerning the meaning of this metaphorical dialectic. On the one hand, Jaspers concedes that Plotinus superficialized Plato's transcendental-intuitive awareness of the reality of *chorismos* and *methexis* by too quickly moving from existential to cosmo-ontological imagery: "Plato looked upon philosophizing as an activity through which man comes to resemble the divine and never thought

---

[13] Cf., *Republic*, 533, and *Parmenides*, 241ff.
[14] *Great Phil.*, I., p. 136.
[15] *Ibid.*, p. 146.

which man comes to resemble the divine and never thought of bridging the gulf between them. But for Plotinus, philosophizing was a union with the divine whereby the distance between God and man was annulled." [16] Yet, on the other hand, Jaspers also perceives a strength in Plotinus, missing in Plato, that derives from the existential force of specific cosmomythic imagery. Thus, even though the becoming of possible Existenz is basically a transcendental or cognitive process for Jaspers, this is never to imply that it is independent of a basis in ordinary sensory experience. Such a suggestion would violate what Jaspers perceives to be the reality of mytho-poetic ciphers as the "intervening bond" between the material and the intellectual dimension of experience. It is, therefore, precisely with respect to the *communication* of the dialectic of *chorismos* and *methexis* (separation and participation) that the language of myth is indispensable, for imagery which has both material and noetic reference points beyond itself to the greater reality of the Encompassing. [17] As Jaspers puts it speaking of Plotinus, "When authentic transcending is present, then . . . in images of the All . . . there is no cleavage between mythical vision and logical clarity. Just as the image becomes metaphor for what cannot be stated in terms of rational thought, so thought itself becomes a logical myth." [18] In Augustine, on the other hand (and in spite of the "natural" or experiential character of transcending-thinking present to Augustine with which Jaspers is in agreement), Jaspers believes that the mythic imagery of Plotinus is hardened and mundanized. The ciphers suspended at either end of the *chorismos-methexis* dynamic are historicized: "Plotinus' Above Being is degraded into being, the spiritual cosmos is elevated to become God's thought, and the two merge into a personal God." [19]

Jaspers therefore believes it imperative that one recognize that the *chorismos-methexis* relationship of classical Platonism is not the basis for a metaphysical dualism nor is it the basis for the kind of irrationalism found in much theology where moral differentiations between *flesh* and *spirit* invariably seem to spill over into an ontology. Even though the phenomenon of a "boundary situation" is envisaged as a kind of spatial

---

[16] *Ibid.*, p. 89.

[17] This "presence" of Transcendence-Itself is also by poetic allusion to be sure, but it is precisely the reason why Jaspers repudiates the Bultmannian project of *Entmythologisierung.* Cf., Part III.

[18] *Great Phil.*, I., p. 69.

[19] *Ibid.*, p. 91. This again seems to be the basis of Gordon Kaufman's argument; cf., *God the Problem, op. cit.*, p. 52ff.

field, it is, of course, strictly transcendental, and its meaning can only be communicated in a symbolic image or conceptual metaphor. [20] The long standing tradition of negative theology and more recently "dialectical" theology which bases much of its reflection on an ontological interpretation of Kierkegaard's "infinite qualitative difference" is for Jaspers not only a misreading of Kierkegaard but a perversion of the transcendental insight intrinsic to the speculative works of both Plato and Plotinus. A good deal of what is known as *dialectical theology* is obviously guilty of mixing metaphors, so to speak, whereby one moves in and out of the "city of God" and the "city of man" at will; i.e., boundary situations are understood as indicators of absolute ontological divisions which can be bridged by Divine revelation alone understood gratuitously as an *ephapax* historical-empirical event.[21] When this happens, the hypostatic-mythic emanations of Plotinus are transformed into historical dispensations and what is fundamental to the structure of experience is made to appear as subjective, synergistic caprice. For Jaspers, as we will see, this is not only an uncritical, self-serving understanding of myth but is tantamount to *bad faith*– at least bad "philosophical faith". While, on the one hand, the critical subject knows how such metaphors are formulated, theologians frequently attempt to underwrite their authority on the basis of an atomistic historical revelation. By contrast, a philosophically constructive understanding of the phenomenon of *chorismos-methexis* and the "boundary situation" implicit thereto is one which is fully cognizant of the transcendental nature of the mythical imagery in *dialectic*. As Jaspers puts it: "A dialectic of mere opposition remains aporetic and serves only as an indicator. However, dialectic by intermediate concepts elucidates the divergent by establishing an intervening bond (*desmos*). Hence the importance of the between (*metaxy*), whereby separates are joined, whereby the one is present to the other or has a share in it. Hence the importance of the moment (*exaiphanes*) of the transition, the juncture of the past and the future in the present. Hence also the Being of what is not, which in a certain sense has being . . . For

---

[20] Anders Nygren, as neo-Kantian, misses completely this very central differentiation. Cf., *Method and Meaning* (Philadelphia: Fortress, 1972), pp. 21-25.

[21] A classic example of this can be found in Barth's reply to Tillich on the "lack of authority" present to Tillich's apology for the paradoxical "Boundary" situation. Cf., *The Beginnings of Dialectical Theology*, ed. James Robinson (Richmond: John Knox Press, 1968), pp. 133-162.

Being and non-Being are not ultimate opposites but are both present at every step, though in different ways." [22]

This view is clearly inspired by the dialectical conceptualizations of Plato in *Sophist* and *Timaeus*. In the former dialogue, it will be recalled, Plato is convinced that a dualist interpretation of *chorismos* must be put to the test and has the Stranger say, "In self-defiance I must test the philosophy of my father Parmenides and try to prove my main force that in a certain sense non-Being is and that Being, on the other, is not." (241) This mediatorial existing-non-being is a primordial awareness for Plato and a point of everlasting confusion for many subsequent interpretations which largely derive from the more mythical language of *Timaeus*. What is interesting to note for our purposes is that the mediating dialectical matrix of the "soul" in the latter dialogue has moments exactly corresponding to Jaspers' three formal modes of transcending-thinking. For example, first there is "pure" Being, " ... always the same, uncreated and indestructible ... of which contemplation is granted to intelligence only," (Jaspers' *Transzendenz*), secondly the Being of sense perception, "always in motion" and utterly contingent (Jaspers' *mögliche Existenz*), and thirdly this "existing-non-Being" which is apprehended by a "spurious kind of reason and is hardly real" but which "provides a home for all created things" (Jaspers' *das Umgreifende*). [23]

In sum, apart from the centrality of lived experience, Jaspers believes that Platonic insight into Being dissolves into the nonsense of a stratified cosmology which today cannot help but appear ludicrous. [24] But given the posture of "participation," that is, *mögliche Existenz*, one is able to both comprehend the boundary situation and also to appreciate the prayerful attitude of authentic metaphysical philosophizing. To be sure in the case of Plato and Plotinus (as in Jaspers' own), these are not prayers of supplication to a personal God, but rather the *awe* which characterizes an individual's participation in Eternalization and the authentication of reflection in freedom. "It is in prayer itself," Jaspers states, regarding the mysticism of Plotinus, "alone with the One, where one hopes to gain presence which can enable a man to speak meaningfully of the Supreme. This way of knowledge does not begin with a theorem from which corollaries are derived, but with a vision which remains its sole

---

[22] *Great Phil.*, I., p. 147.

[23] Cf., *Timaeus* 52a. Cf., also *Perennial Scope of Philosophy*, pp. 24ff., for "shifts" implicit in such differentiations.

[24] This, of course, was Lessing's reaction to the same extrinsicism. Cf. *Theological Writings, op. cit.*, pp. 51ff.

source and goal. It does not select an object to be examined, but in the objective world of appearances finds a fullness that transcends both subject and object." [25]

Freedom itself, then, is the primary means of verifying this experience, for, on the one hand, freedom is unthinkable apart from subject-object distinctions and sustains itself on the basis of these divisions. However, at a deeper level one is aware that if there were only disjunctiveness and division the question of freedom as both reality and possibility would not even arise. Thus far from being an occasion for resignation to a form of dualism, "boundary experience" – as freedom's space – is the necessary pre-condition for transcending-thinking beyond mere disjunction and cleavage; that is, it is precisely that "between" (*metaxy*) which serves as the "bond" (*desmos*) of transcending in relation to Transcendence-Itself. For further consideration as to how this decisive, albeit fragmentary, resolution takes place, we turn to a comparative analysis of the Platonic *One* and Jaspers' *Transcendence-Itself*.

TRANSCENDENCE-ITSELF AND THE ONE

If one can say that for Plato the *Good* is the enlightened life of reason, and that in Plotinus consciousness of the *One* is the cosmo-ontological apex of the intellectual life, so also in Jaspers the *Good* has to do with a sense of the All-Encompassing (*das Umgreifende*) reality in which the act of transcending and the Being of Transcendence co-join without confusion in the project of *mögliche Existenz*. So considered, the *Good* has to do with an experiential reality which is simultaneously within and without; with, as he puts it, a "possible impossibility," with that "thinkable Unthinkable" that is the goal of philosophical faith. [26]

Jaspers does not understand transcendental unity in the Platonic tradition as the result of a trans-logical predication of an hypostatized *Idea* but rather as the result of a fundamental philosophical intuition which has the quality of being all-encompassing or "comprehensive." As fundamental philosophical experience, it is existentially transforming, " ... a deepening of knowledge – self-realization in the purity of mind – an attainment unto the vision of the highest." [27] Speaking of Intelligence and its transcendent analogue, the One, Plotinus says, " ... one

---

[25] *Great Phil.*, p. 45. Cf., also II, pp. 56ff., and *Phil.*, III, pp. 195ff.
[26] *Phil.*, III, pp. 8-10, 43.
[27] Cf., *Great Phil.*, II, pp. 79-80.

must think of it as quiet, unwavering movement; embracing all things and all Being, and that in its multiplicity it is both indivisible and divisible." [28] Because of the descriptively ineffable character of this experience, Platonism and all true metaphysics *founders* at the task of specifying the exact nature of the *One* or Transcendence-Itself. Indeed in Jaspers this foundering is central, for "the freer our grasp of transcending being, the more decisively will its objective supports be destroyed." [29] For Jaspers, however (and not least as philosophical psychologist), what is important in this foundering is that the subject clearly intends what is beyond its capacity to describe. [30] Plotinus, however, is not merely content with the psychological characteristics of the intended Other, but gives quite specific analyses concerning its nature. Therefore what Plotinus says is especially germane in relation to Jaspers who maintains similarly that the act or experience of transcending in relation to Transcendence must be kept distinct from the Being of Transcendence-Itself. Without this differentiation, what Jaspers describes as transcending-thinking would really be no different from process philosophy or what Walter Schulz refers to as the "wholesale reduction of metaphysics to subjectivity . . .with God as just another form of subjectivity." [31] In Jaspers' frame of reference, neither a cosmic process nor existential reflection in themselves can provide the end of transcending-thinking, namely Eternalization. Jaspers' proclivity for theo-philosophical imagery, therefore, is not without its design, for his work from start to finish moves toward that which can only be termed the "objectivity" of Transcendence-Itself as the Encompassing even though it can never be hold of as "object." One might say that just as theology is incomplete apart from a phenomenologically cogent understanding of the process of transcending, philosophy is equally deficient without an understanding or apprehension of that extra-subjective reality which can alone grant *Eternalization*, namely God. [32] As in the case of his own notion of the Encompassing, Jaspers believes that what Plotinus affirms concerning the One is beyond both materialism and gnosticism; that as the pristine apprehension of authen-

---

[28] *Ennead,* IV, 9, 5.
[29] *Phil.,* III, p. 17.
[30] Cf., *Chiffren der Transzendenz,* p. 21ff., *Psych. der Welt., passim.*
[31] *Der Gott der neuzeitlichen Metaphysik* (Pfullingen: Neske, 1957), pp. 111-112.
[32] Here, as well as in the previous section, one immediately thinks of the influence of Plotinus' "God above God" on the theologian Paul Tillich. If it can be said that Tillich is the theologian of the "boundary situation," then Jaspers is his philosophical counterpart. Cf., *Systematic Theology,* I., p. 233ff., for Tillich's interpretation of Plotinus' "Highest".

tic philosophizing, the All-Encompassing outstrips all reductionism. While materialism represents a strictly "this-worldly" resignation, gnosticism, in the process of renouncing the world, "objectifies Transcendence" through esoteric claims to direct and unimpeded knowledge of Transcendence-Itself. What Plotinus offers, according to Jaspers, is not a dialectic between two different worlds between which one must choose, but rather "a fundamental operation of thought . . . something radically different, namely the striving to go beyond both groups of categories, beyond the sensory world and the cosmos of the intelligible to Above-Being and Non-Being."[33] In other words, authentic metaphysical transcending utterly dissolves oppositions in the vision of Unity: "There is no differentiation . . . (The One) does not think, it is not mind, for since it is unwanting and related to nothing outside itself, it does not need to think; nor does it think itself, for in it there is no differentiation or multiplicity, hence it has no self-consciousness. However, and this is all important, what is not thought in thinking must not be interpreted as nothingness, but as superabundance . . . It is that from which everything else is and lives." [34] In sum, "What Plotinus discovers is the summit of thinking . . . not an isolated, anomalous state but the completion and confirmation of intellectual life." [35]

As in the cipher of "Absolute Consciousness" (*absolutes Bewusstseins*) – the decisive moment of *Existenzerhellung* – the transcending movement of reflective thinking in both Plotinus and Jaspers is movement towards the Absolute. Just as Plotinus' "intellectual principle" points beyond itself to the One and *is* only because the *One Is*, so also Jaspers' theorem of consciousness rests squarely on the conviction that the origin and goal of transcending-thinking is Transcendence-Itself, [36] i.e., it is Transcendence as the One which underlies primordially and teleologically the reality of both experience and possible reflection on experience. Moreover, just as Jaspers' cipher of Transcendence is not coexistensive with the Being of Transcendence-Itself, neither is there an empirically demonstra-

---

[33] *Great Phil.*, II., pp. 67, 80. Cf., also *Phil.*, III, p. 12f., "Superstition materializes things and positivistic unbelief dissolves them into illusions."

[34] *Great Phil.*, II., p. 49. Cf., Plotinus, *Enneads*, IV, 9, lff. It is the Plotinian notion of the One that undergirds the ontological aspect of Jaspers' Transcendent Encompassing at every turn.

[35] *Ibid.*, p. 49.

[36] Although Heidegger's understanding of this relationship has a great deal in common with Jaspers and has Greek origins as well, he reserves judgment concerning the Being of any Transcendence beyond that of the act of transcending. Both also claim to refine their notion of Transcendence on the basis of the Kantian "Supersensible," as we will see in the next chapter.

ble relationship between Plotinus' intellectual principle and the One. As Plotinus states, "Certainly this Absolute is not any of the things of which it is the source – its nature is that nothing can be affirmed of it – not existence, not essence, not life, since it is that which transcends all these. But possess yourself of it by the very elimination of Being, and you behold a marvel. Thrusting forward to This, attaining and resting in yourself, seek to grasp it more and more, understanding it by that intuitive thrust alone, but knowing its greatness by the Beings that follow upon it and exist by its power." [37]

This, then, is "Eternalization." Once having experienced the "power of Being," as Tillich calls it, [38] questions of verification disappear and what remains is the only appropriate mode of response, viz., the ultimate apophasis of "silent presence." As Plotinus states, "Once you have uttered *The Good*, add no further thought for by any addition and in proportion to that addition, you introduce a deficiency." [39]

Jaspers' affinity to Plotinian and indeed Buddhist metaphors of "silence," however, is altered by the strong influence of Christian mystics like Eckhart and Cusanus who maintain a constructive attitude regarding the apologetical potentialities of *viva vox*. Even though Jaspers is no evangelist, he is sensitive to the inter-subjective and "linguistic" nature of Eternalization. For as he puts it, it is "*language* [that] makes Transcendence intelligible in the consciousness of Existenz . . . the possibility of historic comunity."[40] The exact character of this concern, however, will be a subject of consideration in Part III.

In summary, there can be little doubt that Jaspers' intellectual ancestry, as in the case of so many other German thinkers is rooted in the unique philosophic spirituality of Plato and Plotinus. In drawing these analogies, however, we have in no way tried to minimize the uniqueness of Jaspers' philosophical contribution. On the contrary, we have tried to show how Jaspers himself tries to maintain something of a "boundary position" in the course of his own interpretation which will forcefully interrelate the act of transcending and the Being of Transcendence and yet preserve their separate identities; a boundary situation that is intrin-

---

[37] *Enneads*, V, 9, 8. Because of the utterly apophatic quality of Plotinus' description of the "One," it is impossible (from a theological standpoint) to conclude whether it is basically a negative or positive reality, for it is both and neither.

[38] It is precisely the mystical, neo-Platonic quality of Tillich's attitude towards "Being-Itself" or God that underlies the force of his famous sermon on "acceptance." Cf., *Shaking the Foundations* (Scribners; 1956).

[39] *Enneads*, III, 8, 10. Cf., also *Phil.*, III, pp. 18-19, 204ff.

[40] *Phil.*, III., pp. 7-8.

sic to the Platonist tradition. Through this existential interpretation we
have seen that from the very beginnings of the idealist tradition, Transcendence is grasped actively and intuitively *not* by a leap out of the
world (as is so frequently thought), nor is it the result of resignation to the
organic-sensate world alone. Transcendence is known on the basis of
carefully delineated "thought steps" or conversions in consciousness
which are latent to the potentiality of conscious experience. Therefore,
Transcendence is not known on the basis of a simple induction from lower to higher forms of life nor on the basis of deduction from so-called
higher realms of Being. It is rather the result of clear reflection on the
nature of consciousness as a "dynamic structure," to use Lonergan's
phrase, in which and through which immanence and Transcendence
coincide. Because of the intrinsically *mysterious* nature of the presence of
Transcendence in human experience, its exact character can never be
specified and the philosopher is forced to move into the evanescent language of ciphers, as in Plotinus' poetic allusion to that "Eternal Spring
that has no source beyond itself."[41] Rooted in experiences, the conceptual cipher goes out from itself and returns to itself – a "qualified negativity" – even though in the process traces of Transcendence-Itself remain.

Because of the ambiguity of such utterances one might ask, why,
even granting the possibility of such an experience, say anything
at all? Since philosophical language can never hope to locate
Transcendence with any fixity, why spend one's time trying to speak
the Unspeakable? Wouldn't one be better advised to maintain the
metaphysical humility of a Wittgenstein, on the one hand, or de-
marcate the philosophical and theological enterprises completely as
in the case of a Barth, on the other? Such options, for Jaspers, are unten-
able for they are tantamount to the denial of possible Existenz. Since
Transcendence lies within the purview of human experience as possibility (in fact, as representative of possibility in its most immediate symbolic form) the project of Transcendence is not to be denied whatever the
cost. During the 1930's especially, when Jaspers began his work on the
subject of Transcendence, freedom itself was at stake. With the secular-
ist's reduction of experience to mere technic and function, and with a
plethora of self-generated myths and illusions, the task of "naming the
Unnamable"[42] became a project of desperate urgency. Whether then or
now, one can simply not be content with relinquishing the question of

---

[41] *Enneads*, III, 8, 10.
[42] *Man in the Modern Age*, p. 179ff.

Transcendence to the archives of antiquity and simply go about one's business. The perennial task of philosophy is rather that of making present the reality of Transcendence latent to experience; a presence that accounts for its very possibility. Moreover, for Jaspers, this rendering present is not simply a task for the poet, but the task for rigorous, logical and operational inquiries as well; the perennial task of determining what it means to be human. "Transcendence," as Jaspers asserts eloquently, "strikes me as a *reality without possibility*, as the absolute reality beyond which there is nothing . . . before which I stand mute." [43]

But Jaspers, like most other Western mystical philosophers, does not really "stand mute." Jaspers, as in the case of his famous contemporary Martin Heidegger, spends an entire philosophical career attempting to speak the silence of the Transcendent All Encompassing – the "ancient name of Being." Indeed, it is Kant, for both Jaspers and Heidegger, who is viewed as the critical source for this possibility, and it is precisely this that radically differentiates their interpretations of Kant from the mainstream. What Kant means for Jaspers will become clear in the next chapter. How Jaspers and Heidegger have moved in quite separate directions out of their respectively *creative* and indeed *visionary* interpretations of Kant will become evident in Part III.

---

[43] *Phil.*, III, pp. 8-9.

CHAPTER SIX

JASPERS AND KANT

Jaspers stated frequently that Max Weber influenced him more than any other person.[1] True as this may be biographically, the fact remains that formally and historically Jaspers' philosophy is virtually unthinkable apart from the influence of Immanuel Kant. "Kant," as Jaspers puts it, "is the nodal point of philosophy . . . the absolutely indispensable philosopher. Without him we would have no basis for criticism."[2] For Jaspers, then, Kant is not the psyche-shattering "Robespierre" about which Heinrich Heine mused, and least of all in relation to metaphysics. The critical philosophy of Kant represents rather for Jaspers an essential refinement of the transcending-thinking that is contiguous with the metaphysical spirit of Plato and Plotinus. What is decisive in Kant, however, is the logical purification of this spirit through showing how what is thought and thereby asserted is inextricably conditioned by the way one thinks.[3] In a word, Jaspers believes that in Kant, for the first time in the history of Western philosophy, we are shown that critical philosophizing is necessarily existential; that the imprint of subjectivity upon what is thought is not just accidental but formally inevitable.

The so-called Copernican Revolution of Kant, however, by no means represents the reduction of cognition to subjectivity and relativism. Quite the contrary, Jaspers believes that Kant's critical attitude is based on the insight that neither the phenomenal world nor the world of ideas, neither the physical nor the mental in and of themselves, are sufficient indices to adjudicate the nature of reality. However, when viewed as a dynamic structure or dialectic, these dimensions of experience not only provide the ground of possible experience but refer to an antecedent ground out of which subject-object, mind-body distinctions arise, name-

---

Cf., *Three Essays: Leonardo, Descartes and Weber* (New York: Harcourt, Brace and World, 1964), pp. 189ff., and "Philosophical Autobiography," *The Philosophy of Karl Jaspers*, Schilpp edition, pp. 55ff.
 [2] *Great Phil.*, I, pp. 380-381.
 [3] *Ibid.*, pp. 243, 317ff., 373; *Psych. der Welt.*, p. 471ff.

ly a "supersensible," encompassing, Ground of Being. As in the case of Jaspers' dialectic of *Weltorientierung* and *Transzendenz*, the Kantian formal categories of percept and concept, space and time, represent the dialectical foci of experience within whose boundaries understanding develops. The task of metaphysics, then, is that of delineating the exact nature of the middle ground or "boundary" within these dialectical dualities. For Kant, this synthetic middle ground has to do with the schema producing capacity of the transcendental imagination, and the transcendental imagination for Jaspers, is the crucible of the cipher-language of possible Existenz. Practically all of Kant's philosophizing, Jaspers believes, represents a search for clearer understanding of this middle ground: "Although this middle ground is always found through the operations of understanding, it is never a known object, but rather a mode in which something, which *in itself* remains hidden, is disclosed to us . . . Whenever Kant fixates dualities, he raises the question of the link between them, the middle term. The middle term is present in the actuality of the individual and as the Supersensible One which is disclosed in it. To the dogmatist who considers the dualities as indispensable positions and sources of clarity, the middle term seems to be a leap into the bottomless abyss of a disclosure of a hidden root from which everything springs. But the middle term does *not* negate the dualities. In penetrating the dualities it aims to elucidate the riddle and *not* solve it. Once fully known, the middle term would be meaningless."[4]

Because the self – as the middle, constituting and synthesizing agency of meaning – is involved so intimately in the process of determining what is known, many after Kant (especially the neo-Kantians who focused largely on the formal mechanics of the deduction) developed an utterly skeptical attitude towards the possibility of all metaphysics.[5] This, of course, is not to suggest that the skeptical attitude of much modern philosophy is contingent entirely upon the critical philosophy of Kant. It is rather to suggest that Kant's refutation of the naïve ocular-realist has unfortunately reinforced the nominalist mood of most modern philosophy. In Jaspers, however, the opposite is the case. Adapting the critical epistemological insights of Kant to the language of Existenz, Jaspers recovers what he believes to be the essential intent and purpose of Kantian *Kritik*, namely a disclosure of the *limits* of objectifying thinking which

---

[4] *Great Phil.*, I, p. 315.
[5] Cf., for example, Anders Nygren's *Method and Meaning, op. cit.*, as characteristic of the rapprochement this influential neo-Kantian theologian makes with the most anti-metaphysical advocates of language analysis.

does not put an end to thinking, but permits transcending or true meta-physical thinking to begin at a critical level. Describing the "transcend-ing" nature of Kantian method, Jaspers is really speaking of his own: "This transcending does not take him [Kant] to another realm, but a transcending it remains, because it is a totally different operation from any that we perform in our knowledge of the world."[6] Jaspers therefore suggests that Kantian transcendental philosophy is certainly not cosmo-ontological transcending, if by that is implied a logical and analytical preparation for a leap beyond the world of ordinary experience. It is rather a transcending-thinking which by remaining completely within the world goes beyond the world. While cognition is utterly dependent upon the material for the presentation of sensate phenomena, Jaspers believes nevertheless that in Kant (as well as in Plato and Plotinus) one encounters the conviction that "where cognition stops, thinking contin-ues." Therefore, at the very limits of conscious experience the Kantian "Supersensible" appears, but it is an appearance which, as in the case of Jaspers' transcendence-Itself, can only be captured fragmentarily in the metaphorical ciphers of possible Existenz. Jaspers provides a strong warning to those who would understand Kant's limitation of reason, and therefore consciousness, in any other way: "Misinterpretation of Kantian thinking can result in two perversions: we can slip back into the world, as though Kant were concerned with only a theory of knowledge by which to justify the validity of science; or we can slip back into the old metaphysics. In the first case we lose Transcendence; in the second, we lose the world. But in Kant the two are inseparable; the world is not illusion but appearance; the phenomenal world is not intrinsic being, but the language of Transcendence."[7]

We now turn to the task of explicating in detail some of the basic paral-lels between Jaspers and Kant on the matter of transcending-thinking.

---

[6] *Great Phil.*, I, p. 322. This is not dissimilar from the thesis of Toulmin and Janik con-cerning the motivation behind the "real" Wittgenstein. Cf., *Wittgenstein's Vienna, op. cit.*, *passim.*

[7] *Great Phil.*, I, p. 323. The well-known Kantian expositor H.J. Paton would basically corroborate Jaspers' understanding of the nature of Transcendence in Kant's writings. In-sofar as the noumenon can be identified with Transcendence-Itself, it is neither equatable with idea nor world but rather with a reality not dissimilar to the scholastic notion of the "Known Unknown" even though this apprehension is beyond the objectifying tendencies of ordinary language. Hence both Kant's noumenon and Jaspers' Transcendence-Itself are reminders that the mere choice between empiricism and idealism is inadequate. Paton, however, is much more willing to admit that Kant himself is ambiguous on this matter. Cf. *Kant's Metaphysic of Experience*, I (London: Allen and Unwin, Ltd., 1936), pp. 63-65, 71.

First, we will compare Kant's understanding of reason with that of Jaspers'; secondly, we will contrast the Kantian Supersensible with Jaspers' Transcendence-Itself; and finally, we will deal briefly with the voluntarism of Kant and Jaspers.

COGNITIVE TRANSCENDING AND RATIONALITY

Basic to idealism is the conviction that the common sense orientation of self to world does not produce knowledge of the "real" or Being. The mere fact that sensate world orientation occurs is not in itself decisive since this operation is shared instinctively by both animals and human beings by virtue of simply existing as organisms in the world. Therefore, even though one can predicate some kind of experience of world in all forms of life, only experience together with reflection produces a sense of "being-in-a-world." In other words, critically reflective experience alone asks whether the world that is experienced is the real, essential or meaningful world.[8] For both Kant and Jaspers that which we call experience is meaningful only when it is coupled with cognitive transcending, that is, experience that is experientially self-conscious or reflective. Through critically reflective experience one discovers that things are not necessarily what they appear to be and hence one seeks more reliable methods of attaining knowledge of the real. However, it is not just the quest for reliable knowledge about reality that represents the kind of transcending-thinking Jaspers has in mind, for mere *quest* can take place at a wholly uncritical level. Critical transcending, by contrast, is a transcending in thinking-itself, that is, it is "transcendental" in the Kantian sense of reflection about the possibilities and limitations of cognition.

In such a manner is Kant the "nodal point" of modern philosophy for Jaspers, for it was Kant who clearly and systematically showed that "all thinking includes the *I think* and that some kind of "understanding is present to every perception."[9] Of even greater significance for Jaspers, however, is Kant's discovery that the uniqueness of rationality lies not in a one-to-one correlation of reason with some thing called mind or intellect, but lies rather in the fact that rationality points to an antecedent

---

[8] Stated otherwise, the difference is that of merely "existing" in a world as an entity alongside other entities and "being" in a world as "project." Even though the Heideggerian as well as the Jaspersian notion of "world" sometimes has the force of an abstract "idea," it is always rooted *in-der-Welt-sein*. Cf., *Being and Time*, esp. Section 69.
[9] *Great Phil.*, I, pp. 251-252; *Psych. der Welt.*, p. 455ff.

ground which provides the possibility of any meaning whatsoever; in other words, in the underlying synthetic capacity for a "perpetual separating and combining of concepts and percepts." [10] It is precisely as a synthetic process that rationality can never be understood as static thing or objectifiable event but rather as eventful transcending. The critical idealist's conviction that there is a disjunction or separation between the knower and the known must never be construed as a Cartesian dualism nor even a provisional kind of dualism (except, in Jaspers' case, under the methodological heading of qualified negativity) that can be resolved ultimately by the transcendental ego as in Fichte or absolute mind in the case of Hegel. Mind, for Jaspers, is but an abstraction encompassed by the far more profound reality out of which all abstractions arise. All such abstractions must, for Jaspers, be perceived against the horizon of *das Umgreifende* as the intervening bond between cognition and the possibility of cognition; the bond of *mögliche Existenz*. Hence objectivity and subjectivity, the material and the conceptual, are simply overlapping dialectical modes rooted in the mediational operations of the rational consciousness which is always *more* than the merely rational. The proximity of Kantian rationality and Jaspers' cognitive transcending is clearly illustrated in the following quotation: "What does Kant mean when he repeatedly and expressly says that the common root of cognition, of the two stems, is a mystery? He does not derive the dichotomy of the subject and object from a conceptual One as the source of all things but explains how being becomes actuality for us in this dichotomy and how, through the elucidation of the area in which we think, we can perhaps, in our thinking, pass beyond it, transcend it." [11]

Jaspers believes, then, that the subject-object relation in Kant does not represent a dualism that can be resolved only by some form of absolute idealism, on the one hand, or the metaphysical resignation of various forms of nominalistic empiricism on the other. The task is rather one of becoming aware of the encompassing character of rational consciousness (*Vernunft*) whereupon authentic transcending is understood not as a denial but as an affirmation of the dialectical nature of experience and meaning. If, however, the subject-object relation is construed as an insurmountable formal barrier or an either/or alternative, resolution can

---

[10] *Ibid.* For Heidegger, this *intuitus originarius* is *Dasein* itself as the intentional "for the sake of . . . ," or the "source of possibility as such." Cf., *The Essence of Reasons*, pp. 93-97. For Jaspers, however, it is Transcendence-Itself as the dialectical correlate of Existenz. Immanence alone cannot provide for this synthetic possibility. Cf., Appendix.

[11] *Great Phil.*, I, p. 255.

only come through reductionism of one form or another. But if rational consciousness is understood as more than either matter or idea in isolation, consciousness-itself becomes the basis for cognitive transcending, and one is, according to Jaspers, on the edge of boundless philosophical and religious possibility. For Jaspers as for Tillich, the "dialectical" as well as the "existential" task is one of *auf dieser Grenze zu bleiben.*

Just as concept and percept are inseparable in the act of understanding for Kant, so also for Jaspers immanence and Transcendence constitute the two foci of possible Existenz. To be sure, there is a lengthening of Kantian terminology to fit the existential character of Jaspers' overall work, but as we have seen, it is based on solid epistemological preparation rooted in Kant. In fact, when the commenatry in *The Great Philosophers* is compared with earlier commentary in *Psychologie der Weltanschauungen*, one sees how Jaspers' original attitude concerning Kantian "Ideen als die Ganzheiten der Erfahrungsrichtungen ... und Erfahrungsinhalten" is abandoned for Jaspers' notion of *das Umgreifende* as that through which "all cognitive formulations acquire first meaning."[12] Even though Jaspers, in *Psychologie der Weltanschauungen*, is clearly aware that Kant's "transcendental ideas are not constitutive of objectivity,"[13] this awareness is sharpened in his later works where *Vernunft* is always understood as "rational consciousness," which is not merely the repository of the categories so many commentators regard as arbitrarily Newtonian, but rather the encompassing ground of Transcendence-Itself. Just as consciousness, since Freud, has been frequently divided into the conscious and the unconscious, so also false polarity is sometimes introduced into the Kantian distinction between the manifold of sense intuition and the transcendental categories. What both Jaspers, Heidegger, and H.J. Paton (see footnote no. 20) find in Kant is an insistence on the compossibility of rational consciousness and experience and that for experience to be experience it must be reliable and intelligible. Transcendental philosophy therefore is, falsified the moment one relies *only* on a logical, psychological or methodological interpretation. It is the "existential" dimension which, as we will see further in the next section, permits one to apprehend the "Supersensible" reality that is, in fact, the ground and possibility of transcending-thinking.

---

[12] *Psych. der Welt.*, pp. 471-478, and *Great Phil.*, I, p. 255ff.
[13] *Psych. der Welt.*, p. 446.

For those who regard Kant's transcendental turn as the first act in a philosophical movement which finds its logical completion in Fichte and Hegel, Jaspers' interpretation of Kant (as well as Heidegger's)[14] is bound to sound arbitrary because it is quite unconventional. Nevertheless, Jaspers offers sound warning as to the outcome of failing to read Kant's first critique existentially. If Jaspers is wrong, that is, if Kant's critique of rationality does not itself provide the mediational possibility for transcending-thinking, then one has, on the one hand, no option other than scientific positivism, absolute idealism or some other notion of a preestablished harmony between self and world; or, on the other hand, irrational subjectivism and other forms of uncritical emotionalism. But such options are precisely what Jaspers wished to avoid and what he believes Kant, for the most part, avoided.[15] The task of critical-transcending-philosophizing is rather that of rational investigation into the dynamic ground of experience even though the philosopher is faced with the impossible task of communicating that which can only be known non-objectively within the confinements of objectifying language. To this end, then, and aware of the internal limitations of both language and cognition, Jaspers designs his cipher-script as the existential complement to Kant's paradoxes, antinomies and paralogisms; linguistic devices which, as metaphorical substantives, become an appeal to that Encompassing of rational consciousness which can never be formally or empirically captured but which underlies the very possibility of critique in the first place.[16] Whether through the highly formalized and analytical investigations of Kant or through the poetic and literary tenor of Jaspers' *Existenzphilosophie*, the purpose of critical and therefore existentially au-

---

[14] Cf., Heidegger's *Kant and the Problem of Metaphysics*, trans. James Churchill (Bloomington: Indiana University Press, 1962), esp. pp. 7-25.

[15] This reservation holds for Kant who, after the first *Critique*, Jaspers believes, became increasingly a dogmatist. Cf., *Great Phil.*, I, pp. 367-370.

[16] One cannot give enough emphasis to Jaspers' particular slant on Kant, for if one loses sight of the fact that Kant's transcendental critique of reason is first and foremost an existentially transcending philosophy which strives toward a comprehensiveness which is both morally and analytically sound, one will be led down the road of a long and laborious search for the *Ding-an-Sich*. Pseudo-scientific philosophizing, according to Jaspers, can never understand Kant or the idealist tradition, for it is always looking for "objects within the whole rather than perceiving the whole within the whole." *Great Phil.*, I, pp. 267-268. By "perceiving," of course, Jaspers means "intuiting," and the notion is not without its own ambiguities for in Jaspers as in Kant the term *Anschauung* in various contexts sometimes refers to the "act" of intuiting or "taking in" and other times to the "content" of that intuition. Cf., *Critique of Pure Reason*, A 20B 33-34; A 190B 235-236. We will deal with this problem further in Part III when we take up the notion of "cipher" in detail. In brief, the English equivalent term "intuition" simply does not have the integrative force of the German term *Anschauung*.

thentic philosophizing is that of elucidating the limits of language and cognition and discovering that at these very limits – and beyond – thinking somehow continues. As in the case of the metaphor, the reality of Transcendence is captured "indirectly" by permitting it to be a lie, that is, through "foundering", whereupon the Encompassing ground of Consciousness-Itself is apprehended. As Jaspers puts it, "From understanding as a faculty spring the categories of definite objects; from reason as a faculty spring the Ideas of a non-objective, indeterminate totality." [17]

In summary, there can be little doubt that Jaspers' method of transcending-thinking is firmly rooted in Kant's understanding of rationality. Because of the transcendental capacity of reason to reflect on its own operations, that is, to become fully cognizant of both its potentialities and limitations, "thinking transcends." But contrary to Heidegger, this transcending capability is not merely the intrinsic possibility of *Dasein* because for Jaspers Transcendence is more than time understood as the realm or "region" (*Bezirk*) of the "question" about world and Being. [18] Jaspers believes that there is a sense in which Transcendence-Itself as non-objective "Other" impinges upon consciousness as *intuitus originarius* (what Kant call the "Supersensible"), and that this impingement is both dependent on and independent of experience. To a fuller consideration of this exceedingly difficult notion we now turn.

TRANSCENDENCE-ITSELF AND THE SUPERSENSIBLE

The driving force behind Kant's transcendental deduction of categories, according to Jaspers, is his awareness of the reality of the "Supersensible" (*das Übersinnliche*). In the quest for the knowledge of Being, Jaspers stresses the Kantian observation that univocal propositions concerning the nature of reality – when pressed – result in antinomies, paralogisms and tautologies; that these paradoxes are not the result of extra-mental disjunction but arise out of the nature of cognition itself. At first impres-

---

[17] *Great Phil.*, I, p. 273; cf., also Paton, *op. cit.*, p. 71f.
[18] Cf., *The Essence of Reasons*, Part II, p. 34ff. Written in reaction to Husserl, Heidegger, sharply differentiating between the transcendental "idea" and the transcendentally "Ideal," says that the latter "as the highest plateau of Kantian metaphysics" demands a "waiver" of interpretation (p. 73). The implication, of course, is that Heidegger is not willing to follow Kant "beyond" that point where he believes that he stops being "critical" and lapses into Christianity. The degree to which Jaspers becomes a "champion of supersensible reason," as Kant himself warns, will be a subject of further consideration in Part III. Cf., *Critique of Pure Reason*, A 639 = B 667.

sion this would suggest that reason is totally unable to arrive at anything resembling ontological knowledge. But for Jaspers, as we have seen, the discovery that reason cannot operate as metaphysical realists once claimed does not put an end to metaphysics but only ontology. As in the case of Kierkegaard, the logical paradoxes of transcendental reflection point to a deeper reality through paradox whereby one apprehends a reality which can only be termed haltingly the "Supersensible" or Transcendence-Itself; a reality which is not known as an object but which beckons as "cipher." Ontology, then, is reconstituted as existential metaphysics; the kind of metaphysics which has characterized authentic philosophizing from the very beginning, including, Jaspers contends, the critical philosophy of Kant.

Jaspers believes, therefore, that the numinous "Supersensible" hovers at the boundaries of everything Kant wrote and is Kant's abiding philosophical motivation.[19] It is against the evanescent horizon of the "Supersensible" that Jaspers considers the Kantian delimitation of metaphysics as a positive and not a negative philosophical development. By indicating as clearly as possible the boundaries and limitations of human cognition, Jaspers believes that Kant already performed the first step in an intellectual conversion away from metaphysical speculation erroneously conceived as pseudo-science, and towards the existential foundering metaphysics that is his own. Whatever credence metaphysics may have surrendered as a science through its transcendental turn is really no sacrifice at all but a long needed catharsis. Just as Kant felt cleansed of the mental cobwebs of Wolffian metaphysics, so also Jaspers believes that Kant restored to metaphysics its originating depths within human experience. It is in this sence that Jaspers regards his own philosophizing as a continuation of the basic "intention" of Kant[20], an intention driven and sustained by the reality of Transcendence, but which stands in need of a conceptual clarification and a concretization that can be provided in *Existenzphilosophie*.

---

[19] *Great Phil.*, I, pp. 284ff., 311ff.

[20] Although Paton agrees that Kant's critical philosophy is scarcely intelligible apart from the realization that an awareness of the non-objectifiable reality of noumena is decisive in the formulation of the first *critique*, he would also call attention to Kant's warning that "What *limits* must be kept distinct from that which is *limited*." Cf., *Critique of Pure Reason*, A 515 = B 543. Paton, to a much higher degree than Jaspers, believes that "we must not delude ourselves into the supposition that this negative and necessary limitation (of reason) is at the same time a positive knowledge of a world beyond." *Kant's Metaphysic of Experience*, Vol. II, *op. cit.*, p. 461f. Jaspers, of course, would agree concerning any "positive knowledge" concerning a "world beyond" but not as nullification of the experience of "Otherness." It is precisely in the context of a purist interpretation of Kant that Jaspers warns "Kantian scholasticism is the most threadbare scholasticism of all."

What then is the Supersensible of Kant and how is it related to Jaspers' understanding of Transcendence? The first clues, according to Jaspers, are the Kantian Ideas as the formalizing principles underlying the functional schematisms of the transcendental imagination. One must discern the manner in which these Ideas are demonstrably linked to and ultimately dependent upon the existence of a Supersensible Absolute. [21] It is not, therefore, the *quid juris* function of the transcendental deduction of categories which is of decisive significance for Jaspers nor is it their psychological function concerning the nature and identity of the self. It is rather the objective status of these Ideas that is sought. In relation to the operations of transcending-thinking, these Ideas point to an "indeterminate totality" which is beyond ideation but upon which ideation rests and which presents that which is present to experience. Jaspers puts it this way: "Kant, as Plato, was well aware that our faculty of knowledge feels a much higher need than merely to spell out our experience according to a synthetic unity in order to be able to read them as experience. He knew that our reason naturally exalts itself to modes of knowledge which so far transcend the bounds of ordinary experience that no given empirical object can ever coincide with them but which are by no means mere fictions of the brain." [22] Summarizing the Kantian movement of transcending-thinking and its relation to the Supersensible-Transcendent, Jaspers continues: "The structure of knowledge begins with sensibility and its chaos of sensations, rises to space and time as the forms of intuition, then to the categories which provide the objectivity determined from the intelligible, and lastly to Ideas whereby knowledge progresses toward synthetic unity. *In this existence of knowledge which in itself cannot be concluded but remains open, the Supersensible makes itself felt by acts, not through any known content. In the phenomenality produced by the understanding, the Ideas are the breach through which the Supersensible enters into knowledge.*" [23]

Kant, therefore, according to Jaspers, is not only concerned with delineating the limits of knowing but with laying the foundations for what might be called a metaphysics of Transcendence. An elucidation of the limits of knowing is the first and essential step toward this end. By paying close attention to the implicitly Socratic dimension of Kant, Jaspers sees

---

[21] The same question, of course, applies to the "eternal objects" of "prehension" in Whitehead.

[22] *Great Phil.*, I, pp. 284.

[23] *Ibid.*, (emphasis, mine). This "breach" to which Jaspers refers is elsewhere described as the "rupture of immanence," *Phil.*, III, p. 13.

that the proper route towards an authentic metaphysic is not that of imposing an ontology on experience but rather permitting a metaphysic to grow out of experience. In the process of elucidating experience and understanding, the transcending subject discovers the Supersensible foundation of experience and thinking which, although it cannot be fixated as an object, is nevertheless experienced as a presence "closer to me than I am to myself," to use the language of the mystics. Again Jaspers states: "This transcending of the understanding with the understanding does not permit any isolated faculty to operate without the understanding. But from other sources the understanding derives functions it could not derive from itself alone. The transcending of understanding takes the form of 'reflecting judgment,' which legislates for itself but never defines an object. *This movement implies the divine intuitive understanding, the divine teleological understanding, the union of all our faculties in the Supersensible Substrate of mankind, our intelligible being as freedom – but all this indirectly; they never become objects.* Of this transcending of the understanding Kant says, 'The transition is not to another thing, but to another way of using reason.' But in each case, there is a leap; from correct knowledge to essential truth, from the action that is correct to ethical action, from the correct judgment of taste to the aesthetic idea – in each case, from a conditioned to an unconditioned, from finite to infinite, from the endless to the meaningful, self-contained Whole." [24]

In his *Critique of Pure Reason*, Kant says, " . . . our intuition of spaces as limited presupposes the existence of an all-encompassing space," and "the infinitude of time signifies nothing more than that every determinate magnitude of time is possible only through limitation of the one single time which underlies it." [25] Thus, for Kant, as Jaspers, while knowledge appears to be disjoint, while the subject-object structure of human experience presupposes the tension of this relationship, and while this disjointness can never be overcome in-the-world, it is nevertheless a disjointness which is both operationally and ideally rooted in Unity. Jaspers further insists that this experience of "Divine Unity" is not due to blind

---

[24] *Ibid.*, p. 285, (emphasis, mine).

[25] *Critique of Pure Reason*, A 25 B 39; B 48. One finds a similar parallel in the transcendental Thomism of Bernard Lonergan who, in his philosophy of understanding and judgment, speaks about the dialectic of the "virtually unconditional" and the "formally unconditioned" or, obliquely, the scholastic dialectic of the "Known-Unknown and the Unknown-Unknown, as the only way in which knowledge of any kind can take place. In other words the "question" about reality itself has a "heuristic structure" even though it is not very frequently recognized or understood. When it is, one not only becomes partisan to epistemological "insight" but engages in the first step towards a constructive metaphysic. Cf., *Insight* (New York: Philosophical Library, 1956), and *Method in Theology*, p. 105f.

faith based on a leap into irrationalism, but rather due to a sense of the mystery intrinsic to the unfathomable limits of experience, for "the unfathomable is not the irrational; it is rather something which reason experiences at the limits of reason and draws into the light of reason." [26] Transcending for Kant, as for Jaspers, is always cognitive transcending, a transcending through thinking.

What then is the experiential connection or link between this transfigured or converted understanding of understanding and the Divine Ground of reason? Is it intuition? Jaspers maintains that in Kant as well as himself, the existence of the Divine is not based on logical and epistemological demonstration alone but one which is also existential, or, following Kant, a moral proof from within. But here also, as in more formal metaphysical speculation, one can only speak about ciphers of the Divine and not cogent demonstrations of the Divine-Itself. One is then led to ask if the Supersensible, so essential to Jaspers' overall system, is incapable of being demonstrated except by poetic allusions having to do with overlap of cognitivity and affectivity (something which I touch in ciphers at the outer reaches of my experience), and in what sense can I ever interpret this as the existence of Transcendence-Itself apart from propositions arising out of religious belief and faith? It is one thing to speak of the *intuitus originarius* of an *intellectus archetypus* and quite another to move from this to an affirmation of a Transcendence that is non-identical with the act or experience of transcending. Heidegger similarly speaks about "Transcendence as the realm of the question," but emphatically denies that it indicates anything beyond the basic structure of Dasein. In other words, in making the case for *Dasein als Transzendenz*, one does not advance hypotheses concerning that which is beyond the boundaries transcended. Thus in English translation, the Heideggerian usage of *Transzendenz* is strictly verbal with none of the substantival resonances Jaspersian usage implies. [27] How, in short, can one say with any kind of authority that the "breach" created by transcendental Ideas in the process of self-critical reflection is an "opening" through which the Supersensible "appears," rather than simply conclude that such *Spalten* are logical and structural rifts. It is clear that Kant himself is much more cautious in the way he uses the terms "transcendent" and "transcendental" suggesting that they are not interchangeable terms since the former refers to the illusion that a transcendent category has validity in and of

---

[26] *Great Phil.*, I, p. 313; in short, a logically induced "logical collapse." Cf., *Phil.*, III, p. 16ff.
[27] Cf., *The Essence of Reasons*, p. 37ff.

itself apart from the manifold of sense intuition.[28] An unqualified or even loosely associative usage of transcendence therefore violates the limits of reason since it claims for itself an ideal repository of Truth independent of the phenomenality of being-in-a-world. Thus even though there is a universal validity for the transcendental categories of understanding in Kant, it is a validity exercised only in relation to empirical data and not independently. Strictly within Kantian limits it would seem that a philosophy *of* Transcendence has clearly exceeded *quid juris* limitations and lapsed into the old supernaturalist metaphysics. Thus strictly within the framework of Kantian theory, the transcendental has only to do with method and not with some *thing* that can be named "Transcendence-Itself" as in the sense of the object of religious faith and belief. Jaspers, although he is frequently prone to stretching Kant through his existentialist interpretation, is also aware of this danger and rarely uses the objectively inferential term *Transzendenz* apart from its dialectical counterpart, *das Umgreifende*, aiming, as he does, at a substantial use which simultaneously involves both experience and its referent. One must also say that Jaspers is very sensitive to the fact that if Transcendence-Itself can only be thought as limit, it cannot itself be that limit, for that would be a contradiction, just as Kant said, "what limits must be kept distinct from that which is limited."[29]

These questions, however, are ultimately impossible to answer from strictly the Jaspersian perspective for, as we have seen, he continually relegates them to the cipher language of Existenz refusing to objectify what is nevertheless asserted to be objective. In the later Kant as well as in the development of absolute idealism in Fichte and Hegel, Jaspers notes the diminution of this refusal and hence the perversion of the initial "transcendental-existential" insight of Kant through asserting that existential apprehension of the Supersensible could provide the basis for a "world-constituting" transcendental ego or an absolute logic.[30] Marx, in Jaspers' view, makes an even more drastic mistake by reducing the dialectic of transcending-thinking to instrumental theories of material and historical causation; by, as he says, "transforming faith into science" whereby true philosophizing becomes "anti-reason."[31] One is left, then, with a tentative conclusion that the Supersensible foundation of both

---

[28] Cf., *Critique of Pure Reason*, A 296ff; B 352ff.

[29] *Ibid.*, A 515 B543. In Part III, we will ask whether or not Jaspers' "ciphers" can actually operate as the "empirical" correlate of Transcendence-Itself or even the transcendental categories of understanding and hence be faithful to transcendental method.

[30] *Great Phil.*, I, p. 313.

[31] *Reason and Anti-Reason*, pp. 8, 16-18, 37ff.

thought and reality is apprehended through more than mere intuition and less than logical demonstration. As the horizon of the middle term the Super-sensible (Transcendence-Itself) seems to hover as that quasi-objective Other within which freedom grounds itself; an Encompassing that provides the possibility of coherence and intelligibility, and also is the origin and goal of the continuous project of possible self-Being.

In sum, there can be little doubt that Kant's rather oblique notion of the Supersensible has a direct bearing on the manner in which Jaspers fashions his philosophy; that in this symbol there is a coalescence of Transcendence and the Encompassing in their epistemological and onto-logical aspects respectively. In the same manner, Kant's notion of the transcendental imagination is transformed out of its schematic-func-tional role and identified with that dimension of human consciousness within which the coalescence of Transcendence and the Encompassing take place. The transcendental imagination, in short, is the matrix of transcending-thinking; the matrix within and through which mere cogni-tion becomes transcending-thinking. In Heidegger, by contrast, and in spite of the similarities of his interpretation of these same points in Kant, there is a notable reserve to read directly, as it were, the Supersensible into the ontologically implicative language of ciphers. On the contrary, "we are," as Heidegger puts it poetically, "too late for the gods / too early for Being." Heidegger, thereby, distends rather than ameliorates the dis-tance between experience and Being even though Being remains the goal. Heidegger's caution also extends to Jaspers' notion of transcending-thinking, namely "The most thought-provoking discovery about our thought-provoking time is that we are still not thinking," and he is forthright to include himself as first among those who cannot so think. [32]

One of the reasons for this apparent difference, we suspect, is the de-gree to which Jaspers both participates in and extends the voluntarism of Kant. To this feature of Jaspers we now turn. It is a problem that will reemerge in Part III in our analysis of transcending-thinking as her-meneutic philosophizing.

---

[32] Cf., Heidegger, *Kant and the Problem of Metaphysics*, trans. James Churchill (Bloom-ington: Indiana University Press, 1962). Also: *Poetry, Language, Thought*, trans. Albert Hofstadter (New York: Harper & Row, Inc., 1971), pp. 3-14; *What is Called Thinking*, trans. Fred Wieck and J. Glenn Gray (New York: Harper & Row, Inc., 1972), pp. 3-19.

POSSIBLE EXISTENZ AND VOLUNTARISM

As we have seen, Transcendence, for Jaspers, does not further scientific advance or insure technological progress, is not the gnostic key for an esoteric and other-worldly vision of ultimate reality, provides no psychoterapeutic formulae for the development of mental health, and is not a substitute for the sanctifying immediacy of a religious sacrament. To what end then, one asks, is the awareness or experience of Transcendence any value at all?

The answer lies at the level of *praxis*. Here also there is a parallel for Jaspers is completely in agreement with Kant that the critical-speculative question "What can I know?" is intellectualistic and self-indulgent in the worst sense apart from the questions "What am I to do?" and "To what end do I live?" The veracity of any philosophy of Transcendence and all metaphysics is determined in the crucible of *Lebenspraxis*: "We cannot transcend this world by our knowledge of something, but solely by the course we take within it, by the experience of the Ideas in systematic knowledge, by the play of all our cognitive faculties in the intuition of the beautiful, and truly and decisively, through our freedom in ethical action." [33]

Existential freedom, then, is the reality which cuts across all the boundaries and limitations one encounters in the formal delineation of transcending in relation to Transcendence, for in freedom both the reality and the objectivity of Transcendence is affirmed through actual self-transcendence. As Bernard Lonergan puts it, "True objectivity is the fruit of authentic subjectivity." [34] Within the constraints of Jaspers' first two formal modalities one beholds the brute force of necessity; the capricious world of Schopenhauer where freedom seems internally contradictory and absurd. However, within the context of a dynamic interplay between world and self, percept and concept, one begins to understand the reality of freedom (as Transcendence) not as a thing but precisely as "possibili-

---

[33] *Great Phil.*, I, p. 290. Jaspers also states, "In der Besinnung denkender Aneignung wird Klarheit gewonnen für das, was Wirklichkeit nur hat in der Lebenspraxis. Philosophie führt dorthin, wo jeder Einzelne sich geschenkt wird, nicht durch Philosophie, sondern durch Transzendenz, und wo er durch seine Existenz entscheidet." *Chiffren der Transzendenz*, p. 107.
[34] *Method in Theology*, p. 292.

ty,"[35] and the dialectical tissue of intellectual vis-à-vis moral conversion begins to unfold as a philosophy of will.

If our experience of world were direct and nonproblematic, willing would be unnecessary and of no account. One would not experience the exigency of moving from knowing to doing, for one would find oneself, as Heidegger puts it, "an object alongside other objects" in a barren mechanism called nature that is devoid of the dynamics of growth as possibility. In such a situation Transcendence, whether considered as self-transcendence or the object of transcending, would be meaningless. The moral conversion that is intrinsic to Jaspers' philosophy of Transcendence, however, militates against the staticism of Transcendence considered only from an epistemological standpoint. Precisely in relation to *Lebenspraxis*, freedom becomes the middle ground between Kant's manifold of sense intuition and the categories of understanding; the living *fondement* of possible Existenz in relation to Transcendence.

Of course Jaspers is aware that Kant did not develop fully the existential implications of his own insight, namely that the freedom of the subject is not nullified but affirmed through understanding the phenomenality of experience. In fact Kant's subsequent development of the moral "ought" under the specificity of a categorial imperative very quickly leads to dogmatism and, from a Barthian perspective, to the excesses of liberalism generally.[36] It is rather from the standpoint of *Lebenspraxis* that the foundations of Kantian theory provide clear and certain evidence for the "freedom" intrinsic to Jaspers' notion of *mögliche Existenz*. There are only two alternatives, as Jaspers sees it: "Either we may, with Kant, transcend all objectivity in order to attain self-awareness through a consciousness of being grounded in freedom; or else we may assert a being in itself, and inherent objectivity and reality, and through such thinking, lose our freedom."[37] The real issue at stake, then, is not clear and certain knowledge of the ontological status of Transcendence, but the reality of freedom. Apart from the reality of freedom there would be no quest and hence no reason whatsoever to inquire into the formal, categorial problematics of the will. Thus against someone like Jean-

---

[35] Cf., *Phil.*, III, p. 14; *Great Phil.*, I, p. 300; *Philosophy of Existence*, pp. 12-29. This is a fundamental point of agreement among all those who might be called "transcendental existentialists." Cf., Karl Rahner's *potentia obedientalis* and its intrinsic "freedom" as the underlying possibility for the "luminosity of Being," *Hearers of the Word* (New York: Herder, 1969), p. 31ff; Heidegger, *Being and Time*, pp. 53-58, *The Essence of Reasons*, pp. 84-85.

[36] Karl Barth, *Protestant Theology from Rousseau to Ritschl* (New York: Harper & Row, 1959), pp. 150-196.

[37] *Great Phil.*, I, p. 303. Cf., also *Philosophical Faith and Revelation*, p. 118ff.

Paul Sartre who suggests that since neither my cognition nor my freedom is absolute in the sense of being God-like, both are illusions insofar as they might illuminate Being,[38] Jaspers concludes just the opposite. Freedom, for Jaspers, is the very foundation of transcending-thinking not because it rids us of the perplexing task of philosophizing by resolving all questions having to do with Being, but because it engenders "philosophical exploration which transcends the understanding and transforms our awareness of Being, leaving us richer in our thinking and open to new thinking."[39] A philosophical transcending that is fully aware of its basis in freedom, Jaspers states, *"hat die Gewissheit des ewigen Ursprungs, dann ist sie in erfüllter Gegenwärtigkeit, dass solange wir da sind, immer noch und immer wieder möglich."*[40]

While Jaspers' philosophy of freedom is not identical with Kantian voluntarism, neither is cognizable apart from common rootage in a philosophy of will that fulfills critical inquiry. In short, the brokenness of being-in-a-world is reconciled in the moral act of the individual, and authentic – in this case "willful" - transcending is authentic only to the degree that it transforms the world in *Lebenspraxis*. So for Jaspers, as in the case of Kant,[41] the final resolution of the moral dimensions of critical philosophizing is the development of rationally grounded religious belief or philosophical faith – mature or "complete religion," as Kant put it.[42] The possibility of such a synthesis, for Jaspers, is "grand volition," that is, willing that derives its power from "the inexhaustible Encompassing within which it is embedded. "For this is what the will is: "The presence of Eternity in the moment."[43]

In concluding this chapter we might ask whether, owing Jaspers' adulation of Kant, he has anything expressly negative to say concerning his mentor. The answer is "yes" but always within the constraints of recognizing fully the historical advantage of living in the age of modern science; something which Jaspers, in other contexts, fails to do. Within this context, however, Jaspers spends little time impuning the apodictically "Newtonian" flavor of the transcendental categories of Kant (so frequently the subject of criticism), for this limitation is historically acci-

---

[38] Jean-Paul Sartre, *Philosophy of Existentialism* (New York: Philosophical Library, 1965), pp. 31-74.

[39] *Great Phil.*, I, p. 321.

[40] *Chiffren der Transzendenz*, p. 109.

[41] Cf., Kant's *Religion Within the Limits of Reason Alone* (New York: Harper, 1960), esp. Part. II, Book Four, p. 156ff.

[42] Cf. Book IV, *Religion Within the Limits of Reason Alone*, trans. Theodore Green and Hoyt Hudson (Open court, 1934).

[43] *Phil.*, II, p. 140-143.

dental and is of only marginal significance when measured against the magnitude of the "transcendental" achievement of Kant's critical epistemology. Jaspers' primary criticism has rather to do with that sin to which all flesh is so vulnerable, namely the creeping dogmatism of system builders. On this score, transcendental method does not lead to rigorous science for Jaspers, but rather systematically and formally articulates the structures and possibilities of true or authentic philosophizing. In short, critical epistemology serves as the necessary propaedeutic to *Existenzphilosophie* apart from which so-called "existentialism" evaporates in subjectivism. [44] Full participation in transcendental method requires nothing less than an intellectual conversion concerning the boundaries and limitations implicit to any kind of thinking – a conversion concomitant with existential decision. Jaspers puts it this way: "To grasp the greatness of Kant's thinking presupposes a basic existential decision. Kant leaves many men dissatisfied as though deprived of food and air. They yearn for a transcendent content and are unprepared to live by Kantian reason with the imageless God." [45] Such a philosophy, as Jaspers says, "cannot pronounce, cannot establish, cannot show absolute reality in the world. It remains hovering in ciphers (*Sie bleibt in schwebenden Chiffren*)." [46] Any claim to an essentialistic or "old" metaphysics for Jaspers, as for Kant, is out of the question; "*All unser Erkennen bleibt immer in der Welt; erreicht niemals die Welt.*" [47]

But to be in-the-world does not mean being confined to the world of skeptical empiricism, and this for Jaspers is the decisive point of Kantian critical theory. While a philosophy of limits (*Grenzen*) fully recognizes what cannot be said – that is, what cannot be predicated in the manner of natural science, it does not repudiate the possibility of the existence or the veracity of that which is beyond the limits of objectifying language but is *present* to experience. It is precisely this boundary positioning so essential to all authentic metaphysical philosophizing that Jaspers finds present cryptically in the writings of Kant but which it is the task of *Existenzphilosophie* to develop. "Between the imageless God, the range of worldly experience and the contemplation of the beautiful, there exists a world in which symbols speak to us, or rather where the particular becomes a symbol of the universal. This is the world of each man's struggle for the historical meaning of his own Existenz. There are possibilities of

---

[44] *Von der Wahrheit* is just such a preparation; esp. Part I.
[45] *Great Phil.*, I, p. 373. Cf., also Paton, *op. cit.*, p. 51.
[46] *Chiffren der Transzendenz*, p. 103.
[47] *Ibid.*, p. 7.

elucidating Existenz which, without negating or even restricting reason, go beyond it. This brings us to something which is not to be found in Kant, and which, where it appears in another philosophy does not refute Kant but complements him and complements his purifying reason."[48]

Inasmuch as Jaspers has set for himself the task of "breaking the silence" which envelops, as it were, the Kantian noumenon, it is necessary to inquire further concerning the historical origins of the goal of Jaspers' philosophizing. We contend in the next chapter that this goal is avowedly mystical; that it is a goal which can be elucidated through an analysis of Christian mysticism generally and of Nicholas of Cusa in particular; that it is Jaspers' affinity with Rhineland mysticism which provides him not only with a definitive horizon for the interpretation of the history of philosophy but also deciding who, among *die grossen Philosophen* are truly "Great." Having delineated the source and medium of Jaspers' historical retrieval of Transcendence, we turn now to its goal, namely the knowledge of Transcendence-Itself or God as understood in the philosophy of mysticism.

---

[48] *Great Phil.*, I, p. 373.

CHAPTER SEVEN

UNFOLDING THE ENFOLDING:
JASPERS AND MYSTICISM

That Jaspers does not consider himself a mystic is not at all surprising since the term *mystic* is so poorly understood and almost always misused. "All our knowledge," he states repeatedly and emphatically, "remains in the world; we never reach the world."[1] Such a position obviously rules out other-worldly or world-negating forms of mysticism. But what about the *world* that the transcending subject can never reach? Jaspers' rejection of mysticism, therefore, is qualified inasmuch as his notion of *world*, as in the case of Heidegger,[2] is itself mystical. That is, the world is not something that merely stretches about us as an environment, it is not identified with geography and physical matter, but symbolizes that toward which we strive or transcend as project. But neither is the world merely an idea or mental picture. It has rather the character of a symbol or cipher which, as in myth, has to do with a known and lived unity; a *Weltanschauung* that is not merely an academic exercise, but something that is unfathomably connected to what we have previously discussed as the *Supersensible*. In other words, the world is not only that from which I come, within which I am, and apart from which I could have no being. It is also that which draws or *calls* me as the idea of possible Unity. In terms of Transcendence the world is something which I simultaneously am and am not. In terms of the Encompassing the world is, as in Cusanus, the *Enfolding* which I, in the project of possible Existenz, *Unfold* through authentic philosophizing. The word *World*, then, has a mystical resonance that transcends both mere objectivity and mere subjectivity.

Jaspers, therefore, falls within the purview of Jean-Paul's wry comment regarding the character of German philosophy: "To the French God has given an Empire of Land; to the British, the Empire of the Sea.

---

[1] *Chiffren der Transzendenz*, p. 7.
[2] "Wir nennen das, *woraufhin* das Dasein als solches transzendiert, die *Welt* und bestimmen jetzt die Transzendenz als In-der-Welt-sein." *Vom Wesen des Grundes, op. cit.*, p. 40. Jaspers, of course, refuses to identify *transzendieren* and *Transzendenz*, and hence preserves a more traditional sense of the mystical.

But to the Germans, God has bequeathed the Empire of the Air."[3] By the term *air* we do not here understand merely abstractionism but rather the ontological domain of *Geist*. And the ontological and religious preoccupation of German thought is no artificial and contrived academic pastime. *Sein* and *Wortmystik* are rather involuntarily etched into the lifeblood of German philosophy and theology. As such, they represent the scarlet thread of reflection in its intellectual tradition from Albertus Magnus in the 12th century to the present day. Indeed, literary German is inconceivable apart from its origin in mystic-religious visionaries like Meister Eckhart and Martin Luther who, not surprisingly, invest its simplist words with resonances of Transcendence.[4]

One cannot underestimate the significance of these linguistic origins, for there is a very real sense in which the sedimented meanings of language guide and even dictate subsequent reflection and expression. "We do not so much speak language," Gadamer is fond of saying, "as language speaks us." How language speaks us, of course, is in large measure determined by the manner in which we receive what it gives. This is the sense of Heidegger's *es gibt*; the same sense that informs Ricoeur's notion that "the symbol gives rise to thought,"[5] and about which we shall have more to say in Part III.

Suffice it to say the preponderance of neologisms and the unconventional usage of traditional words in modern German philosophy and theology is ample indication of the degree to which German intellectuals feel compelled to both free themselves from the historical bondage of certain words and also to communicate somehow their inherent richness. It is no accident, therefore, that *Word* theology should have its most profound expression among German-speaking peoples, for it was the Word which, as *sola scriptura*, in large measure displaced the Sacraments after the Protestant Reformation. Due to the long-standing mystic-tradition of *viva vox*, neither is it an accident that *das Wort Gottes* should bear an altogether different intensity than its English counterpart. In German Protestantism *die Predigt* has quite literally the force of a "Proclamation" *(Verkündigung)* or an "event" or happening (as in Heidegger and Gadamer's notion of *Wahrheit als Ereignis*) in which truth appears out of the primordiality of its concealment in mere words. The Oxford English

---

[3] As quoted by Josiah Royce in *The Spirit of Modern Philosophy, op. cit.*, p. 108.
[4] Cf., Lewis White Beck, *Early German Philosophy* (Cambridge: Harvard University Press, 1969) for an excellent development of this motif. See also Hans-Georg Gadamer, *Hegel's Dialectic: Five Hermeneutical Studies*, trans. P. Christopher Smith (New Haven: Yale University Press, 1976), esp. Chapter Five, "Hegel and Heidegger," pp. 101ff.

Dictionary, by contrast, describes the term "homily" as "tedious, moralizing discourse." While the Oxford sense is probably closer to the truth in practice, we note quite simply that in German there is a compossibility of God or Being and Language that seems to transcend – in force and intensity – most other linguistic traditions.

In Jaspers one finds a continuation of this pious awe and reverence before language as a potential cipher of Transcendence, continuation of the belief that the Word (in both the Johannine and Pauline sense) is the agency (*Logos*) and vessel (*oustrakon*) of Transcendence. Nowhere is this inclination better elucidated than in Jaspers' understanding of Cusanus and the latter's notion of "Unfolding the Enfolding." Moreover, it is important here to note that Jaspers considers Cusanus a mystic in the *authentic* sense, i.e., the sense that Jaspers is himself a mystic. In Cusanus Jaspers sees a "Renaissance Kant;" in other words, a mystic who maintains and does not nullify the subject-object relation. Moreover, it is precisely through his maintenance of the subject-object polarity – and indeed, its extenuation – that Transcendence appears. We will have more to say about the hermeneutical implications of this notion in Part III.

The fundamental differences between Jaspers and Cusanus, however, must not be slighted. Cusanus' metaphysical speculations are fully grounded in the authoritative mediating symbols of the Medieval Church. Jaspers, owing his peculiar sense of universal history (which also serves to set him apart from Heidegger and Gadamer and also to identify him with Ricoeur in a somewhat curious way), does not confine himself to any single religious tradition even though he fully recognizes his dependence on Christianity. Therefore, he frequently gives the impression that it is not only possible but desirable to bracket out the religious and doctrinal peculiarities of Cusanus and thereby preserve through such *purification* the formal structures of an instance of transcending-thinking that stands independently of any theology. What Jaspers admires in Cusanus, in short, is the development of a mystical philosophy based entirely upon rationally self-conscious reflection on the mystery of experience.

In the following, we will attempt to show first that there is a fundamental connection between Jaspers' notion of conceptual "foundering" and *docta ignorantia* as it develops in the writings of Cusanus. The notion of "learned ignorance," to be sure, has antecedent expressions in John Scotus Erigena, Dionysius the Areopagite, Plato and Socrates. In Cusanus, however, the doctrine has epistemological sophistication and this is what appeals to Jaspers. Second, we will focus on the relationship of Jaspers' Encompassing and the *coincidentia oppositorum* of Cusanus and how they differ with respect to Transcendence-Itself or the Being of God. Finally, we will summarize briefly Jaspers' relationship to philosophical idealism, and outline the problems with which we will deal in Part III.

COGNITIVE TRANSCENDING AND LEARNED IGNORANCE

The paradoxical has always played an integral role in the religious consciousness and by now it should be obvious that it is central to Jaspers' philosophy as well. There have been religious epochs when the paradoxical dimension of religious experience has found rich and profound expression and countermovements in which it has been suppressed and almost eliminated. During the height of the Medieval period when the power and doctrinal authority of the Roman Church were virtually uncontested, the paradoxical dimensions of religious experience were so formalized and refined that the paradoxical itself became the rational. The maxim *inter finiti et infiniti non est proportio* and the theological conviction that revelation had overcome this disproportion decisively, was translated into a sacramental system within which ontology was domesticated as soteriology.

It was precisely the rationally ordered and habitually schematic character of the manner in which scholasticism handled the interrelationship of transcending and Transcendence which gave rise to dissenting positions, most notably nominalism in the 14th century. Very few to be sure, including the nominalists, questioned the supreme authority of revelation during this period, but increasing numbers of philosophers and theologians began to doubt the veracity of formalizations in which the divine and human mind coincided as unproblematically as the institutional hierarchy would have it. One of the curious aspects of the high medieval period, therefore, is that at the very time Aquinas was solidifying scholastic realism in its most impressive form, internal signs of decay and protestation were also under way. Under the influence of the Dominicans, Aristotelian logic and metaphysics had forced the Platonic-Augustinian tradition off centerstage, but it was by no means extinct. On the fringes of the Holy Roman Empire, particularly to the north of Europe, the Franciscans, the establishment of German universities and the fascinating developments in Rhineland mysticism, all contributed to the carefully reasoned challenge to scholastic realism which finally emerged in William of Ockham in the 14th century and the Protestant reformation that followed.

Although Nicholas of Cusa was not a nominalist (nor a realist in the traditional sense, for that matter), his position represents one of the truly prophetic philosophical movements in the late middle ages. Cusanus, as in the case of Jaspers, envisaged the major philosophical task as that of contending for the middle ground between nominalism and realism; in short, the recovery of the integrity of experience that makes formalized characterizations of that experience both unnecessary and superfluous. The project of Cusanus, then, is analogous to what Heidegger called "fundamental ontology," and Jaspers' "periechontology," viz., a *philosophische Grundoperation* that seeks the encompassing ground of experience antecedent to the origin of one's alienation from it.

Cusanus' method of dealing with this primordial ground is his version of *docta ignorantia*; a notion which bears striking similarity to Jaspers' description of the experience of the foundering intrinsic to cognitive transcending. This notion encompasses an intriguing blend of realism, nominalism and Plotinian mysticism which, in Cusanus as in Jaspers, is as enigmatic as it is insightful. By zealous Thomists, Cusanus is regarded a thoroughgoing pantheist; by Jaspers, Cassirer, Tillich and Gadamer, among others, a renaissance Kant. The transcendental aspect of *docta ignorantia* rests on Cusanus' observation that "all concepts are concepts of comparison." [6] The exception to analogical reasoning, however, is theological metaphysics because there is *nulla proportio* "between the measurer and the measured" when the measured is the Eternal God. [7] Contrary to the Aristotelianism of the scholastics, Cusanus believed that the *analogia entis* could not even approach the Divine Essence. All propositional claims to exacting and cogent knowledge concerning the nature of God are therefore *conjectura* and not formal demonstrations of the Being of God.

This, however, is only the nominalist side of Cusanus which by itself would scarcely be capable of arousing the enthusiasm of Jaspers. As in the case of Descartes, cognitive *dubito*, for Cusanus, is only the first step to constructive metaphysical insight; the occasion, as it were, for a movement into interiority which transforms the manner in which the question about reality is formulated. The key to metaphysical insight is not ordinary objectifying thinking (or what one might call "cataphatic" logic in the case of Aristotle and the scholastics), but rather what Cusanus calls transcending in "philosophical non-knowledge." In place of the *analogia*

---

[6] Cassirer, *The individual and the Cosmos*, p. 12ff.
[7] Jaspers, *Nikolaus Cusanus* (München: Piper Verlag, 1964), p. 37.

entis and the ontological language of proper proportionality, Cusanus substitutes the apophatic, paradoxical and indirect language of learned ignorance through which he is able to make assertions about the nature of reality *not* on the basis of what he knows but, as in Jaspers' "qualified negativity," on the basis of what he knows he does not know: "When we are able to see that God transcends every concept we form of Him, we see that we cannot know Him; we see that our knowledge of God is a knowledge of our ignorance of Him." [8]

Docta ignorantia in this instance, however, is removed considerably from the intellectual resignation of certain nominalistic Protestants in the face of the *deus absconditus* and for whom, as Bonhoeffer characterized it, "Revelational Positivism" became the only answer. Cusanus' method represents rather a decisive transition away from the emotive mysticism of a *devotio ritus* and cultic confessionalism with its implicit dogmatism, and, as in the case of Eckhart, the beginnings of a *devotio intellectus* within which transcending-thinking discovers the Divine Absolute present to consciousness-itself. As Jaspers puts it: "Das Unendliche der Gottheit ist zwar nicht durch Verstandeswissen, wohl aber in Nichtwissen des Verstandes durch Vernunft berührbar. Dieses Nichtwissen ist nicht das leere Nichtwissen, das nicht weiss, dass es nicht wissen kann. Es ist vielmehr das wissende Nichtwissen, das sich denkend entfaltet und sich erfüllen lässt." [9]

While the metaphorical abounds in mystical literature, and while Cusanus does not refrain from metaphor in the least, [10] Cusanus' metaphoric imagery is decidedly conceptual or "noetic" and for that reason he is the perfect historical *Verbindungspunkt* for Jaspers' notion of conceptual or "cognitive" transcending. Not only is all metaphysical discourse metaphorical and indirect for both thinkers, but the mind itself is regarded as the primary metaphor. What is understood as mind, then, is not simply the formalizing, abstracting ability of *ratio* but the encompassing power of consciousness as *intellectus*. Aware of its multi-dimensionality as both immanence and Transcendence, the fully self-conscious mind knows its limits and in so knowing it "sees by not seeing" [11] therefore beholding "transcendental truths." As Jaspers puts it, "Die Vielheit der Dinge ist die Entfaltung (*explicatio*) der Einfaltung (*complicatio*) des

[8] *Of Learned Ignorance*, trans. Germain Heron (New Haven: Yale, 1954), p. 63.
[9] *Nikolaus Cusanus*, p. 23.
[10] Cusanus' *The Vision of God*, trans. Emma Salter (New York: Julian Press, 1960), is nothing less than a continuous "conceptual metaphor."
[11] Cusanus, *Of Learned Ignorance*, p. 31.

unendlichen Geistes." [12] Although Jaspers is here considering Cusanus' understanding of the Divine Mind, human consciousness for Cusanus (as for the Romantics) is a microcosm of the Divine Consciousness. [13] In Cusanus, however, the analogy is based on thinking and not extrinsic cosmological data; in other words, it is transcendental. [14] What Jaspers finds in Cusanus, then, is a cogent epistemological differentiation between the "encompassed" (*ratio*) and the "encompassing" (*intellectus*) originating in Plotinus but not developed in the modern period until Kant and Hegel. As an "unfolding of the enfolding" the mind is understood by Cusanus as the encompassing ground for the possibility of both the knowledge of God and of self-Being; a transcending power which in its perfectness, outstrips all perceptual imagery. At the level of *ratio* (or the objectifying thinking operative within Jaspers' first formal mode of transcending, *Weltorientierung*), there is only an extrinsic sensory awareness of the object outside or external to consciousness. But at the level of *intellectus* (and really *Vernunft* as in the second modality of *Existenzerhellung*), the reality of mind is heightened and not diminished through the consciousness of external limit as simultaneously the internal limit. This positive intuition of *Grenze* as the existential boundary situation also was perceived by Cusanus, Jaspers believes, as the "moment" of metaphysical elucidation for the first time, viz., as "das wissende Nichtwissen das sich denkend entfalten und sich erfüllen lässt." [15] Through this careful differentiation between the operations of *ratio* and *intellectus*, consciousness-itself is seen to be the ground and possibility of transcending-thinking: "Aber wo Erkenntnis aufhört, hört das Denken nicht auf, und wir haben die Möglichkeit, durch Chiffren uns des Menschseins wenigstens heller bewusst zu werden als ohne." [16]

One must note that the significance of Cusanus' *docta ignorantia* for Jaspers is *not* based on the supposition that this conversion of consciousness is from a lower to a so-called higher ontological level. As a clearly existential conversion, both dualist and monist reductionism is

---

[12] *Nikolaus Cusanus*, p. 33.
[13] *Ibid.*, p. 34. Cf., also Walzel, *German Romanticism*, trans. Alma Lussky (New York: Ungar, 1965), p. 22f.
[14] Cf. *The Vision of God*, pp. 52-53, 110, 122.
[15] *Nikolaus Cusanus*, p. 23. Cf. also *The Vision of God*, pp. 59-60.
[16] *Chiffren der Transzendenz*, p. 17. Cassirer similarly regards Cusanus' *Docta ignorantia* as the recovery of the "essential Plato," namely, as a thinking which grasps the "whole" not through a series of "cosmological leaps" but rather through a differentiation of the act of thinking-itself: "In Kantian language, Cusanus shows that while our knowledge is bounded by insurmountable limits, within the domain assigned to knowledge, there are no limits placed upon it." *The Individual and the Cosmos*, p. 23. This is what Wittgenstein also regards as the authentic mysticism of the "Limited Whole" at the end of the *Tractatus*, 6.45.

avoided. Transcending-thinking thinks through and not at the expense of opposition because first, it understands itself as polymorphous, and secondly, it therefore realizes that consciousness is not exhausted by any one of its many operations, i.e., it knows that where "cognition ends, thinking continues." In this context the mind as rationality self-consciously apprehends its non-formalizable character as *Geist*. Thus, for Cusanus, the rational consciousness is a "limited Unlimited;" limited because one's cognition is always bounded by the reductionistic exigencies of objectification, but Unlimited precisely because it recognizes this objectifying limit as limit [17] just as Jaspers' Transcendence-Itself is apprehended as a "possible impossible." [18] Intrinsic to this recognition, then, is an intellectual conversion whereby one's conscious understanding of the nature and potentialities of experience is transformed through the "foundering" (*Scheitern*), as Jaspers puts it, that is concomitant with metaphysical insight. The task of transcending-thinking, for both Cusanus and Jaspers, is not to somehow manage this conversion by charting formally the *aporia* between *ratio* and *intellectus*, *Verständnis* and *Vernunft*, as though it were a once and for all kind of conversion, for that would be to lapse into blatant gnosticism. As Jaspers puts it, one must rather understand that all "speculative thinking remains a thinking of the unthinkable and it must preserve an unresolvable tension wherein its fundamental concepts remain paradoxical . . . We are repeatedly caught up as in a vortex; things are not as I think of them in objective terms . . . I am made aware of them as a non-objective reality." [19]

Transcending-thinking methodically guided by the "qualified negativity" of *docta ignorantia*, then, necessarily expresses itself in the conceptual-metaphorical cipher, for "the experience of metaphorical Being and the production of enigmatic images are the substance of speculative philosophizing." [20] And not only the expression but the origin of the experience of *docta ignorantia* is metaphorical, for it is analogous to the Plotinion One or Transcendence-Itself which Jaspers characterizes as "the origin that has no origin and is the origin of the origin." [21] Transcending-thinking as *docta ignorantia* is nothing less than a continuous self-transcending metaphor f for "If everything that is, everything we imagine and think is metaphorical, then this statement itself is a metaphor.

---

[17] Cf., *The Vision of God*, pp. 106ff., for Cusanus' development of a quite amazing Christology on the basis of just these epistemological conditions.
[18] *Phil.*, vol. III, pp. 45-47.
[19] *Great Phil.*, II, pp. 125-126.
[20] *Ibid.*, p. 136.
[21] *Ibid.*, p. 170.

Only thinking which grasps the metaphorical character of all thinking results in the perfect state of suspension (*die vollendete Schwebe*) which enables us to move freely within every type of symbolism. But as long as we express ourselves with words, we cannot go beyond metaphor." [22]

As a heuristic device, however, *docta ignorantia* is not a solipsistic methodology, but is always referential in the sense that it both originates and ends in Cusanus' cosmo-ontological notion of the *coincidentia oppositorum*. To be sure a coincidence of opposites is the paradoxical aspect of learned ignorance, but for Cusanus it is also referential in the way that the doxology, "Preserve us O Lord in Thy Truth, all things begun and ended in Thee," is referential, viz., a philosophical faith that is simultaneously Pythagorean and Catholic. As we investigate the relation between Cusanus' *coincidentia oppositorum* and Jaspers' *das Umgreifende* we must, therefore, ask whether Jaspers' philosophy of Transcendence – if it is to be both internally and externally consistent – must not be bounded by a similar kind of faith.

THE ALL ENCOMPASSING AND THE *COINCIDENTIA OPPOSITORUM*

According to the Psalmist, "The fear of the Lord is the beginning of wisdom." From the Jaspersian perspective one might say, an awareness of "limit" yields the same result. In the Biblical context, however, respectful fear has to do with the wisdom of knowing the consequences of transgressing a divinely established Law; that the Way of Torah is the only possible basis of possible Existenz. In the context of Jaspersian *Existenzphilosophie*, the knowledge of limit obviously no longer has anything to do with something as empirically and cultically specific as a law-giving Lord but rather with the transcendental relationship of thinking to itself. Can one, then, regard the learned ignorance of noetic limitation as the knowledge of something which has an extra-subjective existence, and in what way can such a knowledge be called "saving" in either a theological or existential sense? Does the apophasis of foundering in learned ignorance generate a cataphatic theological claim or is it merely the propaedeutic to a *credo quia absurdum* and salvation by ambiguity? If the result of self-critical "transcending-thinking" is not merely an end in

---

[22] *Nikolaus Cusanus*, pp. 43-44. Cf., also *Von der Wahrheit*, p. 276ff, where the subject of *Gleichnis* is discussed in detail.

itself, how does one move from the knowledge of limit to that "origin without origins that is itself the origin of the origin," as Jaspers puts it, which, in the Judaeo-Christian tradition, is the Transcendent God of Abraham, Isaac and Jacob?

There can be little doubt that this final transcending to Transcendence-Itself demands a kind of "leap" whether it be the Christian faith of Cusanus or the philosophical faith of Jaspers. Whatever it is that ultimately engenders this leap, it should be clear by now that it is a leap with considerable preparation. One might not be crystal-clear concerning the nature of that towards which one leaps, but one is at least familiar with both the subject and ground from which one leaps. As in the case of Kant, the knowledge of limit does not lead to phenomenalism, but to a full, participating consciousness deeply rooted in the freedom intrinsic to the constitution of meaning. To be sure, there is a great deal of risk incumbent upon and within this act, and its salutary feature is that of being altogether "open." But as in the case of Camus' "Sisyphus," the absence of any support structures in such a model of transcending has differing effects on different subjects. Jaspers formulates an interesting comparison between Cusanus and Nietzsche contemplating the discovery that one leaps from one abyss to yet another: "In Nietzsche, the astronomical conception becomes the symbol of an entirely different and very important experience; that of existential nihilism which has been steadily growing in modern times under the cover of superficially retained traditions. The idea that astronomical and other scientific discoveries determine men's faith instead of serving him by broadening the horizon of his knowledge presupposes a general intellectual flattening. But in Cusanus, we are dealing with ideas which from the outset transcend the narrow-mindedness that chains men to matter, to material cosmos and to mere technical skill."[23]

Jaspers' own career was similarly dedicated to freeing men from scientific and metaphysical narrow-mindness and the delimiting belief that one merely has to set various scientific mechanisms into motion in order to effect "true faith, true art, true poetry, true happiness and true Being."[24] Extrinsically held convictions such as these are really no different than the mythical cosmological beliefs that Cusanus rejected in his own epistemological anticipation of the astronomical conception. A failure to come to an awareness of the limits of all the polymorphous dimensions of

[23] *Great Phil.*, II, p. 190.
[24] *Ibid.*, p. 251.

human experience, then, always results in "scientific superstition" (*Wissenschaftsaberglaube*) and a perpetuation of the myth of the objectifying consciousness which precludes the discovery of authentic science. Authentic metaphysics, on the other hand, has always been aware "of its limits and does not transgress them and does not leave the world disenchanted. It clears the way for new ciphers and does not destroy the old ones when it shows that they fail to provide us with tangible real knowledge; it does not destroy the miracle which underlies everything we call meaning." [25] Authentic science, then, offers no *Weltbild* whatsoever and, " ... zum erstenmal in der Geschichte haben wir durch die Wissenschaften selber Klarheit darüber. Früher waren Weltbilder, die das Denken ganzer Zeitalter beherschen konnten, wundersame Chiffern, die uns heute noch ansprechen. Das sogenannte moderne Weltbild dagegen, begründet auf die Denkungsart, die in Descartes repräsentiert ist, das Ergebnis einer Philosophie als Pseudowissenschaft, hat nicht den Charakter einer Chiffer für Existenz, sondern einer mechanischen und dynamischen Apparatur für den Verstand." [26]

But does the conclusion that the critical point of view does not leave the world *disenchanted* mean that it is or ever was *enchanted*? In a sense the answer for Jaspers is yes, for enchantment here has to do with meaning; that is, the possibility of meaning is itself *miraculous*. Again, this does not bespeak mere pragmatism on Jaspers' part as though just any meaning will do, for he believes that one can move from the knowledge of limit to an awareness of that which both underlies and is beyond limit, that this knowledge of limit itself provides the means to negotiate this most difficult *aporia*.

As we have noted, the paradoxical effect of *docta ignorantia* is that while one comes to an awareness that Being-Itself cannot be known on the basis of sense, mind or an aporetic combination of the two, neither can it be known apart from this dynamic relationship. The knowledge of Being is therefore somehow coterminous with the very movement of transcending-thinking which, as movement, apprehends Transcendence-Itself as both the origin and goal of itself. Here Jaspers is advocating a position which is analogous to that of Kierkegaard, namely that the "motion" intrinsic to Existenz is also its "telos," inasmuch as " the *telos* is not outside but in the movement itself and even behind it as in the case of an immanent progression." [27] The process position, as in the case

---

[25] *Nikolaus Cusanus*, p. 213.
[26] *Chiffren der Transzendenz*, p. 98.
[27] *Philosophical Fragments*, p. 66.

of Whitehead, is not without its difficulties; that is, even though the reformed subjectivist principle" reconstituted as "prehension" is construed as that which touches the primordial ground of reality, we must have a basis of somehow determining that this is the case. Thus even though hybrid conceptualizations are understood to "alienate" life from its ground, the "Eternal Object" is necessary to provide intelligibility to process. [28] The question is, how, qua existentialist, is Jaspers able to move beyond the "moving center of Existenz" to something which is more than mere process? In Cusanus, by contrast, we have an epistemological anthropology which is both preceded and succeeded by a belief in a creator God who both initiates and fulfills the historical process including that of the subject's own historicity. But since Jaspers is no apologist for the Christian understanding of creation, [29] how can he get beyond *docta ignorantia* as a mere epistemological exercise?

In several of his writings, Jaspers alludes to a conviction that all periods of "creative advance" in history are the result of a "monistic" principle or what one might regard as an attunement to the existence of an "ordered Other" that renders intelligible what is *not other*. [30] Moreover, as we have seen, Jaspers believes that it is the encompassing or comprehensive character of Transcendence which makes human experience both possible and intelligible. Needless to say, there is a good deal of what Lewis White Beck calls the "isotropic" present to these contentions, namely, the belief that there is an equivalence of proportionality between the greatest and the least, the heights and depths of Being; that the macrocosm is accurately mirrored in the microcosm. On the basis of this isotropism, Beck states, the idealist "supplies a cosmology proportionate to the measure of his Pythagoreanism." [31] Certainly it is such a conviction which is preeminent in Leibniz and that informs the *Lebensphilosophie* of the Romantics as well. [32] Moreover, it is something analogous to this isotropism which leads Cusanus to conclude that the "soul" is no better "gateway" to knowledge of the Divine than a "geometrical figure." [33] Can the Ordered Other of Jaspers' Transcendence-Itself and that Ultimate Reality "beyond the wall of the coincidence of opposites" in Cusanus be accounted for on the basis of monistic isotropism?

---

[28] Cf., The Appendix for a scheme analogous to Whitehead's.
[29] Cf., *Philosophical Faith and Revelation, passim*.
[30] Cf., *Origin and Goal of History; Reason and Anti-Reason, passim*.
[31] *Early German Philosophy*, p. 58.
[32] Cf. Jaspers' *Schelling, Grösse und Verhängnis* (München: Piper Verlag, 1955); Walzel, *op. cit.*, pp. 3-33; Walter Schulz, *op. cit.*, pp. 12-30.
[33] *Of Learned Ignorance*, I, 5ff.

It is the conviction of Cusanus that in spite of the disjunction and duplicity of human experience, everything comes together – apophatically, eschatologically – in God. While at the level of *ratio* or objectifying thinking, black can never be white, two parallel lines can never intersect and a polygon can never become a circle no matter how many times its sides be multiplied, *intellectus* – on the basis of its Divine Ground – is able to apprehend the resolution of all paradox and opposition in God. This resolution, however, is not Aristotelian (in the scholastic sense), but transcendental, i.e., neither the coincidence nor its resolution is cognizable apart from thinking about some empirical thing. Again we are dealing with the conversion of consciousness intrinsic to Jaspers' *philosophische Grundoperation* which, although it does not nullify the subject-object structures of experience, it transforms the inconclusive status of this dialectic by thinking *through* opposition in ciphers *to* the Ground of Being: "We touch it (namely, Transcendence-Itself) by thinking, not by ecstasy and not by *mystic unio*, not by abolishing the subject-object dichotomy, but by preserving it." [34] By no longer differentiating the infinite and the finite, the qualitative and the quantitative on the basis of an extrinsic ontology of substance, but determining transcendentally the plurality of realms of experience within consciousness, Cusanus only gives the impression that he is pantheistic (as in Anaxagoras' famous statement, "Everything is in everything"). In Cusanus, however, there is a demarcation between that resolution which is "transcendental" (owing the nature of consciousness) and that which is "eschatological" (owing the nature of Grace). The two modalities of interpretation are separate even though mirrored in each other because of the compossibility of God and experience. As Cassirer observes of Cusanus in a similar manner: "By denying any overlapping of the two realms and by teaching us to see the One in the Other and the other in the One, the separation itself guarantees the possibility of true participation of the sensible in the Ideal." [35]

This differentiation, however, is not always detected. In a stinging criticism, Vincent Martin, for example, notes that Cusanus' notion of a *coincidentia oppositorum* is a "subtly disguised form of anthropomorphism" and that what Cusanus' God resolves is a "limitation peculiar to the human mind and not a limitation in nature," i.e., Cusanus confuses the

---

[34] *Great Phil.*, II, p. 158.
[35] *The Individual and the Cosmos*, p. 24. In other words, "*Ontos on* and *onta*, *logoi* and *pragmata* can never be joined, only thought." *Ibid.*

modus rei intellectae and the *modus intelligendi rem ipsam.*[36] On closer examination, however, one sees that the Transcendence of God is not sacrificed to pantheism nor is it resolved by so-called pan-en-theism. The coincidence of opposites, in Cusanus, is not *itself* God but is present to consciousness *because* God is "beyond the wall of the coincidence of opposites."[37] In other words, God is that Transcendent reality which "draws" consciousness unto itself because God himself is its origin. For example, in Cusanus' famous essay *The Vision of God*, the term *vision* is itself double-sided since it not only refers to the transcending subject's object of quest, but equally to the fact that the icon of Christ itself symbolizes vision that is "omnivoyant" as in the sense of the Psalmist when he says, "Whether shall I flee from Thee, O Lord?" The experience of *unio* is therefore dependent on being-in-the-world amidst other phenomena, and consciousness-itself is understood as the ensemble of subjectivity and objectivity, which, in knowing what it means to be-in-a-world, is able, qua *fondement*, to transcend to a consciousness of the Transcendent Ground of its origin precisely in experience. Jaspers describes this experience well in the following passage: "Through transcending-thinking we arrive at the point beyond all ciphers. Our thinking outdoes itself. It is unseemly for thought to stammer but not to outdo itself in full lucidity and in so doing to become certain of itself and that which it seeks. In extreme situations of human life, when Existenz becomes actuality, we say 'the rest is silence.'"[38]

Here, we believe, we can clearly perceive both the potentialities and shortcomings of transcending-thinking as a method of doing metaphysics. On the one hand, transcending-thinking is aware of the intentional nature of consciousness; that is, it is aware that experience is always experience of an intended object and that, as such, it is grounded in the dialectical relation of knower and the known and in the constitutive act of meaning and meaning as constituted. Both naive realism and skeptical relativism are precluded as options which do not seriously entertain the implications of this dialectic in its fullness. However, in the case of religious experience the intended object is not an object nor is it merely an Idea, but a reality with some kind of ontological status beyond mere

---

[36] *The Dialectical Process in the Philosophy of Nicholas of Cusa*, Extrait du Laval Théologique et Philosophique, Vol. V, No. 2 (Quebec: Editions de L'Université Laval, 1949), pp. 216-268.

[37] *The Vision of God*, pp. 39-50. Cf., esp. closing doxology.

[38] *Great Phil.*, II, p. 172.

Idea. At this point consciousness "founders," as Jaspers puts it, and similarly the two alternatives of this theorem, namely, that reality is present to experience "either as object or idea." [39] The final *aporia* between critical epistemology and metaphysics cannot be transcended apart from that eschatological element theologians call Grace. Thus while transcending-thinking has the virtue of being unrestricted and open-ended by virtue of its intentionally epistemic relationship to a formally unrestricted Unconditioned, it cannot transcend this boundary except in "ciphers." [40] The "Otherness" of Transcendence-Itself at this ultimate level of transcending-thinking is similarly voided as "Non-Otherness" (*non aliud*) as all descriptive categories fail – even the paradoxical. Freely editorializing on this motif in Cusanus, it appears that Jaspers is also speaking for himself in the following passage: "Das Nichtanders aber ist kein Gegensatz zum Anders, da es dieses dadurch *definiert* dass es ihm vorhergeht . . . Gott ist ohne Gegensatz. Er ist das Nichtanderssein, dem weder das Andere noch das Nichts entgegensteht, da er auch dem Nichts vorhergeht und es definiert. Daher Dionysius: Gott sei in Allem alles und in Nichts – nichts." [41]

In sum, both Jaspers and Cusanus are driven and sustained by Plato's "Good beyond all being," but Jaspers more than Cusanus. That this is the case can be drawn out from the statement of Ricoeur that "Only he who can address Transcendence as Thou can speak of Transcendence as It," for in Jaspers allusions to the "nameless, imageless God" of the Judaic-Christian tradition tend to be dissolved in ciphers, whereas in Cusanus speculation is always doxological in the face of the *deus revelatus* he adores in faith. In sum, it is Christian and not philosophical faith that shields Cusanus from a monism of the Encompassing. This, it would appear, is the fate of purely speculative metaphysics and, indeed, all philosophies of reflection, viz., a situation in which the *coincidentia oppositorium* is coterminous with the *deus absconditus* and about which one can say nothing. The consequences of Jaspers' rather dramatic demarcation between philosophical and theological faith [42] are far-reaching and highly problematical as we will see in Part III when we scrutinize transcending-thinking as a hermeneutics of symbol.

---

[39] *Phil.*, I, p. 87.
[40] As Jaspers states, "Without the world there can be no transcendence," and the word "Transcendent [viz., Transcendence-Itself] has to do with that which lies beyond all objectivity." *Phil.*, I, pp. 83, 77.
[41] *Nikolaus Cusanus*, p. 91.
[42] *Ibid.*, pp. 88-89, 98ff.

SUMMARY: JASPERS AND PHILOSOPHICAL IDEALISM

Concerning existentialism, Jean-Paul Sartre once said: "What complicates matters is that there are two kinds of existentialists; first, those who are Christian, among whom I would include Jaspers and Marcel, both Catholic; and on the other hand the atheistic existentialists among whom I would class Heidegger, and then the French existentialists and myself. What they have in common is that they think that existence precedes essence, or, if you prefer, that subjectivity must be the starting point."[43]

While Sartre's typology has some credence it is far from being wholly accurate. In the first place, Jaspers is neither Catholic nor Lutheran, for that matter, but a German Protestant and with wholly non-confessional connections to his tradition. Secondly, Heidegger is far from being atheistic in the sense that Sartre is atheistic. Heidegger's relationship to religion is far more comparable to that of Nietzsche – albeit less violent – in that both Heidegger and Nietzsche were deeply nurtured by the Catholicism and Lutheranism which both later rejected or, more properly, transformed through deeply religious reflection and speculation. Sartre's comments, however, are understandable from the standpoint of 1947 when they were first uttered, for at that point the so-called later Heidegger had not as yet surfaced. Indeed, the religious dimension of Heidegger is at least as pronounced if not more so than the religious dimension of Jaspers which makes all the more curious Sartre's demarcation of existentialism into its religious and non-religious dimension. Only recently, through scholars like Hans-Georg Gadamer, has it become clear that the preeminent motif in Heidegger, at first latent and later manifest, has always been fundamental ontology with a profoundly mystical and religious aspect.

This makes it clear that Sartre's axiomatic suggestion that "existence precedes essence" and that "subjectivity" is the only legitimate starting point perhaps applies to himself alone. It certainly does *not* apply to Jaspers who insists first that one starts to philosophize as a subject, to be sure, but a subject who finds himself first of all as "Existenz." And Existenz is always construed as a dynamic possibility that is possible only in relation to something, and this for Jaspers, is its relatedness to Transcendence. What Transcendence is more precisely, as we have also seen, is not altogether clear. At this point, however, we can most assuredly say

[43] Jean-Paul Sartre, *The Philosophy of Existentialism* (New York: Philosophical Library, 1965), p. 34.

that the meaning of Transcendence for Jaspers is substantially different from the way Sartre understands it, viz., as a formal or epistemological aspect of consciousness with no extra-mental veridicy whatsoever. [44]

This is why we have presented Jaspers' philosophy of Transcendence as a retrieval with a double aspect. In Part I, we described the formal-phenomenological aspect of this retrieval, that is, we described how Jaspers reaches deeply into the nature of experience in order to uncover and disclose the structure and modalities of transcending-thinking. Through this analysis we noted that Jaspers, in a manner contrary to both Sartre and the early Heidegger, refuses to identify Transcendence with the act of transcending, that is, he neither identifies Transcendence with "the region of the question of transcendence," nor with unfulfilled potentiality, nor with the essential constitution of Dasein as "temporality." While historicity is of the essence of possible Existenz, it is not *the* essence. In short, the term Transcendence retains the character of a symbol with an *overplus* of signification much in the sense of Rudolf Otto. The experiential dialectic of Existenz and Transcendence is not reduced to an immanental existentialism, and even though the foci of this dialectic are known only in the experience of active transcending, Transcendence retains a definite, albeit unspoken, intentionality that harks back to the so-called *old* metaphysics of the Tradition.

Because one senses in Jaspers a reluctance to sacrifice to modernity all of the traditional meanings of Transcendence, we have sought to delineate the second or *historical* aspect of its meaning. It is, of course, Heidegger who is most famous for this *Wiederholen* and, to be sure, his project is far more radical that that of Jaspers. Contrary to Heidegger, Jaspers does not believe that the history of metaphysics must be destroyed or "unthought" in order to reconstruct an authentic ontology. Nor does Jaspers locate "the ancient name of Being" primarily among the pre-Socratics. While the "passions of the night," the archaic, and the unconscious are for Jaspers important (qua psychologist, if nothing else), he is not as romantic and mystifying as Heidegger. Indeed, the *mediational* character of the history of Western thought is viewed constructively by Jaspers. Transcending-thinking, then, is an historicist hermeneutic

---

[44] Jean-Paul Sartre, *The Transcendence of the Ego: An Existentialist Theory of Consciousness*, trans. Forrest Williams and Robert Kirkpatrick (New York; Noonday, 1957). There is for Sartre neither an objectifiable transcendence from without (God) nor from within (Ego), that is objectifiable as entity or substance or essence. In fact, both are radicalized as project even moreso than in Jaspers.

of Transcendence. It may be this aspect of Jaspers that has influenced to a considerable degree the hermeneutic philosophy of his successor at Heidelberg, Hans-Georg Gadamer, who, himself mediates, as it were, Jaspers and Heidegger. Certainly it was for the purpose of rehumanizing the history of Western philosophy that Jaspers turned to his "great philosophers," and this turn to the tradition, we suggest, was guided by the primary project of recapturing the meaning of Transcendence.

In turning to Plato and Plotinus, Kant, and Cusanus we have attempted to elucidate the source, medium, and goal of Jaspers' retrieval. All are principal figures in the critical idealist tradition and all share in the conviction that Transcendence is not only that toward which Existenz strives, but that which undergirds the very possibility of meaning. It is this shared conviction, we suggest, that similarly underlies Jaspers' contention that Transcendence is a *cipher* of inexhaustible significance. It is a conviction that is, quite obviously, also faith; *philosophical* faith, to be sure, but also *religious* faith inasmuch as Jaspers is hard-pressed to very strictly maintain the parameters of philosophical faith as, indeed, has also been the case with many of his idealist predecessors.

Jaspers hovers, as does Paul Tillich, at the boundary between idealism and realism. The critical idealists, and especially Kant, guide and in many ways govern Jaspers' reflections concerning the nature of reality. But there is also a kind of restraint at accepting the consequences of a thoroughgoing nominalism, the present effects of which, as Gadamer similarly laments, are all too evident. Like Paul Tillich, Jaspers wishes, it seems, to preserve the best of two possible worlds: the grandiose metaphysics and ontology of the Tradition, on the one hand, and modern, critical epistemology, on the other; the development of what Tillich once termed a self-transcending critical realism. At the matrix of this boundary situation one finds Jaspers' philosophy of ciphers just as, in Tillich, one finds a theology of symbol. For it is through the cipher that Jaspers wishes to move beyond the confinement of the subject-object relation, still preserve its critical limits, and yet affirm the reality of a Transcendence that clearly surpasses these limits.

This brings us directly to the problem of hermeneutics, and the task of obtaining a clearer understanding of how transcending-thinking interprets specific ciphers of Transcendence.

PART III

TRANSCENDENCE AND HERMENEUTICS

PART III INTRODUCTION

In Parts I and II, we delineated the phenomenological and historical aspects of Jaspers' philosophy of Transcendence. We noted that for Jaspers Transcendence is not only present to experience, but underlies its very possibility. Transcendence, therefore, is known through the dialectic that experience-itself is. However, Transcendence is not simply experience; that is, Transcendence is not reducible to *merely* an immanent explanation of experience. If this were the case Transcendence would lose its force altogether as signifying a dimension of reality that is ultimately non-objectifiable. It was, in fact, the immanentalist reductionism of early 20th century philosophy against which Jaspers reacted as we have seen. Therefore, if placed into the position of having to opt for immanence or Transcendence as a "way" of doing philosophy, Jaspers would certainly choose the latter. Of course, such a choice is strictly hypothetical and in practice impossible for a dialectical thinker like Jaspers. The point here is simply that from the standpoint of Transcendence the immanent is utterly real as the only possible context of transcending-thinking, whereas from the standpoint of a philosophy of immanence dogmatically avowed the reality of Transcendence is nullified *a priori* as denoting anything other than the mental character of epistemological categories. Indeed, it is precisely in this regard that Jaspers dissociates himself from pure existentialism saying that "The unfathomability of the whole, of the One that defies cognition, forbids me to take Existenz for all there is – as I would in the narrowness of an existential philosophy secluded on the basis of self-being." [1]

What we have termed Transcendence-Itself, then, is more than merely the intentional object of the act of transcending. In Jaspers the intentionality of Transcendence takes on special characteristics, for Transcendence-Itself is neither simply a mental construction, nor is it a reality

---

[1] *Phil.*, III, p. 201.

that perdures in the world apart from experience. Transcendence-Itself rather has the character of a symbol or, to use Jaspers' terminology, a *cipher* which itself, as *das Umgreifende*, encompasses a double meaning in terms of its referentiality. On the one hand there is that Encompassing which, as a transcending subject, I am, and on the other that Encompassing which, as transcended, I am not. Were one to identify the Encompassing with immanent Transcendence only, it would no longer have the metaphysical quality Jaspers clearly intends through its use. In fact, Jaspers' notion of the Encompassing is introduced in his later writings precisely, it would seem, to reinforce the mystical character of Transcendence. This intention is also present in *Philosophie* inasmuch as it is clear that the object of transcending is not merely the quantitative *more* of immanent experience but an *Otherness* that can be communicated only in the language of ciphers.[2] A certain ontological restriction is therefore inevitable if experience is viewed from the standpoint of immanence alone, and a metaphysics of Transcendence is precluded. As we have seen, however, it is precisely this experience of restriction or "disjointness" at the level of immanent experience which is Jaspers' starting point and the first clue toward the possibility of a philosophy of Transcendence.

Thus, contrary to many attempts to speak meaningfully about Transcendence from a point beyond experience (as in the case of various theologians), Jaspers begins both with and from experience. For Jaspers, the phenomenologically critical philosopher must deal first with the tendential phenomenon that man himself is, viz., the experiential force of "overcoming" or "going beyond" in the face of an Otherness which is simultaneously within and without. Jaspers' claim concerning the reality of Transcendence, then, is made neither on the basis of acquiescence to infallible theological authority nor ontological presuppositions, but is confirmed, he believes, through an analysis of the meaning of experience qua experience through deepening our understanding of its structures, its grounds, its limits and its possibilities.

Of course, there are those who would question the veracity of Jaspers' description of experience on the basis of what appears suspiciously to be a particularly religious understanding of both the philosophical task and the idealist tradition. In Part II, we hope we have succeeded in demonstrating that while Jaspers indeed is firmly rooted in the historic lan-

---

[2] *Ibid.*, pp. 119ff. Cf., also Emmanuel Levinas, *Totality and Infinity: An Essay on Exteriority* (Pittsburgh: Duquesne University Press, 1969), pp. 33ff, for an argument even more insistent in this regard.

guage of idealism, he is by no means guilty of merely repristinating it. Jaspers' reading of the idealist tradition through the conceptuality of *Existenzphilosophie* in fact opens a horizon of possibilities for understanding idealism precisely in terms of a mystical quest for Transcendence. At the same time, this does not absolve Jaspers from the serious question as to whether his reading of the Idealist Tradition is superficial for this very reason and whether, in fact, what Jaspers regards as philosophizing is not another form of subjectivism which subverts altogether the demands of critical analysis. Certainly there are those for whom it would appear that Jaspers' description of transcending in relation to Transcendence is circular argumentation in its worst and most offensive form; that the Kantian antinomy becomes for Jaspers an end in itself, and what Jaspers describes as Eternalization is salvation through what Ryle calls "category confusion." Metaphorical circularity, however, is not either unproductive or logically invalid. Speaking hermeneutically Jaspers states that the philosopher's task is not one of escaping circularity but "ascertaining the depth or shallowness, the adequacy or inadequacy of a given circle."[3] Mirroring the life process, the phenomenon of circularity is utterly essential to understanding and communication and hence the development of any metaphysic that does not ossify into ontology. In Jaspers' case we have seen that the circularity which develops reflectively in the modalities of transcending-thinking is described ultimately in terms of a "foundering" (*Scheitern*). In the process of trying to fixate and objectify that which can never be objectified, cognition founders in the face of a reality which "hovers" (*Schwebe*) as something that can only be communicated indirectly in ciphers.

The structural dynamics of transcending-thinking, then, has a great deal in common with theological hermeneutics and the circular dynamics intrinsic to Anselm's *credo ut intelligam*. This dialectic of creative insecurity, far from representing a *theologia gloriae*, is analogous to *theologia crucis* inasmuch as it is the *hubris* of formalism, on the one hand, and emotionalism, on the other, which one avoids by remaining within the circle.[4]

As we analyze further transcending-thinking as a hermeneutic of cipher several questions arise. First, is the cipher the bearer of specific metaphysical content and if so how is its meaning comprehended and

---

[3] *Myth and Christianity*, p. 46. Cf., also *Phil.*, III, pp. 129ff.
[4] *Phil.*, III, p. 208. Cf., also *Great Phil.*, I, for an analysis of Augustine's understanding of *questio mihi factus sum*, pp. 180-182.

appropriated? What is the relationship between the cipher and the faculty of intuition? Can this relation be properly differentiated experientially or is an extended use of intuition proportionate to the rather extended metaphors that ciphers are in Jaspers' view? Do ciphers only appear to have the appearance of logical meaning as mere fictions of the transcending imagination? Inasmuch as Jaspers himself states that the veracity of his "foundering metaphysics" depends on the attainment of the "purely suspended consciousness", [5] what does this have to do with elucidating the truth-claims of the metaphorical cipher?

After dealing with the relationship between intuition and ciphers we will turn to an analysis of Jaspers' hermeneutic of the principal ciphers of God in Western religious experience. In this connection we will turn to an analysis of Jaspers' own hermeneutic of the principal ciphers of God in western religious experience. In this connection we note that throughout his writings there is the pronounced tendency to speak about Transcendence and the Encompassing in general and very rarely in relation to what might be regarded as concrete examples of their symbolization. This is particularly disturbing in view of Jaspers' continuous insistence on the historic character of Transcendence; a concern that motivated our inquiry into Jaspers' relation to idealism. The allegorical character of Jaspers' interpretation of the cipher of God in his final work lends credence, indeed, to the much earlier contention of Mikel Dufrenne and Paul Ricoeur that in Jaspers' *philosophie a deux foyers* it is the foci of a highly noetic and disembodied Transcendence that is won at the price of particularity; that the lived specificity of Jaspers' existential *dialectic* ultimately *collapses* because of its lack of specificity. [7] Thus we ask, is there a fundamental difference between the conceptual cipher and the pre-philosophical fullness of mythic-religious symbols? For this question, the Bultmann-Jaspers debate is of special value. Charged with polemics that must not be overly emphasized, this discussion nevertheless raises issues having to do with Jaspers' claims concerning the "immediacy of comprehension" which, on the one hand, reinforces our theory previously advanced having to do with the mystical goal of Jaspers' philosophizing, and on the other, exposes transcending-thinking as its most vulnerable point, namely, the charge of aestheticism. Because Jaspers isolates the aesthetic and the historical in a manner directly contrary to someone like Gadamer, for example, the result is a blurring of

[5] *Truth and Symbol.*, p. 61.
[6] *Karl Jaspers et la philosophie de l'existence* (Paris: Edition du Seuil, 1947), pp. 363-371.

the formal and the historical that leaves the issue somewhat confused. As Paul Ricoeur says, "the cipher replaces the miracle, contemplation replaces prayer, and communication replaces the church." [7]

It is simply impossible, we will contend, to "purify transcendence," as Jaspers puts it, of all its presumably histrionic *accoutrements* and still have Transcendence that is convincing. As in the case of most of the values human beings cherish, symbols of Transcendence are invariably wedded to involuntary contexts over which we have little or no control, and when the contexts of these symbols are mitigated superficially for the sake of formal coherence, Transcendence disappears. Jaspers' drive to "purification of Transcendence," then, is reminiscent of the later Hegel. Excessive preoccupation with the deep structure of symbol – its purified strata, as it were – is won at the price of minimal attention vis-à-vis the initial horizon of the primary and largely unreflective naiveté that accounts for the production of religious symbols in their first instance. Of course we are not here suggesting that it is possible either to generate or to understand religious symbols and myths apart from reflection and speculation, or that such symbols come "plummeting down from above" as Karl Barth tended to suggest. We are suggesting rather that apart from a careful analysis of the rich textures of the mythic-symbolic in its historic givenness, the specificity of Transcendence is nullified through reification in the conceptual abstractions of cognitive transcending. When one interprets a given symbol or myth strictly from the standpoint of *Existenzerhellung*, one is faced with a much too facile *Horizontverschmelzung*, to use Gadamer's term, and comprehension and appropriation are achieved at the expense of the symbol and not through it. Indeed, this charge is somewhat ironic inasmuch as it was Jaspers who, over against Bultmann's project of Demythologizing, called for a "remythologizing" of religious language. But, as we will see, Jaspers fails to do what he himself calls for and it is to this extent especially that the subsequent work of both Gadamer and Ricoeur can be viewed as a "filling out" of Jaspers' intention. On the one hand, it is Gadamer, who insists that the gulf which seperates the contemporary interpreter and the ancient text is far greater than historical-critical science has assumed, and that it is a gulf that cannot be bridged through the disclosure of the latest method. On the other hand, there is Ricoeur who, against all purely speculative hermeneutics, warns that interpretation must begin from the "fulness of language" if it is to be authentic. For this to happen, one must participate in a "sympathetic reenactment" of myth far more rigorous than either the romantic-

---

[7] Schilpp, p. 624.

existential approach which views the extrapolation of personal meaning as one's first and primary task.

Indeed, inasmuch as we have spent a good deal of time delineating philosophical influences on Jaspers, it is well to mention here the debt that Gadamer and especially Ricoeur, as the two most prominent hermeneutical philosophers today, owe to Jaspers. Both Gadamer and Ricoeur, we contend, are in fundamental agreement with the goal of philosophizing as we have encountered it in Jaspers, viz., an "unfolding of the enfolding." Both men, I am suggesting, are driven by the mystical dimension of philosophizing by maintaining that reality makes sense not merely on the basis of pragmatic and functional necessity, but at the level of Transcendence. Therefore, both Gadamer and Ricoeur share with Jaspers the anti-nominalistic inclination that we are *Enfolded* by a reality that is symbolic of both that towards which human beings aspire and that reality which makes aspiration possible. *The authentic task of philosophy, then, is to unfold the meaning of that which enfolds, but not to unfold it too quickly.*

CHAPTER EIGHT

TRANSCENDING-THINKING AS HERMENEUTIC PHILOSOPHIZING

Although Jaspers rarely refers to his philosophy as hermeneutical it is hermeneutical throughout, for it is an *interpretation* of Existenz in relation to Transcendence. There are perhaps two primary reasons why he is reluctant to use the term and why he never aligned himself formally with the so-called hermeneutical movement that has exerted so much influence during the past thirty years. First, when Jaspers wrote his primary philosophical works during the 1930's and 1940's, the term hermeneutics, in its modern significance, was identified largely with Martin Heidegger's *Daseinsanalyse* as a rigorous science of existence. Insofar as the early Heidegger was dependent on Husserl, Jaspers considered *Daseinsanalyse* as a pseudo-science inasmuch as it intends a *Wesensschau* of Dasein's being-in-a-world which, on Kantian grounds, Jaspers believed impossible. Also, since the early Heidegger was commonly regarded as being an existentialist in the Sartrean sense (and for reasons we have already mentioned) Jaspers rejected *pure* existentialism which, he believed, led to voiding of authentic Transcendence and the substitution of surrogate forms of Transcendence. Jaspers also dissociated himself from Heidegger's "hermeneutics of Dasein" and what has come to be known as hermeneutic phenomenology or philosophy because he believed that with the development of his own *verstehenden Psychologie* (modeled in part on his friend Max Weber's *verstehenden Soziologie*) he had anticipated Husserl or, at the very least, implemented the legitimate "descriptive" domain of phenomenology in his early psychological writings. Thus Jaspers felt unobliged to come to terms with either Husserl or Heidegger. [1]

---

[1] Cf. Schilpp, p. 18; and Herbert Spiegelberg, *Phenomenology in Psychology and Psychiatry: A Historical Introduction* (Evanston: Northwestern University Press, 1972), pp. 96, 191. In Maurice Natanson's lucid analysis of Husserl, he contends that the speculative side of philosophy is not as foreign to rigorous phenomenology as so many have contended, and does not understand why someone like Jaspers, for example, failed to understand this. I would offer two reasons. First, Natanson contends that the *Ur*-Husserl is the Husserl of the *Krisis*. This is an assumption which had little currency in the 1930's.

Another equally important aspect of Jasper's strained relationship with Heidegger, of course, has to do with the latter's questionable politics, for during the time that Heidegger had made his peace with the Nazis Jaspers was in exile. Moreover, if one demarcates between the earlier and the later Heidegger, Jaspers would be of the opinion that the mystical archaism of the later Heidegger is directly attributable to an immanentalism which voids moral decision in the first instance. Jaspers, in brief, is far more Kantian than Heidegger when it comes to ethics. However, Jaspers himself does not come out of the turmoil of the 1940's unscathed as we will see when we turn to his interpretation of the cipher of God.

Perhaps the most significant factor, however, as to why Jaspers is not directly associated with the hermeneutical movement is its association with the Biblical theology of Rudolf Bultmann. Jaspers, to be sure, enters this discussion briefly and with fury in his exchange with Bultmann in 1953, and we will deal more with this in chapter ten. Suffice it so say here that Jaspers always viewed theology (especially in its liberal genre) as a kind of parasite, picking and choosing what it liked from philosophy, but neither contributing anything original nor entering philosophical discussion openly and without reservations. Moreover, and for reasons articulated above, Jaspers did not appreciate the Heideggerian flavor of the Bultmannian discussion which, on ontological grounds, he viewed as a wholly incommensurate coincidence of opposites. Indeed, Heidegger for similar reasons discontinued his formal association with hermeneutics even though, after 1950, his work is more hermeneutical than ever. In this respect Jaspers anticipates somewhat, although for different reasons, Heinrich Ott's reassessment of Heidegger and theology. [2]

Heidegger and Jaspers, however, do share a great deal in common,

---

when Jaspers was publishing his *Philosophie* and after he had already limited phenomenological method to its descriptive function as a means to *verstehenden Psychologie*. Second, this delimitation is informed by the fact that Jaspers from the outset regarded the subject-object relation in its Kantian setting as entirely adequate to the project of *Existenzphilosophie*, and therefore does not believe that a radical *démontage* of the subject-object relation is necessary. Had Jaspers grappled seriously with Husserl, however, he may well have come to a conclusion close to that of Natanson. Cf., *Edmund Husserl: Philosopher of Infinite Tasks* (Evanston: Northwestern University Press, 1973), pp. 160-161.

[2] Cf., James M. Robinson and John B. Cobb, Jr., *New Frontiers in Theology*, Vol. I, *The Later Heidegger and Theology* (New York: Harper and Row, 1963), pp. 77-114. It is not that Jaspers would agree with Ott's contention that Heidegger's ontology has more in common with Karl Barth whose position he would similarly reject. It is rather that Jaspers was among the first to see that the enthusiastic alliance being fashioned by Bultmann's followers between Heidegger's method and Christian theology was wholly incongruous.

especially the general *mood* of philosophizing in which both ask whether philosophy in its traditional horizon is possible anymore. When Hölderlin says "Man / Not unhappily measures himself / Against the godhead," both Jaspers and Heidegger question whether this 'measuring" can any longer be a "gay science," to use Nietzsche's phrase. "Long is the time," Heidegger muses, and perhaps we are at last drawing near to the "midpoint of our time of need."[3] Jaspers' sense of anguish is similar when he poses what he terms the "final question," namely, "what sort of a cipher of foundering is still possible today," and indeed, "Is it still possible for some sort of Being to still shine out of a total darkness?"[4] Like Heidegger, Jaspers does not provide the last word nor does he believe that such a word can be offered. His metaphysics of foundering issues only in what he terms "active sufferance" whereby one still "clings to Being *in spite of* one's foundering when the cipher of foundering itself disappears."[5]

When Heidegger speculates on the nature of "thinking" saying repeatedly that "the most significant thing that we can say about thinking is that we have not yet begun to think,"[6] Jaspers has a similar understanding of his own *transzendierenden Denkens*. One does not in the attempt to attain a knowledge of Transcendence *transcend thinking*; one transcends *through* thinking, and even then one does not transcend to *something* but to *silence*, and "if we break the silence, we speak without saying a thing."[7] Transcending-thinking, then, as a hermeneutic of Existenz is akin to Heidegger's "letting-lie-before-us and taking-to-heart also."[8] Transcending-thinking effects a kind of *seinlassen* in which the Being of beings appears even though these are "vanishing moments" that can never be fixed.[9] However, if transcending as the dynamic possibility of thinking is not present, thinking is no longer reflectively present to that which presences itself, and thinking is reduced to mere cognition.

Hence, for Jaspers as for Heidegger, the necessity of the poetic cipher or metaphor as the primary language of Transcendence or Being, for the poetic can never be fixed as *object* and a poetics is the only language proper to a foundering metaphysics. Cipher language is the language of

---

[3] Martin Heidegger, *What is Called Thinking?* Trans. Fred Wick and J. Glenn Gray (New York: Harper and Row, 1968), Lecture I.
[4] *Phil.*, III, pp. 205ff.
[5] *Ibid.*, p. 207.
[6] Heidegger, *op.cit., passim.*
[7] *Phil.*, III, p. 205.
[8] Heidegger, *op.cit.*, pp. 229-244.
[9] *Phil.*, III, p. 207.

das Zwischenreich; the only symbols appropriate to man's situation "between" earth and sky – the region surveyed by "the upward glance;" [10] the only *measures* that can communicate the reality of Transcendence in the form of an *appeal* to transcend.

Let us, then, once again look carefully at the nature of cipher and then at Jaspers' interpretation of the cipher of God.

ON THE READING OF CIPHERS AND INTUITION

As Paul Tillich once put it following Schelling, all ontological and metaphysical speculation presupposes the reality of the *Unvordenkliche* as the self-revelatory context within which what is thought may itself unfold. [11] Since "thinking the unthinkable" for Jaspers is clearly a paradox which both cries out for and simultaneously nullifies every formulation and expression of its object, it is a reality which can only be addressed indirectly in the form of an "appeal" (*appellieren*) to ciphers. We have already spoken briefly concerning the nature of "ciphers" and about how a sense of "foundering" is intrinsic to the determination of their meaning. It is now necessary to focus more sharply on the nature of the relationship between the two highly problematical and mystifying terms *cipher* and *foundering* and their relationship to the immediacy of *intuition* because upon their opperational coherence and intelligibility the possibility of a Jaspersian metaphysic clearly rests.

We have indicated that Jaspers prefers the term cipher to symbol because a symbol can be existentially neutral or, as in the case of sheer aestheticism, the meaning of symbol can be "lost in favor of the free contemplation of forms, [whereupon] life becomes aesthetic contemplation and action becomes the enjoyment of feelings." [12] In either case, symbols are no longer really ciphers but empty signs, because the existential dimension of "transcending" is no longer the compelling factor in interpretation and "apart from Existenz, there can be no ciphers." [13] Furthermore, the reason why ciphers of Transcendence have reality only for Existenz is that Existenz alone is caught up in the exigencies of freedom. In contrast to Heidegger, *Dasein*, in and of itself, is not

---

[10] Martin Heidegger, *Poetry, Language, Thought*. Trans. Albert Hofstadter (New York: Harper and Row, 1971), pp. 219-220.
[11] *Theology of Culture* (New York: Oxford, 1959), pp. 87-88.
[12] *Truth and Symbol*, p. 27.
[13] *Philosophical Faith and Revelation*, p. 117.

the problem. For Jaspers, as for mystics like Jacob Boehme, it is the *Abgrund* of freedom that makes *Dasein* a problem. While *Dasein* is objecable either as subject or object because freedom is not objectifiable and it is freedom that provides that ground antecedent to all subject-object differentiations. Hence, both Existenz and freedom can only be known from Transcendence.

At the level of common sense then, symbols simply point to or indicate something which they themselves are not as in the case of the functional transmission of information. But for Jaspers, and here very similar to the Johannine incarnationalist understanding of *semeion*, the symbol as cipher not only serves the function of indicator but somehow participates in the reality which it signifies. Thus in the case of ciphers of Transcendence, Being-Itself is present to the symbol even though as Transcendence it cannot be objectively or materially localized. The "presence" of Transcendence, therefore, is qualified severely because the ciphers that are their vehicles are, for Jaspers, "bottomless ... defying conclusiveness." In the cipher the "objectness of Being is suspended" even though "through" the cipher Being is somehow "transparent" as the "presentness of its content". [14]

The circularity of Jaspers' reasoning is here clearly manifest, for rational consciousness must founder prior to knowing the content of ciphers – indeed, to know the symbol as cipher at all – and then founder again in the very act of knowing. In fact the interpretation of ciphers (understood in the narrow sense of "valid" interpretation as E. D. Hirsch puts it) [15] is for Jaspers impossible. One does not "cognize the meaning of a cipher," for in relation to cipher interpretation is "a metaphysical act, a game," and their content as Transcendence is "nameless." [16]

Is then the inconclusiveness of foundering in the cipher language of metaphysical transcending an end in itself? And if so, does not Jaspers' foundering metaphysics dissolve in solipsism? Jaspers would say no, for the purpose and goal of transcending-thinking through ciphers is the knowledge of Being-Itself even though "[Being-Itself] ... is not what is thought of as something to be rounded off as a work of thought, as something available as objective truth, as something existing in itself without

---

[14] *Truth and Symbol*, pp. 33, 38.
[15] Cf. the neo-Artotelian hermeneutics of E.D. Hirsch, *Validity in Interpretation* (New Haven: Yale, 1967).
[16] *Truth and Symbol*, p. 42.

me. Being is not in function; it is not in the thinking of the subject as only a present reality of this accomplishment. On the contrary. Being is that which, through the reality of myself, I understand as that which is in itself even without me, but which is possible for me to perceive only through my entire nature as the organ, as it were, of the knowledge of Being." [17]

While the Being of Transcendence is reducible neither to object nor subject nor the dialectical relationship between subject and object as Kierkegaard similarly observed, [18] Transcendence for Jaspers can still be known. Moreover, it is the exclusive function of ciphers to mediate Transcendence and Existenz in a way which simultaneously encompasses and transcends all mediation, for "the cipher is neither the object nor the subject but an objectivity permeated with subjectivity in such a manner that Being becomes present in the Whole." Therefore the "consciousness of Being lies simultaneously in the grasping of the object [of Being] and the consummation of subjectivity . . . I complete Being when it is Being-for-me." [19] In the *chifferwerden* of the world we are, therefore, "plunged into the unfathomable, catching ourselves as something incomprehensibly catches us." [20]

We must note, however, that the *a priori* inconclusiveness and incomprehensibility of the Transcendence present to ciphers is based on an ontological presupposition present throughout Jaspers' discourse on ciphers, namely, that although the phenomenal order is fundamentally contingent and disjoint, it is disjointness arising out of an antecedent completeness – "*den tiefen Grund in dem alles Sein ein Sein ist.*" [21] Therefore, even though the act of transcending is motivated initially by the brokenness of being, Being-Itself is not fragmentary since, as both the origin and goal of Existenz, Being is an Encompaasing which, as in the case of the God of Cusanus, is "Infinite and boundless, the unity of opposites, the affirmation and negation of all." [22] All dogmatic interpretations of the content of ciphers of Transcendence ultimately must fail; a failing that sometimes generates skeptical "anti-reason" that would consign to absurdity all talk of ciphers. Hence, failure to maintain the "boundary" position represented by *Existenzphilosophie* leads, as

---

[17] *Ibid.*, p. 34.
[18] Cf., *The Sickness Unto Death*, (Princeton, 1941), pp. 17-19.
[19] *Truth and Symbol*, pp. 23, 34.
[20] *Philosophical Faith and Revelation*, p. 116.
[21] *Von der Wahrheit*, p. 260.
[22] *Philosophical Faith and Revelation*, p. 260.

Jaspers puts it eloquently, "to the world of hazy ideologies which offer themselves as authentic truth, to the unreasonable, to absurdities which claim to be profundities, to aesthetic license and poetic anarchism, to hyper-intellectual constructions which mean nothing at all and to the dialectic which enables every decision to be abandoned, everything to be contradicted and everything justified. It leads, in a word, to the witches' sabbath of metaphorical talk, dogma and absolutes, to an endless retracing of one's step, ever-changing interpretations of life, for which interpretation is no longer important as the way to the source but as a fathomless end in itself, the dead end of interpreting interpretations." [23]

Strong words indeed manifesting the seriousness with which Jaspers would have us view his project; words reminiscent of theologians like Karl Barth and Anders Nygren, and philosophers such as Bertrand Russell and Alfred Jules Ayer. Neo-orthodoxy, however, made no claims for Transcendence apart from belief in *Heilsgeschichte* and the enabling *testimonium spiriti sancti internum*; and the logical empiricists, having well and enough of Transcendence in all its forms, made no such claims at all. Jaspers clearly stands midway between these two extreme forms of neo-Kantianism. How then are ciphers of transcendence to be known, and once known *what* is known?

Jaspers clearly does not count himself among either the philosophical or the theological dogmatists, and neither does he regard himself as a skeptical nihilist or relativist condemned to "the dead end of interpreting interpretations." How then does he propose to interpret ciphers of Transcendence in a way that is both critically respectable and existentially constructive? And once the meaning of these ciphers is known, what, precisely, is known?

Here we get to the crux of the matter, for Jaspers maintains that the reality and meaning of Transcendence cannot be known apart from "a certain intuitive element." [24] Indeed, the term *intuition* is central for, as we saw throughout Part II, Jaspers extends consistently the prevailing neo-Kantian understanding of intuition reinvesting it with what might be termed the crypto-Platonic, metaphysical resonance that intuition enjoyed among the mystics. The metaphysical-religious potentiality of intuition, however, is never asserted to be a fact directly but only on the *a priori* condition that one is philosophizing *aus möglicher Existenz*. In other words, the metaphysical potentiality of intuition is something

---

[23] *Reason and Anti-Reason*, p. 70.
[24] *Myth and Christianity*, pp. 24, 77-78.

which, as in the case of Paul Tillich, is a *latent* possibility which becomes *manifest* through the series of existential and intellectual conversions we have outlined in Part I. In every instance the reality of Transcendence present to intuition is perceived to be rational and not irrational, for Transcendence is the precondition of reason.

Jaspers' position on the relation between Transcendence and rational intuition, it would seem, has strong resemblance to the view of John Findlay when he says of the Absolute that "it is an intentional object unique among cave-objects in that it brings into one focus all recognized values and leaves no room for an alternative synthesis beside it: it is also unique among cave-objects since it cannot be thought of in full seriousness except as existing, and as existing with necessity." Findlay further states that there seems to be something "inevitable" about this conclusion by virtue of the fact that we are "living and conscious;"[25] that is, the inevitability seems to derive from the very nature of rational intuition which, for Jaspers, is the presence of Transcendence to *Vernunft* as its antecedent ground of its possibility.

Thus in Jaspers the truth value or objectivity of Transcendence is completely contingent upon an intelligible elucidation of the experience of Transcendence; that is, upon demonstrations of the conversions intrinsic to cognitive transcending and not on the basis of *a priori* claims whether emotive or gnostic. If one does not accept Jaspers' phenomenology of experience together with some rather unconventional epistemological presuppositions, what Jaspers has to say concerning the reality of Transcendence can easily appear either as nonsense or yet another form of gnosticism. Moreover, even if one concedes the kind of cognitive and existential transcending Jaspers outlines, one must ask, as in the case of Dufrenne and Ricoeur, whether a project which tries to establish some kind of "equilibrium" between Kierkegaardian "Transcendence" and Nietzschean "Immanence" does not result in an "aestheticism of Transcendence" and whether it is not from the outset motivated by a kind of "vanity."[26] Indeed, there is a sense in which any kind of appeal to an undifferentiated intuitive power is bound to sound like mystagogy analogous to the contemplative warning to take stock carefully of one's life before entering into psyche-shattering interstices of the "cloud of unknowing," or even the apocalyptic pertubations intrinsic to Jesus' statements that "Many are called but few are chosen," and "Strait is the

[25] Cf., *The Transcendence of the Cave* (London: George Allen & Unwin Ltd, 1967), pp. 77ff. It must be noted that Findlay's argument for the Absolute is "axiological" whereas Jaspers' is strictly "intuitive" and "experiential."
[26] *Karl Jaspers et la philosophie de l'existence*, pp. 363ff.

Gate, and Narrow the Way." But in the case of Jesus, such warnings are of a decidedly moral nature, and in the case of the ascetic, a warning which reminds the novice of the *discipline* one must muster in order to survive the indeterminacy of the contemplative life. Can one say as much of the manner in which Jaspers frames a project of transcending-thinking and reflection about reflection which sometimes sounds like a comfortable drawing room activity? Does the language of Existenz and its presuppositions make the same kind of demand upon the subject or is it, as in the case of a good deal of existentialism, as Barth suggested, a bourgeois *cor curvum in se*? Critical questions of ethics aside, can intuition alone serve as the medium of Transcendence or does it merely compound the problem, particularly the task of hermeneutics, as Bultmann asserted when he disdainfully referred to Jaspers' intuitive ciphers as a "magical language." [27] Even though there is clearly an Otherness present to the intuition of ciphers, intuition, as we have stated repeatedly, makes sense only with reference to an object-Other that can be intuited. Yet within the constraints of Jaspers' *Anwesenheit*, there can be no elucidation of a cipher of transcendence through reference to an interior reality, whether psychic, conceptual, theological or empirical. "Ciphers," Jaspers states, "do not permit interpretation with regard to an 'Other'." Here we must ask whether the fundamental "alterity" of transcendence, so eloquently developed by Levinas, [28] is not lost or at least sacrificed to Jaspers' method of transcending-thinking precisely for the sake of ontological agenda that Jaspers himself both rejects and claims to avoid.

Before we can answer these questions and others concerning the meaning of intuition and its relation to the mytho-poetic we must attempt to focus more accurately on the symbolic function of cipher-language, that is, upon what it is that ciphers transmit by way of a specific content that can be transmitted or communicated in no other way.

THE CONTENT OF CIPHERS

Although the notion of cipher is central to the philosophy of Jaspers' writings, he does not provide the rigorous and detailed analytic of symbol one finds in the writings of Cassirer, Ricoeur and Gadamer. As we have seen, Jaspers makes extensive use of phenomenology as a descrip-

---

[27] *Myth and Christianity*, p. 61.
[28] *Totality and Infinity* (Pittsburgh: Duquesne University Press, 1972), Part One.

tive tool, but he does not believe that it is capable of laying bare the eidetic structures of experience, as in the case of Husserl's *Wesensschau*, nor does he use phenomenology to elucidate the symbolic nature of language, whether by way of a phenomenological hermeneutic, as in the case of Gadamer and Ricoeur, or by uncovering a presumed mythical substratum of language as the propaedeutic to philosophical anthropology as in the case of Cassirer and Jung.

For the neo-Kantian, Ernst Cassirer, objectivity of whatever kind, whether artistic, scientific, religious or philosophical, is possible only on the basis of presentation through symbolic form. Whatever meaning man is able to derive from these areas of inquiry and expression is possible only on the basis of reflexive re-presentation through symbolic form. In sum, the symbol not only stands at the matrix of human experience but at the very matrix of reality. Thus it is possible, in Cassirer's view, to reduce all questions concerning the nature of reality to the symbolic form of their content.[29] If one's intention is that of laying hold of Truth, one will not find it by either addressing the object as subject nor the subject as object but by closely scrutinizing the phenomenon of language because whatever Truth, is through language. What Cassirer finds at the level of primal linguistic experience is not an elucidation of Being through abstract differentiations or the ability to so abstract, but rather a "concentration" of experience that gives rise to language. This process is most clearly illustrated in the language of myth. As Cassirer puts it, "It is here in the intuitive-creative form of myth and not in the formation of our discursive-theoretical concepts that we must look for the key which may unlock for us the secrets of the original conceptions of language."[30] It is at the heart of the intuitive-creative symbol, then, that Cassirer finds consubstantiality between man and world, subject and object; a primordial, undifferentiated "presence" which is simultaneously material and dynamic. It is the pre-predicative, nascent awareness of "presence" or what Heidegger terms the "at-home-ness" of "dwelling" that gives rise to the search for formal means of differentiation and apart from which the latter would be impossible.[31] What differentiates Cassirer from Jaspers is

---

[29] Cf., Ernst Cassirer, *The Philosophy of Symbolic Form*, Vol. I, trans. Ralph Manheim (New Haven: Yale, 1973), especially chapter two and following.

[30] *Language and Myth*, trans. Susanne Langer (New York, 1946), p. 34.

[31] For example, in the wide and for us undifferentiated sense of the use of the term *Wakanda*, by the American Indians, Cassirer finds a symbolic form "so manifestly protean that it is not susceptible to translation into more highly differentiated languages of civilization," inasmuch as the term can alternatively signify power, divinity, age, grandeur, etc., and hence a much more encompassing manner than our own use of the term "mystery." *Ibid.*, p

the latter's insistence on non-objectifying thinking that more definitively separates him from the neo-Kantians. What differentiates Jaspers, Heidegger and Gadamer from Cassirer is that Cassirer is after a genetic theory of language and Being.

Cassirer also offers a distinction as to the nature of the symbolic metaphor by differentiating between the "conscious" and the "radical" metaphor in a manner that is analogous to Jaspers' distinctions between "symbol" and "cipher," "cognition" and "thinking." Whereas the conscious metaphor involves conceptualization and categorical interpretation, the radical metaphor involves no such conceptual transfer of meaning through the evocation of "supporting" symbols. As in Plato, the radical cipher effects a *metabasis eis allo genos*, i.e., "not merely a translation to another category but the creation of the category itself." [32] Both Cassirer and Jaspers would be in agreement with Ricoeur that the meaning of the symbol cannot be approached by the hermeneut equipped only with the linear-bound tools of symbolic and modal logic. [33] As Cassirer puts it, ordinary logic is operative on the basis of "concentric expansion" – placing as much as possible within the aegis of the simplest and most economic categories of explanation – whereas the form of logic appropriate to the comprehension of the mytho-poetic must "be able to comprehend the compression of experience to a single point." [34] Jaspers, as we have seen, is less inclined towards the formal possibility of any such logic, for an experience of the "single point" is cognizable for the transcending subject only in the particular "lived" existential situation which, a priori, is itself non-objectifiable. [35] Hence, the development of a "philosophy of symbolic form," for Jaspers, is precluded by the very nature of its object. As Jaspers states: "Ciphers are listened to, not cognized. All talk about them . . . is already mistaken in its roots. For this reason the character of the cipher is only encircled but not reached if, in metaphor, we call it speech." [36] Cassirer's philosophy of symbolic form

67. This does not in any way signal a weakness in reason, for Cassirer, but rather the strength of experience; what Heidegger would no doubt regard as an altogether different sense of *Da-sein*. Cf., *Poetry, Language, Thought*, pp. 143-162.
Cf. *Poetry, Language, Thought*, pp. 143-162.
[32] *Language and Myth*, p. 88.
[33] Cf., *Freud and Philosophy*(New Haven: Yale, 1971), p. 56, and also Ricoeur's article "The Hermeneutics of Symbols and Philosophical Reflection," *International Philosophical Quarterly*, II, No. 2, 1963, pp. 192-193.
[34] As an example of this "single point," Cassirer cites the principle of *pars pro toto* or comprehending the "whole in the part" which has a long history in the fetishism of various shamanistic religions. *Language and Myth*, p. 90.
[35] *Von der Wahrheit*, pp. 24-27.
[36] *Truth and Symbol*, p. 41.

also brings to mind Whitehead's notion concerning the "fallacy of mis-placed concreteness." Certainly both Jaspers and Cassirer would agree that it is precisely the drive to fixity within the Western analytical mind which militates against appreciating the "prehensive" ground out of which mytho-poetic expressions arise. Thus the task for Cassirer as in the case of Whitehead, is somehow to get back to this primal ground by mapping out the landscape of intuitive feeling. [37] The difference however, and it is by no means inconsequential, is that primordialists like White-head, Cassirer, Jung and to some extent Heidegger, tend to be romantics, for, as Ricoeur observes in the case of Freud, the romantic always seeks truth on the basis of a drive of the "always anterior" regions of experience. [38] Jaspers, who sometimes manifests similar tendencies, nevertheless recognizes the danger of the reductive-archeological tend-ency which he believes is almost always based on the intention of ex-tending metaphysics to ontology. The sole purpose of interpreting ciphers or symbols for Jaspers, by contrast, is the elucidation of the re-gion "between" (*Zwischenreich*) the universal and the particular, that is, the mediational nexus that always retains its ethical mo-ment. Therefore, Jaspers is reluctant to regard cipher-script as some kind of primordial *Urgrund* upon which one may de-velop an ontology of symbolic form, as in the case of Cassirer, or a cos-mology, as in the case of Whitehead's philosophy of experience. In either case, what is intended is the discovery of some kind of objective given or empirical substrate however concealed it might be in conceptual meta-phors, and what is lost in the process of objectivation is the *sui generis* and spontaneous character of ciphers, the metaphysical contents of which are cognizable only to a particular Existenz. If, however, Jaspers fails to provide a descending analytic of mytho-poetic language as in the manner of either Cassirer, Whitehead or Ricoeur, he does very definitely provide his own version of an ascending dialectic or teleology in the form of a periechontology of transcending-thinking. In fact, it is Jaspers' con-tinual invocation of the term Transcendence and all its conceptual cog-nates which militates against any primordial reduction. It is the dialectic of Transcendence and Existenz which takes place within the "embattled realm of ciphers" which has disavowed the glorious quest for categorical absolutes – whether primordial or eschatological – and the dialectic which points beyond itself to that All-Encompassing ground "beyond

---

[37] *Process and Reality*, esp. pp. 238-279.
[38] *Freud and Philosophy*, p. 423.

dialectic." [39]

If it sometimes seems that Jaspers rather indiscriminately invokes the language of intuition in order to firm up and somehow validate what is in fact merely an intended reality, it must also be said that he does not disguise in the intuitive language of ciphers a project as large as either that of Cassirer or Whitehead. In Jaspers the content of ciphers always has to do with transparency to *freedom* as the ground of possible Transcendence. Thus the task of Existenz is *not* to go *beyond* ordinary experience but to remain completely *within* it. This is clearly evidenced, as we shall see, in Jaspers' interpretation of the cipher of God.

THE CIPHER OF GOD

As the bearers of Transcendence, ciphers are agencies of mediation immediately given to human experience; *Anknüpfungspunkten*, to use the term of Emil Brunner, between the act of transcending and the Being of Transcendence. Anything within the horizon of possible experience can be a cipher of Transcendence, and while some ciphers are more revelatory than others, all presuppose the active participation and reflection of transcending-thinking. [40] Jaspers develops no hierarchy of ciphers, for the cogency or presence of Transcendence to a particular cipher is utterly contingent upon the historical, cultural and religious situation of an individual Existenz. Consequently, Jaspers insists that the religious ciphers of the Judaeo-Christian tradition or any so-called developed religion are not superior to other religious ciphers or non-religious ciphers, for that matter. [41] Ciphers, according to Jaspers, are to be differentiated according to their performance at a particular level of consciousness. Stated differently, that which is of decisive metaphysical and existential significance concerning a particular cipher is not its historical givenness, but the quality of its mediation of Transcendence as it effects the ethical and aesthetic quality of the transcending subject. In a word, it is *Lebenspraxis* that authenticates the cipher as experienced, interpreted, understood, and appropriated.

---

[39] *Philosophical Faith and Revelation*, pp. 200-203.
[40] This is what Fritz Buri, in a similar way, terms *Thinking Faith*, trans. Harold Oliver (Philadelphia: Fortress, 1968).
[41] Cf. John Findlay, *op. cit.*, pp. 81ff., where he suggests that the acid test of the name of a religious Absolute is whether or not "it is an expression of *Vernunft*."

While Jaspers states that "Transcendence is not known in general but only through historical experience," [42] and that "it is historical experience which provides the first and direct language of ciphers," [43] it is not the first or *material* language of ciphers that really concerns Jaspers. Here, as in most of Jaspers' work the term historical has to do with epistemological differentiation; that is, Jaspers is talking about historical consciousness and not immediate sensory experience. At the level of non-historical immediacy, experience (especially *religious* experience) is undifferentiated and only dimly understood. As in the case of a child, one does not think beyond the first or primary language of ciphers; one rather "exists in their glow," [44] as it were. However, at the second or *reflective* level of experience, the term historical assumes a partially critical function whereby the rationale for the organization of a specific body of myths can be produced from ciphers. With the existential element introduced the process of interpretation begins; an "unveiling by veiling things anew" or a "remythologizing" of our experience, as Jaspers puts it, [45] that frequently results in the development of a canon of myth whereby the true is separated from the false. Because of the subjective character of this level of reading ciphers, however, one can easily be trapped in orthodox dogmatism unless the third or *speculative* language of ciphers is introduced. Left to itself, the orthodox attitude, according to Jaspers, is unaware of the fact that the cipher of Transcendence is "non-identical with itself;" that the Transcendence intended by the first or primary language of ciphers intends a meta-reality that cannot be manipulated into dogma based on so-called *objective* historical facts. Orthodoxy's claim to historical objectivity, then, is but a disguised form of uncritical subjectivism. Without the third or critically speculative level of differentiation, the mythic symbols espoused by various religions ossify into the heteronomous shells of empty religiosity, their Transcendent contents having long since vanished.

While the first two levels of cipher language, for Jaspers, are somewhat objectifiable both methodologically and functionally, the third or metaphysically speculative language of ciphers is not. As consciousness of the

---

[42] *Phil.*, III, p. 114.

[43] *Ibid.*, p. 115.

[44] Cf. *Chiffren der Transzendenz*, p. 65, where Jaspers speaks at length about the "*wundersame Geborgenheit*" and "*Naivität*" of one's initial experience of ciphers of Transcendence. It is precisely the notion of *naiveté* that is developed by Ricoeur as the counter-measure against Jaspers' philosophy of reflection.

[45] *Phil.*, III, p. 116; *Myth and Christianity, passim.*

Absolute, this level of interpretation demands a kind of intellectual conversion. Such knowledge is known only out of a consciousness of the depths of freedom and is doxologized as *gift*: "It is like a gift from the source of Being. As a mundane ascertainment of Transcendence it seeks out the light from the roots of possible Existenz and its content is not an advancement of knowledge but the historic truth of transparent existence." [46] Jaspers' triadic conception of the reading and interpretation of ciphers (not to mention the three primary modalities of transcending-thinking upon which they are based) are close, if not identical, to the triadic movement or "activity" of Hegel's Absolute Spirit. Hegel speaks of his stages as those of "manifestation" (nature religion), "development" (through the emergence of individuation), and finally "determination" (through theology and philosophy of religion). [47] Whether largely historical and logical, as in the case of Hegel, or existential, as in the case of Jaspers, both thinkers presupposed as the antecedent reality to this gift an *intuition* of the cipher of God which tests in an ultimate way the boundaries and limitations of knowing. However, it is a paradoxical testing for from it knowledge discovers its non-objectifiable source. As Jaspers puts it: "The cipher of God is that which points me beyond all ciphers transcending to the true Transcendent abyss and ground of all mysticism; to the ground which I cannot mythicize anymore." [48] Jaspers' "Transcendent abyss" clearly has its origins in Rhineland mysticism – especially the *Abgrund* of Jacob Boehme, and can also be perceived as undergirding Hegel's Absolute Spirit: "That Spirit, as it does in all else, must in religion also run through its natural course, is necessarily bound up with the conception of Spirit. Spirit is only Spirit when it exists for itself as the negation of all finite forms, as this absolute ideality." [49]Transcendence is, therefore, the "original cipher."

Jaspers' final university lectures delivered during the summer semester at Basel in 1961 provide us with a case study for examining his mystical idealization of the cipher of God. [50] In these lectures we find not only

---

[46] *Ibid.*, p. 120. See also Schilpp, *op. cit.*, p. 139.

[47] G.W.F. Hegel, *On Art, Religion, Philosophy: Introductory Lectures to the Realm of Absolute Spirit*, ed. J. Glen Gray (New York: Harper, 1970), pp. 182-206.

[48] *Philosophical Faith and Revelation*, p. 123.

[49] Hegel, *op. cit.*, p. 205.

[50] *Chiffren der Transzendenz* (Munich: R. Piper, 1970). See also the essay by John N. Findlay, "Religion and its Three Paradigmatic Instances: Jesus, Buddha, Socrates," in *Religious Studies*, II, 1975, pp. 215-227, for a similar rendering of the primary instanciations of the Absolute, but in a way much more favorable to the "cipher of Incarnation."

the obvious traces of the mystics but also stern pronouncements against confessional Christianity and the cipher of the Incarnation. Here Jaspers, in fact, departs from Hegel's notion of the necessary incarnate instantiation of Absolute Spirit. Thus we ask, is the anti-incarnationalism of Jaspers motivated strictly by epistemology and ontology or are there other reasons, perhaps of a moral and political character, that inform his apparent hostility to the cipher of Jesus as the Christ. Here we will address briefly the political horizon against which, in part, Jaspers' interpretation may be viewed.

Western tradition, Jaspers states, has generated three basic ciphers of the Divine: God as "One," as "Personal" and as "Incarnate." [51] The cipher of God as One presents Transcendence through the rational will to unity which, as One, can overcome the multifariousness of experience and provide a foundation for life which is secure and unassailable to the onslaughts of contingency. The radical monotheism of the Hebrew experience provides what Jaspers considers to be the most profound mythic form of the will to unity: "Yahweh," he states, "is simultaneously the Absolute One of Transcendence and the One in the direction of my historical realization . . . therefore the infinitely distant, inconceivable, unrecognizable Ground of all Being, and on the other hand, very near as it is given to me in my freedom and on the way of my becoming identical with myself." [52]

Whenever the cipher of the Transcendent One is reduced to a "numerical one," it is no longer a cipher of God but a basis for ideological dogmatism and fanaticism which demands conformity on the basis of a single, prescriptive notion of unity. [53] All periods of dogmatic religious orthodoxy destroy Transcendence and in its place divinize a form of immanence. True unity, by contrast, is always "the gift of Transcendence apart from which no one can prove that he has it. If one advances prescriptive judgments on the basis "having this Unity, then these judgments become pernicious (*ein verderbliches Urteilen*) and destructive of that which is truly human." [54] Jaspers, like Bertrand Russell, does not hesitate also to show that most of the atrocities in history have been committed by crypto-religious ideologies in the name of the One which are both perversions and transmutations of the qualitative Other-

---

[51] *Chiffren der Transzendenz*

[52] *Ibid.*, p. 52.

[53] Jaspers' reflections on the "numerical one" are clearly informed by Cusanus. Cf., *supra.*, Part II, Ch. Seven.

[54] *Chiffren der Transzendenz*, p. 56.

ness present to authentic experiences of Transcendence. In contrast to the numerical, quantitative one, "the qualitative One maintains itself in a state of hovering (*in der Schwebe*) pointing the way. The numerical one fixates, rapes and interrupts the way. It leads to that which is senseless and nonsense in relation to the One and is against God even more so when it refers to God."[55] The cipher of the One, then, is that which has simultaneously produced the great monotheistic religions of the world (including a-theistic Buddhism) as well as that which has provided the unifying force of speculative metaphysics – particularly metaphysical idealism dating from Plato and Plotinus. Clearly it is the *idea* of the Transcendent Yahweh in Hebrew religion that appeals to Jaspers, and not the *substance* of this deity. This has long been the case in the Platonist tradition of Christian metaphysics, and Jaspers is no exception as we shall see in his interpretation of the cipher of Incarnation.

The second great cipher of the Divine in the West is the notion of a "Personal God." As in the case of the cipher of Unity, the idea and mystery of the person, according to Jaspers, is fundamental to human experience and will continue to be so long beyond the endurance of any particular religion. Nevertheless, Jaspers believes that through the biblical experience the cipher of the person has been elevated to an uncommonly profound and serious level of existential and metaphysical expression through the notion of the numinous but historical encounter with a "Transcendent Thou." Furthermore, it is the quality of biblical personalism which bears along by sheer force a great deal of testimony concerning the historic objectivity of Transcendence; an observation close in its intent to Lonergan's notion that "true objectivity is the result of authentic subjectivity."[56] Therefore, in opposition to those who, like Feuerbach and Freud, would demystify the notion of encounter with a personal God, Jaspers affirms that "If one knows that one is given one's freedom by Transcendence, this means that in our consciousness we are always directed towards something, that we are split into subject and object, then I suggest that *there is an objectivity to Transcendence* to which the subjective freedom of self-Being seems to be opposed. Therefore, one can in no way state that the personal God is an illusion, something which man simply produces because he needs it. This suggestion would perhaps have some validity if it could be shown that this creativity in man really can produce something like God and not merely state it . . . One can just

---

[55] *Ibid.*, p. 58.
[56] Cf., Bernard Lonergan, *Method in Theology* (New York: Herder, 1972), p. 297.

as validly assert the personal deity as that through which man comes to his humanity – becomes a *personal* man ... Therefore, one can say that to the degree that Transcendence assumes the cipher of the personal God, to that extent the personal character of man increases. Because human beings can become persons or personalities, they become as the objectivity of Transcendence in the Encompassing which opens itself in the cipher of the Personal God." [57]

The cipher of the personal God, then, is precisely that which prevents the objectification and hence the reduction of human existence to mere function and process. Even though the cipher of the personal God is not unique to the Judaeo-Christian tradition, nowhere, for Jaspers, is it developed with more power and presence, for it is precisely the God of the Bible who is supremely active within and known through history: "The God who is angry and full of passion, who loves, who punishes, who makes irrevocable demands, who directs history and all this in pictures and mandates which appear in the Bible and which imprint themselves on the Westerner. However, the multiplicity of these images illustrates the overpowering indefiniteness of the Whole, or, so to speak, the formless form of God. The people that permitted Moses to go up Mount Sinai knew that man is not allowed to see God for he will die immediately and Moses sees God only from behind and Isaiah only his feet. These are ciphers which show the overpowering indefiniteness of the Divine as both something conceivable and inconceivable." [58]

While Jaspers reveres the moral and ethical force of the cipher of the personal God, he has grave doubts concerning its consequences when ontological status is attributed to the Transcendent Thou. On the one hand, the force of the Genesis myth of creation makes clear that human life is dignified by virtue of the isomorphism of the creator and the created intrinsic to the *imago dei*. All who would objectify and thereby defile the meaning of human existence are warned that such actions are a fundamental transgression of what is Unconditional. The cipher of the personal God, therefore, can be an effective weapon against all who would, contra-Kant, regard human life as a *means* and not an *end in itself*. But on the other hand the notion of a personalized Thou as Transcendence-Itself is informed by the conviction, as in Hartshorne, that the essence of Transcendence is "relations" which would imply that God qua person "needs other things, persons, and nature besides itself." Here Jaspers'

---

[57] *Chiffren der Transzendenz*, pp. 60-61. Emphasis, mine.
[58] *Ibid.*, p. 64.

mystical theism in its ontological dimension reasserts itself against the cipher of the personal God, for he warns that "Lest man profane the deity – and in order that he may be himself as he should – he must keep Transcendence pure in its concealment, its distance, its strangeness." [59] The cipher of the personal God when avowed uncritically, in short, leads very easily to the corporealizing of Transcendence one finds in the cipher of the Incarnate God.

We detect two basic reasons for Jaspers' severe critique of the third cipher of God, the cipher of Incarnation. First, it is a cipher whose basic meaning is already concealed in the ciphers of Unity and Personality and secondly, it is a cipher which radically immanentalizes the Divine, hence destroying its status as a cipher. The significance of the cipher of Incarnation for Christianity lies in the fact that it is a unique, historical manifestation of the Divine. Moreover it is *ephapax* – once for all time – and not one of the many incarnations characteristic of the mystery religions. This uniqueness, however, is adumbrated by a plethora of Christological conflicts which, for Jaspers, indicate the degree to which man erroneously craves for the corporealization of Transcendence and hence an end to the existential struggle intrinsic to the freedom that both underlies and empowers transcending-thinking in ciphers. Christology, for Jaspers, frequently degenerates into Christomonism if not blatant Christolatry in what he terms the "pretensive" character of much Christian theology: "Here man no longer really wants to be man; he would like to be rid of the tremendous burden which has been laid upon him through the hazardous risk of freedom and the endless ignorance of his ways; to be rid of everything which is imposed upon him as man by possessing the corporeality of God which brings everything into order." [60]

The passion with which Christianity has preserved and perpetuated its highly prescriptive interpretations of the person and work of Jesus is for Jaspers sufficient evidence of a "will to exclusivism" that is not only the major impediment to global religious understanding but the phenomenon which has shattered the very fabric of Christianity itself. This is why Christianity is so frequently willing, as Dostoevsky similarly observed, to exchange "truth" for "order." The either/or attitude of Kierkegaard is, for Jaspers, symptomatic of the radical "decision" the church demands of one over against the corporeal God, Jesus: "Either one falls down in prayer or one participates in his murder." [61] For Jaspers, this *Krisis* for-

---

[59] *Phil.*, III, pp. 146-147.
[60] *Chiffren der Transzendenz*, p. 68.
[61] *Ibid.*, p. 69. See also *Myth and Christianity*, pp. 76-84, where Jaspers does not reflect on

mula is acceptable only if the cipher of Christ is understood as a *single* but not the *only* manifestation of the encompassing cipher of a Transcendence that is transhistorical and transcultural. If this is not the case, that is, if one maintains that "Jesus is the only way," then the cipher of the Incarnation loses its transparency and we are no longer dealing with a cipher at all but yet another hypostatized "myth of the objectifying consciousness" [62] whereby authentic transcending – and faith – have been nullified altogether. The so-called *skandalon* of the Incarnation, then, does not for Jaspers have so much to do with the Jesus of history as with the more traditional Christian doctrines of the atonement (especially the Latin or Anselmian *cor deus homo* formulation) in which "everything has been taken care of, so to speak, by the incarnate god-man." It is in this sense that the claims of *Katholizität* – so frequently the brunt of Jaspers' ire – are considered by Jaspers as both inimical to reason and destructive of true faith. [63]

Jaspers therefore concludes that the Hebrew scriptures and Jewish tradition generally, out of its deep and abiding sensitivity to the tragic and fallen character of the human condition and its familiarity with the reality of exile and "active sufferance," attests to an authentic comprehension of the cipher of God. As the preeminent example of radical monotheism and with ontology bracketed, as it were, Judaism insists that our only comprehension of Transcendence can be through ciphers. Contrary to New Testament thinking, these ciphers are never viewed as being identical with Transcendence-Itself; a precept firmly rooted in the Decalogue which prohibits the immediatizing of the Divine in any "image or likeness" or theory, we might add. [64] It is in this spirit that Jaspers asserts: "Although we can imagine the appearance of seeing beyond images, we cannot be deceived by this. We do not need ciphers in order to contain the Divine but to hear them as ciphers, to see them and read them in order to obtain contact with Transcendence without being forced to believe that what we are seeing as appearance has become reality or the corporeality of the Divine which they never are." [65]

---

the skandalon of the incarnation and atonement, but upon what he considers to be the "scandal" of the Lutheran doctrine of "justification by faith." Noticeably missing from Jaspers' discourse, however, is any attention to "grace" and its visible signs as the agency whereby justification is effected "through faith."

[62] Cf., Fritz Buri, *Theology of Existence*, trans. Harold H. Oliver (Attic Press, 1965), pp. 108ff., for the most direct adaptation of Jaspers' philosophy by a theologian in the Christian tradition.

[63] Cf., *Chiffren der Transzendenz*, p. 43; *Von der Wahrheit*, pp. 850-855; and *Myth and Christianity*, pp. 76-84.

[64] *Chiffren der Transzendenz*, p. 66.

[65] *Ibid.*, p. 44.

PHILOSOPHICAL FAITH AND CHRISTIAN FAITH

The cipher of God, then, is the *axis mundi* of Jaspers' philosophy of Transcendence. It is the cipher of ciphers, the originating ground of all possible ciphers. As such, it is the cipher preeminently transparent to the abysmal reality beyond all ciphers, all dialectic, and all possible formal modalities of transcending-thinking. It is the cipher that passes into the silence of the above-Being and the oblivion of non-Being. In their concrete historicality, ciphers of God, when authentic, evidence what Luther termed the dialectic of the *deus revelatus* and the *deus absconditus* always keeping, as Jaspers puts it, "the essence of the Godhead flatly concealed." [66]

Unlike Luther, however, and in contrast to Christianity generally, Jaspers, as we have seen, does not view the cipher of the Incarnation as admitting the dialectic of concealment and unconcealment in a constructive manner. Needless to say, this is a bit odd for a thinker who otherwise is so firmly ensconced in Western philosophical and religious tradition. Certainly, the cipher of Jesus as the Incarnate Christ is as subject to inspired or perverse interpretations as any other cipher. The question, then, is why, given the ethical and moral dimensions of Jaspers' thought, he is not led to at least appreciate the kind of Christology one finds in his contemporary, Dietrich Bonhoeffer, for example, in whose work the ontological and historical aspects of Christological speculation are so critically and prophetically balanced. [67] Can it be that we are at this very point confronted by the fundamental difference of the "cost of discipleship" and its exchange value between philosophical and Christian faith? Does philosophical faith, in fact, demand anything that might be termed *discipleship*? Is there anything that might be regarded as a kind of *wager* to admit one into the life of philosophical faith? The following passage, so rich in allusion to the imagery of Christianity, would suggest that there is: "As consciousness at large I see nothing but sheer existence. Antinomies are built into my existential relations to Transcendence; through these relations there is as yet no completion in time. But the eye of Existenź, contemplative imagination, makes it possible for me as I read the

---

[66] *Phil.*, III, p. 60.
[67] Cf., *Act and Being*, trans. Bernard Noble (New York: Harper, 1961); *Ethics*, ed. Eberhard Bethge, trans. Neville Horton Smith (New York: MacMillan, 1955); and *Christ the Center*, trans. John Bowden (New York: Harper, 1966).

ciphers to have a sense of completion, of temporal fulfillment, for a vanishing moment. Imagination lets an Existenz find peace in Being; the cipher transfigures the world." [68] Is this the language of faith or is it the language of a kind of romantic aestheticism?

Perhaps this question will come into focus a bit more clearly if we reflect a bit on the political and religious horizon that informs Jaspers' negative reading of the cipher of the Incarnation and, indeed, his choice for the superiority of Judaic over Christian *Chifferschrift*. The political and cultural factors, we contend, are of at least as much significance as the idealistic underpinnings of Jaspers' existentialism in the hiatus he establishes between philosophical and Christian faith.

It is a well-known fact that the moral integrity of many German intellectuals has been questioned severely by the Jewish community since the tragic events of World War II. This suspicion is directed not only at those who, like Heidegger and Karl Heim, quickly and even enthusiastically made their peace with the Third Reich, but even more so at those who capitulated in silence and, *a forteriori*, are viewed as being guilty of an even more insidious complicity in the Holocaust.

On this account it would seem that Jaspers' record is utterly inviolate. During his college days he went on record as being against all forms of exclusivism based on social, racial or religious differences by refusing to join a fraternity. In 1910, Jaspers married the daughter of a prominent Jewish family and was therefore especially sensitive to and highly critical of the rising tide of anti-semitism after World War I. These apprehensions are well documented in *Die geistige Situation derZeit* (1931), a text that enjoyed immediate translation into French, Spanish, Japanese and English within three years, thus attesting to Jaspers' reputation as a prophetic humanist and moralist. Because of its critical character, Jaspers was forbidden by the Nazis to have anything more to do with University administration and, in 1937, he was censored from further publication and divested of his professorship. Given his convictions, it was inconceivable that he would even consent to divorce his wife, Gertrude, when pressured to do so by the Nazis as a sign of so-called "good faith;" a travesty to which virtually thousands of prominent Germans complied. Indeed, it was the impeccable record of Jaspers that led the Allies to sin-

---

[68] *Phil.*, III, p. 135.

gle him out as the first rector of the University of Heidelberg after the war, and also to be editor of *die Wandlung*, the first newspaper to be published by the Germans in the American occupied sector.

It came as a great shock, then, to hear Jaspers called a "crypto-Nazi" by a prominent professor of German literature. Since there was absolutely nothing in the record to corroborate such a charge, it seemed that Jaspers' detractor was simply a malcontent. Two years later, however, in 1975, as a result of an extended conversation with the distinguished Jewish historian and philosopher, Gershom Scholem, it became apparent that he too was less than completely satisfied concerning the manner in which Jaspers conducted himself after the war. Indeed, it was precisely because of Jaspers' inviolate record, that the Jewish community especially looked to him as a scholar-administrator with great political influence.

Scholem's misgivings began, he said, after Jaspers' first public address on the event of his installation as rector. It was a message that the Jewish community anticipated with both expectation and great trepidation. "What now," Scholem mused, "would a great German philosopher say about the disaster of the past decade?" The address, *"Erneuerung der Universität*, delivered in 1945, and thematically preparatory to *Die Schuldfrage* (1946), represented to Scholem, however, a *minimalist* statement considering the circumstances. "Please don't misunderstand me," Scholem said. "It was not that the address was in itself in any way objectionable, for Jaspers insisted that 'because we are today alive is the sign of our guilt.' Still, it seemed too mild and too cautious."

Scholem also confessed that not all Jewish intellectuals felt this way, and that many, including Hans Jonas, viewed Jaspers' comments favorably. Indeed Scholem himself was willing to change his mind and had the occasion to do so two years later when he met with Jaspers on a mission to enjoin his assistance in the retrieval of many important Jewish texts and other scholarly works that had been confiscated by the Third Reich. Professor Scholem recalled in great detail this conversation with Jaspers and his wife, Gertrude, regarding the war in general and the issue of Zionism and the State of Israel in particular. Both Jaspers and his wife, Scholem stated, confessed that whereas they had been pro-assimilationists and critical of Zionism prior to the war, they had now reversed their views completely and now believed that Zionism and Israel were essential to the survival of Judaism in the future.

Pleased to hear this, Scholem confessed that he had to reverse his opinion of Jaspers once again following the Eichmann affair. The event that spurred this reversal was the publication of Hannah Arendt's controver-

sial book, *Eichmann in Jerusalem.*[69] Arendt, of course, was a close personal friend and former student of Jaspers, and he quickly came to her
defense stating, according to Scholem, 'that he had never been a support-
er of the politics of Zionism.' When asked to locate precisely what it was
about the work by Arendt that he found objectionable, Scholem suggested that as an academic thesis it was, of course, entirely respectable. However it was the "tone" of the account, a certain flippant quality that
was, Scholem said, "absolutely the worst thing that could come from a
Jewish intellectual concerning the Jewish experience during the war.
That Jaspers himself could not see this was for me highly disturbing."

The corroboration of this discussion and its inferences one way or
another, of course, is impossible since it is an issue weighted with high
emotion. Nevertheless, it does raise another question regarding the hiatus between philosophical and religious faith and the adequacy of a hermeneutics of transcending-thinking vis-à-vis the cipher of God. In fact, it
is the question raised repeatedly by Paul Ricoeur against Jaspers concerning the "don Juanism" of his interpretive method, viz., that the liber-
al-idealism implicit in his philosophical faith tends to make all things
equal in an attitude that dissolves the crisis of decision into what Ricoeur
terms "disquieting aestheticism." This is obviously aimed especially at
Jaspers' interpretation of the cipher of Incarnation which resists utterly
such an approach.

We will discuss the methodological reasons for Ricoeur's objections in
the next chapter. We can, however, mention briefly here the Barthian
spirit that seems to inform the dismay of both Ricoeur and, in his own
way, Scholem as well. Barth, as is commonly known, was the primary
critic of the presumed bankruptcy of late 19th and early 20th century
liberal interpretations of religion; interpretations that would, for the
sake of intellectual respectability, compromise those aspects of Judaism
and Christianity that seemed necessary. Jaspers, in his "Philosophical
Autobiography" and elsewhere makes it clear that he shared this horizon and that his confessional relationship to Christianity was strained
almost from the beginning. He muses that after the "joke" of Confirmation, he told his father that he was leaving the church for good. However,
his father warned him (even though of a similar mind) that institutional
religion should be maintained as a "regulative force" in society: "if we
simply destroy it, an unforeseeable evil will break through." Thus, the

---

[69] Hannah Arendt, *Eichmann in Jerusalem: A Report on the Banality of Evil* (New York:
Viking, 1963); and see also *Antisemitism*, Part I, *The Origin of Totalitarianism* (New York:
Harcourt, 1951).

liberal must maintain a tolerant and even supportive attitude concerning the church. He adds, however, that "before death, and when we are no longer active in the world, we may clear the deck by leaving the church."[70]

There can be little doubt that Jaspers' harangue against the notion of "Catholicity" is in large measure informed by this attitude and also, justifiably, by what he perceived as the perverse capitulation of the church and its leadership as symbolized by the infamous *Concordat* of Pious XII with Adolf Hitler. Jaspers even mentions that as early as 1924 when he protested the blatant anti-semitism on the faculty at Heidelberg, he received no support from someone as prominent as his theological colleague, Martin Dibelius.[71]

Because of these and other factors of a similar character, we can see that the cipher of Incarnation is read by Jaspers *politically* as well as philosophically. That is, his negative reading is not so much due to the mythical aspects of the cipher as it is to ossification of the meaning of the cipher in the authoritarian structures of the church. Jaspers, then, is an advocate of the Protestant belief in the "invisible" essence of the church in *extremis*. When this is combined with method we have at least two factors that prevent a direct confrontation with the central symbol of Christianity. First, because of the noetic-speculative character of transcending-thinking, Jaspers is more concerned with the dynamics of heightening consciousness than he is with the givenness of the symbol or myth to be interpreted. Second, since a hermeneutics of transcending-thinking is always grounded in Existenz, the meaning of any interpretation is for Existenz and Existenz alone. Given the interrelatedness of these two factors, Jaspers' interpretations of the cipher of God inevitably lack what Ricoeur terms "the consistency of world" that can make them finally convincing. In short, religious symbols and myths tend to be interpreted by Jaspers not as they are given and therefore mediated by the texts and institutes that are their embodiment, but as he believes they should be given in order to be consistent with what he terms "philosophical faith." Indeed, without closer attention to the processes of mediation, transcending-thinking itself dissolves either into solipsism or into the esoteric air of gnosticism. This is what both Barth and Scholem, in their respective and distinctive ways, understand regarding the critical centrality of the historical, textual, dogmatic, and institutionalized instantia-

---

[70] Schilpp, *op.cit.*, p. 76.
[71] *Ibid.*, p. 49.

tions of religion; that is, only *through* these agencies of mediation is interpretation possible and not in spite of them as tends very frequently to be the case in Jaspers. In a similar way, this is why Barth, when faced with the choice of opting for either liberalism or orthodoxy would choose the latter as the only basis upon which one can consistently espouse an ethics that is the emergent consequence of interpretation. For it is precisely the sense of the Unconditional that is absent from a religion based on humanistic liberalism whether it is institutionalized or not. To be sure there are cases when the institution is corrupt. But one cannot build a philosophy and even less an ethics on exceptions when, in the larger view, the dedication of a given institution is clearly to human dignity and truth. The weakness of religion in Germany both before and during the war was not a consequence of its institutional character *per se*, but the weakness of a compromising liberalism both within and without, in short, the weakness of a culture-religion in the service of privatized values.

The hiatus between philosophical and religious faith, then, seems to be localized precisely on the matter of transcending-thinking as an adequate hermeneutic of religious myths and symbols in their historic and communal givenness. In fact, the question arises as to whether Jaspers' philosophy of Transcendence is really dependent on any specific instantiation of Transcendence in symbol, text or tradition. With respect to the cipher of Incarnation, upon which we have here focussed, it would seem that Jaspers' interpretation is even more idealistic than that of Hegel for whom incarnation is viewed as "the essential moment of religion that must necessarily appear in the definition of its object." [72] While Jaspers does not reflect at length on the movements of the Absolute Spirit, dealing instead, qua existentialist with the subject, we can say in a somewhat ironic way that Jaspers is more reductionistic than Hegel. For in his relentless attempt to lay hold of immediate meaning, *aus möglicher Existenz*, the act of interpretation is conceived entirely as meaning *pro me*, but meaning won at the expense of its origin *extra nos*. As Levinas puts it, existentialist hermeneutics by the very nature of its orientation tends to reduce the "alterity" or otherness of Transcendence to the "sameness" of the horizon of the subject. [73]

To be sure, Jaspers, in his notion of the cipher, always insists that the Being of Transcendence-Itself is never identical with the act of tran-

---

[72] Hegel, *op.cit.*, p. 199.
[73] Levinas, *op.cit.*, pp. 19ff.

scending. The luminousity of the Encompassing is merely touched by ciphers, to put it metaphorically, and is never exhausted by the comprehension of any given Existenz. However, there is no basis in Jaspers for ever determining the nature and the character of that surplus of meaning. One must rather, in the act of philosophical faith, believe that it is there. The reason for this, we contend, is that Jaspers pays such scant attention to the agencies of mediation, whether it be the text, as in Bultmann, the body, as in Ricoeur, or language, as in Gadamer. It is ironic that a philosopher so concerned with the dynamics of communication should fail to recognize that philosophical and religious meaning, and therefore *faith*, is always mediated and never immediate. Thus the task of the hermeneutical philosopher and theologian primarily has to do with making sense of the manner in which the transmission of meaning takes place; a transmission that is both transcendental, in terms of a philosophy of understanding, and empirical, with respect to the form in which something is transmitted.

We might say, in summary, that the much heralded "default of the gods," as a genitive proposition, is much more the "default of man" with respect to agencies of mediation. A good many philosophers and theologians that lament "our time of need" tend to overlook the fact that religious faith can only be as vital as the specific religious institutions that nurture and sustain it. In other words, many tend to view the sorry status of culture and value as the result of either the ontological deteriorization of humanity, or as the result of some sort of ideological conspiracy. The fact of the matter is, we suggest, much simpler; namely, the failure of people in general, and intellectuals in particular, to make a concerted and involved commitment to religious institutions as the only possible means of keeping that which *transmits* alive and true to their fundamental purpose. Transcendence, in short, never takes place in a vacuum, but only through a symbol system that manifests within itself a self-critical thickness and density that "invites reflection" as Ricoeur puts it, and therefore provides the basis for possible self-transcendence.

To be sure we have witnessed of late in mainstream religious institutions "a cunning theory of adaptation" [74] to the very secularism it is the task of the higher religions to transform. There can be no mistaking this, for the evidence is everywhere. But the constructive response in view of this situation is not the placement of philosophical over against religious faith as its enlightened opposite for the simple reason that it is, in isola-

---

[74] Theodore Roszak, *Unfinished Animal* (New York: Harper, 1975), pp. 44ff.

tion from the lived community, quite powerless. As Theodore Rozak put it eloquently, but in a privatized context we cannot here accept, "The willful belief of the unbelievable has always been a poor substitute for sacramental experience." [75] Sacramental experience, however, can take place *only* within the context of community; that is to say, the sacramental symbolizes the *mediation* of meaning par excellence, and to this issue we now turn in the discussion of Jaspers and his critics.

[75] Theodore Roszak, *Where the Wasteland Ends: Politics and Transcendence in Postindustrial Society* (New York: Doubleday, 1972), p. 449. Roszak's narrative analysis of religion and culture is sometimes stunning in spite of its flamboyance. His notion of the sacramental, however, is also privatized perhaps due to his enamourment with both romanticism and Eastern forms of mysticism. In short, we agree with his critique of religion but not with his method of correction which seems, at least to this writer, superficial as evidenced in the above cited work. However, that not just philosophers and theologians shoud now be talking seriously about Transcendence, but now social scientists, we find encouraging.

CHAPTER NINE

THE SUCCESSORS AND CRITICS OF KARL JASPERS

It was Jaspers' articulation of "the boundary situation" which, in Hans Gadamer's view, redirected German philosophy in the 20th century more than any other single factor because it asked for a level of "existential commitment" which had at the time almost disappeared. [1] Jaspers' thought, of course, made little impression in the United States until after World War II when some of his writings began to appear in English for the first time. Even then existentialism never made the impression in the Anglo-American world that it did on the Continent. Indeed, during the postwar period when innumerable books, essays and articles were pouring off the press attempting to introduce the American audience to phenomenology and existentialism, it was commonplace to lump Jaspers, Heidegger, Buber, Tillich and Bultmann together with French philosophical and literary figures like Sartre, Camus, Marcel and others as though they were totally homogeneous one with the other. Today, of course, we realize that the differences between these so-called existentialists are frequently greater than with philosophers who are not so labeled.

It is also interesting to note that while Jaspers has enjoyed a wide audience and while his thought has been influential in many fields and subjects, he has never developed the close following that we find in the case of Heidegger, Tillich and Bultmann. The primary reason for this, I believe, is that the philosophy of Jaspers is such a personalized statement that it defies imitation. Since Jaspers did not really set forth a program that invited others to refine or extend he did not attract disciples and, indeed, did not want any. In this respect the mode of Jaspers' highly humane philosophizing is most akin to what we find in Socrates and Nietzsche although he lacks the incisiveness of Socrates and the flourish of Nietzsche. His philosophy is rather, as we have seen, a cogent description of the human condition within the context of freedom with its risks,

---

[1] Hans-Georg Gadamer, *Philosophical Hermeneutics*, trans. David E. Linge (Berkeley: University of California Press, 1976), pp. 137-138.

and an affirmation of the reality of Transcendence. Thus, his primary greatness, as in the case of Socrates and Nietzsche, has been the ability to articulate "the spirit of the times" positively and constructively during a period when hope was in short supply. He has done this, moreover, in a manner which while forceful and brimming with insights and ideas is sufficiently vague so that his students, critics and successors have not always felt obliged to acknowledge their debt to him formally.

Therefore, rather than here catalogue all who have in some fashion or other been touched by Jaspers, we will turn our attention to Bultmann, Ricoeur, and Gadamer upon whose views concerning the nature of Transcendence and the task of hermeneutics the thought of Jaspers has a definite bearing. The famous and bitter exchange between Jaspers and Bultmann will be our point of departure, for it is here that there takes place a reopening of the question as to whether or not religion can exist without myth. The curious feature of this debate, of course, is that in it we find Jaspers, the confessionally marginal philosopher, maintaining against Bultmann, the confessional biblical theologian, that if religion is to remain connected to the Transcendence it avows, it must seek not to *demythologize* but to *remythologize* its message. Both Gadamer, Jaspers' successor at Heidelberg, and Ricoeur, one of Jaspers' most famous students, take up this challenge in their related but distinctive ways. It is our primary intention here to indicate how and in what manner the thought of Ricoeur and Gadamer, the two most prominent voices of hermeneutic philosophy today, are influenced by Karl Jaspers.

THE QUESTION OF MYTH: JASPERS AND BULTMANN

If invective and argumentation *ad hominem* is an index, the bitter exchange between Jaspers and Bultmann on "*Die Frage der Entmythologisierung*" in 1953 perhaps is rivaled in the twentieth century only by the polemic on "*Natur und Gnade*" between Karl Barth and Emil Brunner in 1934.[2] What both treatises have in common is fundamental conflict concerning the relationship between religions and science, faith and reason, and a certain sense of indignant betrayal. On the former issue, both Barth and Jaspers accuse their respective opponents of not understanding the enemies they are presumably seeking to accomodate. Barth sug-

---

[2] *Die Frage der Entmythologisierung* (München: R. Piper Verlag, 1954); published in English as *Myth and Christianity* (New York: Noonday Press, 1956). See also, *Natur und Gnade: Zum Gespräch mit Karl Barth* (Tübingen, 1934).

gests that Brunner's understanding of natural or rational theology is wholly naive, laced as it is with "Kierkegaardianisms," and Jaspers suggests that Bultmann neither understands modern science nor the Heideggerian *Daseinsanalyse* that Bultmann perceives as being consistently "scientific." Moreover, it is Bultmann's perception of *Daseinsanalyse* as a "rigorous science" that prevents him, in the eyes of Jaspers, from comprehending the true nature of mythic-symbolic language as something transcending scientific inquiry completely. But whereas Barth was incensed at a personal level by what he perceived to be the betrayal of his former disciple, Brunner, one senses in the invective of Jaspers a tacit condemnation of Bultmann for being the disciple of the wrong philosopher, namely the early Heidegger. Indeed, there is a certain irony in this, for in his insistence that the meaning of religious language is irreducibly mytho-symbolic, it is the later Heidegger who ultimately "remythologizes" religious and philisophical meaning far beyond anything one can find in either Bultmann or Jaspers. Because of the heat of this debate one cannot regard as definitive the positions set forth by either Jaspers or Bultmann in this treatise. One can, nevertheless, isolate issues that have redirected subsequent hermeneutical inquiry, and for this reason their exchange is a kind of watershed. One can in this text also locate propositions by Jaspers that bring into relief the inherent weakness of transcending-thinking as the methodological foundation of his philosophy in its hermeneutical aspect.

Jaspers' critique of Bultmann hinges on two basic premises. First, Jaspers regards the very term demythologizing as "blasphemous" since, for him, the mythic symbolization of experience is utterly essential for transcending-thinking in speculative metaphysics. We have already seen this in Jaspers' "Kantian" endorsement of Hebraic radical monotheism. It is a position shared by Ernst Cassirer. But secondly, it is Jaspers' conviction that the essential task of hermeneutics is "purifying the splendor of mythical vision" that separates him absolutely from Bultmann.[3] One must at all costs, Jaspers contends, prevent the sacrifice of the mytho-symbolic to the objectifying sciences, no matter what disguises they may be wearing in the name of methodical rigor. The question, of course, is how this or any other project of purification can take place without losing the myth that is, its *raison d'être*, so to speak, in the first place. While Jaspers objects to Bultmann's translation of the meaning of myth through Heideggerian *Daseinsanalyse*, one must ask how it really differs

---

[3] *Myth and Christianity*, pp. 16-17.

from *Existenzerhellung* as a means of interpretation? Is purification effected when one merely translates a presumed naive set of meanings (*intentio recta*) into those less offensive intellectually (*intentio obliqua*)? The movement from first to second level naiveté is still naiveté, as Ricoeur would insist, and not exhaustive *explanation*. Apart from this admission it would seem that Jaspers, just as much as Bultmann, is still caught in the subject-object dichotomy although both, for different reasons, believe that it has been somehow transcended. This can be seen in the following passage where Jaspers says: "While we see, hear, and think in the language of myth conceived as code, while we cannot become concretely aware of Transcendence without a code language, we must at the same time keep in mind that there are no demons, that there is no magic causality, no such thing as sorcery . . . True piety, as a matter of course, eliminates the materialistic, magical and ultilitarian misuse of literal interpretation."[4] This has obvious similarities to Bultmann's project of demythologizing, but there is this important difference. While one must, Jaspers believes, make the above differentiations, the essential task of the hermeneut is not one of opting, *a priori*, for an ontology to which the meaning of the myth must conform. The task is rather, as Jaspers puts it, one of "struggling for true faith *within* mythical thinking."[5] With this insistence, Jaspers is consistently phenomenological recognizing, as does Paul Ricoeur, that the religious symbol or myth "sustains an intrinsic claim to validity;"[6] i.e., the meaning of the mythic-symbolic is *sui generis*, as it were, and does not have to satisfy any extrinsic criteria of verification of falsification. The question is how Jaspers, while remaining "within mythical thinking," proposes to think the myth from the *inside out* as it were. One senses here an intent similar to the *Erlebnisausrück* of Wilhelm Dilthey[7] and an "intuitive art" that always, as Gadamer contends, borders on gnosticism.[8]

Presuming that such a technique is possible, what, one must ask, are the critical norms whereby one is able to avoid the extrinsic interpretation of myth that Jaspers believes to characterize both the literalist and subjectivist positions? Can one, in fact ever grasp the *spiritual essence* of a given myth without falling into subjectivism? Bultmann's injunction to

[4] *Ibid.*, p. 19.
[5] *Ibid.*, p. 19.
[6] As cited by David Rasmussen, *Mythic-Symbolic Language and Philosophical Anthropology* (The Hague: Martinus Nijhoff, 1971), p. 121.
[7] Cf., Wilhelm Dilthey, *Das Erlebnis und die Dichtung* (Stuttgart, 1957; first published, 1906).
[8] Cf., Hans-Georg Gadamer, *Truth and Method* (New York: Seabury, 1975), pp. 192-214.

Jaspers is well put: "To define the myth as a cipher of Transcendence merely describes the problem of interpretation; it scarcely solves it." He also believes that Jaspers' introduction of "cipher language" is really a "magic language" the truths of which are accessible only to Jaspers. [9] Jaspers' rejoinder is that if by a method of hermeneutic one is looking for some kind of "recipe," [10] then their entire discussion is futile, for the meaning of Transcendence or Being does not give itself to a method. This notion, obviously, is thematic in both Heidegger and Gadamer. Jaspers' response, moreover, is quite similar to the insistence of Wilfred Cantwell Smith that "we can never engineer our way into the sacred" and that the task of the interpreter is "not to dominate but to revere." [11] Nevertheless, all interpretive theories, even the most intuitive, demand some kind of formal structures – even if they are structures against structures, as in the case of Jaspers' method of "qualified negativity." Jaspers' comments on the *hermeneutical circle* are of some help here. "We cannot get out of this circle," Jaspers insists, "we can only try to enlarge it." [12] Now to enlarge the circle within which one finds oneself is, quite plainly, to make it more "encompassing;" and to obtain an understanding of the Encompassing, as we have seen, requires agreement on what we have already developed as the modalities of transcending-thinking and the conversions of understanding present thereto. This is an issue to which Bultmann never replies.

Perhaps the degree to which Jaspers' hermeneutics of the Encompassing is different from the hermeneutics of his neo-orthodox theological counterparts might be clarified by contrasting his position briefly with that of Emil Brunner. A Christian theologian midway between the conservatism of Barth and the liberalism of Bultmann, Brunner wishes to extend the ambit of revelation beyond biblicism and yet he repudiates speculative hermeneutics on the conviction that the hermeneutical circle is a "circle of immanence" and therefore a "circle of futility." Brunner believed that the methodological restriction of interpretation theory to referentiality within the circle alone resulted in a solipsistic reduction of truth to various permutations of *Selbstbewusstsein*; a conclusion which Fritz Buri, Jaspers' most faithful disciple in theology, by contrast, accepts with little hesitation. [13] Theologically, the immanentalism inherent

---

[9] *Myth and Christianity*, p. 61.
[10] *Ibid.*, p. 87.
[11] See Robert Baird, ed., *Methodological Issues in Religious Studies* (Chico, California: New Horizons Press, 1975), pp. 19-21.
[12] *Myth and Christianity*, p. 95.
[13] Cf., Fritz Buri, *Dogmatik als Selbstverständnis des Christlichen Glaubens* (Bern: Verlag Paul Haupt, 1956), esp. Erster Teil, *Vernunft und Offenbarung*, pp. 285 ff.

in the hermeneutical circle, especially as it was believed to be avowed by Heidegger, nullifies utterly for the conservative theologian the operation of Grace as the historical breakthrough of the Divine into the circle of immanence. And apart from *breaches* in immanence (the term that Jaspers also uses frequently) created by Transcendence-Itself, knowledge of the Truth and therefore "salvation" is deemed impossible. [14] Contrary to Barth, however, Brunner does not presume to delineate the topography of these breakthroughs, or to restrict them entirely to Christian revelations; i.e., Brunner does not opt for what Bonhoeffer termed the "revelational positivism" of Karl Barth. Brunner rather confines himself descriptively to a language of "encounter" (*Begegnung*), similar to Martin Buber, and to the happenings or events within the life situation within which "the Thouness of God" is experienced. [15] It was for such manifest *Kierkegaardianism* in which there is a blurring of the operations of faith and reason that Brunner incurred the wrath of Barth.

Even though there are some similarities between Brunner's personalistically construed *Wahrheit als Begegnung* and the Jaspersian language of *Existenzerhellung*, the differences between them are far greater. Brunner's metaphoric language, for all of its tolerance, is ultimately dependent upon the particular historical events that surround the work and person of Jesus; precisely the cryptic liberalism that Barth was quick to recognize and denounce. One cannot, for Barth, "have one's cake and eat it too," so to speak, since there is something finally uncompromising about Christian faith and one only deludes oneself if one thinks it can be any other way. Indeed, the problem is either that of remaining entirely transcendental and rigorously phenomenological in one's understanding of hermeneutics, or disguising ontological or even cosmological motives within one's hermeneutics. This concealment, Jaspers believes, is present to the Lutheran underpinnings of Bultmann's position in the form of a subterranean *Heilsgeschichte* apart from which authentic or "eschatological existence" is deemed impossible. "If there is no historicity apart from the Divine Thou [of Christianity]," Jaspers says, "then it is true that I know nothing of historicity." [16] *Daseinsanalyse* notwithstanding, Bultmann's position, Jaspers believes, depends on a historical "corporealization of Transcendence." With this sardonic barb, Jaspers places his finger on an extremely sensitive point in Bultmann's

[14] Emil Brunner, *Revelation and Reason*, trans. Olive Wyon (Philadelphia: Westminster Press, 1946), pp. 43ff, 365ff.
[15] Emil Brunner, *The Divine-Human Encounter*, trans. Amandus Loos (Philadelphia: Westminster Press, 1943), *passim*.
[16] *Myth and Christianity*, p. 92.

position and one that has been perceived by others. [17] The *skandalon* Bultmann perceives to be intrinsic to the Gospel does not, Jaspers contends, have so much to do with the reality to which Jesus is transparent in his life and teachings as it is dependent upon the patently *offensive* features of the Pauline-Lutheran doctrine of justification. The *true* scandal of Christianity for Jaspers, on the other hand, lies in the radicality of its notion of freedom wherein one realizes that "man is given totally to himself" in responsible historicity. To substitute for this an extrinsic doctrinal version of the *skandalon* of faith is to erect a "false stumbling block." [18] For Jaspers, then, the hermeneutics of historicity or authentic existence is not clarified by opting for the neo-orthodox distinction between immanence and Transcendence since these terms are exceedingly fuzzy owing to their lack of epistemological and ontological differentiation. Nor can the problem of hermeneutics be resolved by leaping away from some of the mythically offensive features of the *Old* Transcendence implicit in the God of Abraham, Isaac and Jacob through Bultmann's partial rapprochement with the *Daseinsanalyse* of the early Heidegger. After all, Jaspers states emphatically, "The swamp of Dasein is precisely that from which we seek deliverance." [19] To this extent, at least, Jaspers is in agreement with Brunner that immanence qua immanence is neither satisfactory for a doctrine of salvation, nor does it supply the means for an adequate hermeneutic of myth. Contrary to Brunner, however, Jaspers does not believe that the hermeneutical circle, unaided, as it were, by historical revelations breaking in from the without, is merely a futile circle of immanence. It is this conviction that underlies his plea for widening the circle of interpretation and understanding through a more sophisticated understanding of the dynamics of "comprehension." As we have seen throughout this analysis, the basic motion of transcending-thinking is towards that Transcendence which, in its essence, is *das Umgreifende*. As such, transcending-thinking, as the intrinsic motion of possible Existenz, is simultaneously a heightening and a deepening of experience vis-

---

[17] Cf., for example Schubert Ogden, *Christ Without Myth* (New York: Harper and Row, 1963).

[18] *Myth and Christianity*, pp. 82-84. As Kierkegaard perceived over against Hegel, however, it is precisely the scandal of the "historical" Jesus that militates against any and all conceptual *purifications* of Christ-symbols, and it is this that underlies the pathos of Kierkegaard's notion of *Existenz*. Jaspers fails to integrate this aspect of Kierkegaard in his own adaption of the term and it is not an unimportant feature of his usage.

[19] *Chiffren der Transzendenz*, p. 57.

à-vis its encompassing-comprehensive ground in freedom. Religious myths at their profoundest levels of meaning, then, do not refer to spatial or ontological levels of reality but to the dialectic that is at the center of one's experience of freedom as that "encompassing I am, *and* that encompassing I am not." When this dialectic is lifted out of experience - abstracted from *mögliche Existenz*, then immanence and Transcendence become hypostatized ontologically as one finds in naive mythology and in much theology. Here there is agreement between Jaspers and Paul Tillich inasmuch as Tillich also insists that the symbols of immanence and Transcendence are to be regarded quite strictly as "dimensions" of experience and not "levels of Being."[20] So considered, the hermeneutical task for Jaspers is not that of adapting the early Heidegger's reduction of experience and Transcendence to historicality, nor is it that of somehow escaping from the circle of comprehension to a point of privileged perspective which is precisely what Jaspers finds in the notion of *Heilsgeschichte* built on the rock of "Catholicity."[21] All hermeneutics must be maintained strictly within the transcending-experiential dialectic that Existenz-Itself is, and only here does talk about immanence and Transcendence make sense. Just as Existenz is the *fondement* for Transcendence, so also it is the *fondement* of hermeneutical possibility. In sum, the only authentic hermeneutics is the participatory hermeneutics of transcending-thinking *aus möglicher Existenz.*

Out of his firm insistence on the thoroughly existential character of hermeneutics, Jaspers turns to the language of ciphers as the mediational agencies of the meaning of Transcendence. Yet these ciphers are agencies that remain completely within the subject-object structure of human experience, as they are *for* Existenz and Existenz alone and cannot be dealt with independently from it. Therefore, only within the cipher is there an isomorphism of Existenz and Transcendence that does not violate the subject-object structure of experience. This is because Existenz perceives the dialectical boundaries of experience in a way that is totally different from the objectifying consciousness. For Existenz experience can be likened to: "The luminous crest of a wave surging above unfathomable depths and may be compared to a flame that is nourished by the flow of the inexhaustible Encompassing. If the flow stops, if awareness of the deep ground is absent, if there is only the split between a conscious mind and the objects it intends, then we have no more than a

---

[20] Paul Tillich, *Systematic Theology*, III (University of Chicago Press, 1963), pp. 12ff.
[21] *Von der Wahrheit.*, pp. 766ff.

rustle of withered leaves, the random swirling of dead husks of words, producing a semblance of external order and meaning in endless, arbitrary variation." [22]

These glowing poetics convey what Jaspers considers to be the framework and direction of a participating hermeneutic grounded within the structures of the subject-object relation *and* within the structures of the *mytho-symbolic*. Thus, only when there is both an encounter with and a preservation of *mythos* can one grow in the knowledge of being Encompassed, and herein lies the dynamic aspect of Jaspers' hermeneutic. While the language of the mytho-symbolic is replete with the imagery of immanence and Transcendence, this imagery no longer has empirical or ontological reference beyond the experience itself. Its reality is rather one with what it says and its meaning is intuitively immediate. Thus when Bultmann objects that "mythical thinking is just as objectifying as scientific thinking" [23] and accuses Jaspers of "hypostatizing the language of Transcendence," [24] he does not understand clearly the mystical underpinnings of Jaspers' notion of freedom as the *fondement* of Existenz and its relation to Transcendence. Moreover, when interpretation is construed as the determination of "valid meaning," as E. D. Hirsch would have it out of a neo-Aristotelian perspective, [25] one is hopelessly embroiled in the determination of what, in religion, can be viewed as fact and non-fact. Moreover, a predetermination of so-called facts immediately vitiates participatory hermeneutics and imposes upon the challenge of interpretation yet another form of objectifying thinking. This is why Jaspers insists that "ciphers are to be listened to, not cognized. All talk about them . . . is mistaken in its roots. For this reason the character of the cipher is only encircled but not reached if, in metaphor, we call it speech." [26] Participatory hermeneutics *aus möglicher Existenz* is more akin to a "metaphorical act" or "game" than to a science fashioned after modern notions of *Wissenschaft*. [27] But this does not mean that the so-called *game* of hermeneutics is any less serious. Because it is participatory it is the most serious game one can play because the "spectator" approach is repudiated. So envisioned, the challenge of hermeneutics is not

---

[22] *Myth and Christianity*, p. 13.
[23] *Ibid.*, p. 61.
[24] *Ibid.*, p. 65.
[25] Cf., E.D. Hirsch, *Validity in Interpretation* (New Haven: Yale University Press, 1967).
[26] *Truth and Symbol*, p. 41.
[27] *Ibid.*, p. 42. Gadamer's frequent characterization of hermeneutics as a "game" and as "play" is, in this writer's view, as dependent on Jaspers as it is on Wittgenstein.

to know *what* mythic ciphers are, but to keep ourselves "open" to the truth they "encompass." [28] To comprehend the circularity of the hermeneutical act, then, does not have to do with the development of the definitive method, for "a system of cipher interpretation is impossible." [29] It has rather to do with development of a kind of Vedantic awareness that "what merely passes in time rounds into Being;" [30] in other words, an awareness that is concomitant with the act of *foundering* within the act of interpretation whereupon something "beyond exegesis" [31] catches us even as we founder. To say anything more precise about this event, for Jaspers, is to say nothing at all. For Bultmann, needless to say, this is an extremely frustrating situation and he simply terminates discussion.

The issues arising out of this discussion can be summarized as follows: First, Jaspers makes it clear that the mythic-symbolic character of religious and metaphysical discourse is essential and not at all to be identified with a scientifically deficient worldview. Jaspers simply is not as troubled as Bultmann regarding the conflict between religious and scientific truth and the necessity of bringing into some kind of harmony the religious *and* the scientific dimensions of truth. In fact, it is when theology pretends to be scientific that one confronts, in dogma, the destruction of the authentic insights of myth and therefore religion. To be sure, Bultmann, in his often misunderstood theory of myth, does not believe that biblical literature is invalidated because it is mythical either. Following Feuerbach, Bultmann believes that all talk about God is inevitably anthropomorphic and therefore mythical. Because it is man who talks about God, it is man who must necessarily talk about God within the constraints of language that always objectifies, whether that objectification is scientifically sophisticated or not. But contrary to Feuerbach, and to Freud as well, Bultmann does not believe, as Ricoeur accurately points out, that all myth is projected representation of what can be rationally explained at a strictly mundane level. [32] The mytho-symbolic is rather the attempt to render intelligible truths that have an origin beyond the limits of ordinary knowing. At the same time, Bultmann does not appreciate to the same degree as Jaspers the insistence of Feuerbach that all theology is anthropology *and* physics (in the sense of the Greek

---

[28] *Ibid.*, p. 53.
[29] *Phil.*, III, p. 128.
[30] *Ibid.*, p. 131.
[31] *Ibid.*, pp. 186, 204.
[32] Ricoeur, *The Conflict of Interpretation: Essays in Hermeneutics*, ed., Don Ihde (Evanston: Northwestern University Press, 1974), p. 391.

phusis); that is, truly anthropomorphic talk about God is *natured* or *embodied* talk about God. Therefore, one does not 'believe in spite of the nature of our experience," as Bultmann suggests, [33] but only within and through experience that is at once historic and natured. As Goethe put it, "in man nature and history coincide." It is precisely this realization that leads Jaspers to insist that our primary task is not to demythologize religious language but to "remythologize" it; that is, to restore to religious and metaphysical discourse its power through a reinvigoration of what Nathan Scott, Jr. eloquently terms "the figural imagination" [34] and not through tedious accomodation with yet another objectifying, scientific method of explanation.

Second, Bultmann elicits from Jaspers a contradiction that illustrates the fatal weakness of transcending-thinking as a kind of intuitive hermeneutic of symbol and, indeed, the weakness in all philosophies of reflection, as we will later see in Ricoeur. "Guided by the bible and by Kant," Jaspers brusquely rejoins Bultmann, "I stand in an immediate, non-mediated relationship to the godhead." [35] But if one is *guided* by something, one does not, *a fortiori*, stand in an immediate relation with that to which one is guided. One stands rather within a context of mediation. The excessive mystification of symbol in Jaspers clearly leads to a kind of existential monism which, as Ricoeur recognizes, is its basic weakness. And since Jaspers refuses to clarify further the mystic-intuitive aspect of his hermeneutic of cipher, one really cannot go any further as both Gadamer and Ricoeur recognize. It is, in fact, impossible for Jaspers to say more than he does, for to do so he would have had to re-think the fundamental limits of a philosophy of reflection. To do so Jaspers first would have had to delimit radically the notion that Existenz represents the only legitimate ground of philosophizing. Secondly, he would have had to engage in a far more rigorous form of phenomenological description in which case the ontological resonances of Transcendence would be abandoned. [36] It is precisely this resonance he would preserve, however elusive and metaphorical this preservation might be. In Ricoeur and Gadamer, as we will see, we find a continuation of

---

[33] Bultmann, *Jesus Christ and Mythology* (New York: Scribners, 1958), p. 84.
[34] Nathan Scott, Jr., *The Wild Prayer of Longing: Poetry and the Sacred* (New Haven: Yale University Press, 1971), *passim*.
[35] *Myth and Christianity*, pp. 24-26, 77-78.
[36] In other words, in order to vitiate the charge of ontologism, Jaspers' philosophy of the Encompassing would have to become exclusively a transcendental philosophy of consciousness which it is not. For an approach that does attempt to do precisely this see J.G. Arapura, *Religion as Anxiety and Tranquility: An Essay in Comparative Phenomenology of the Spirit* (The Hague: Mouton, 1972).

Jaspers' firm belief that the mythical, the symbolic, and the poetical play a fundamental role in the preservation of the ontological aspect of religion. But in Ricoeur and Gadamer we find clarification of basic issues in methodology and concerning the nature of language that are prerequisite to a convincing hermeneutics of Transcendence.

THE QUESTION OF METHOD: JASPERS AND RICOEUR

Recent studies of Paul Ricoeur tend to emphasize rather strongly his dependence upon Maurice Merleau-Ponty, Gabriel Marcel and, of course, Edmund Husserl.[37] Given the French context of Ricoeur's phenomenology, this is scarcely surprising. By not also attending to Jaspers, however, Ricoeur's commentator's may be missing his most enduring, albeit problematical, influence. Now this thesis, obviously, is far from revolutionary inasmuch as Ricoeur devotes his first two major published works to extensive studies of Jaspers.[38] What I am contending is that the influence of Jaspers is a rather constant factor and cannot be confined merely to the earlier Ricoeur as some of his followers tend to assume.

At a superficial level it may appear that the existentialism of Jaspers has been left far behind, for in his more recent writings Ricoeur rarely makes reference to Jaspers at all. Moreover, since few philosophers on the contemporary scene are as ranging in their "detours" as the peripatetic Ricoeur, it is extremely difficult to say at any given moment to what or to whom he is directing his seemingly boundless critical energies. Most of the work that has issued from the pen of Paul Ricoeur in the twenty-five year period that has elapsed since the publication of part two of *Philosophie de la volonté*, however, can be viewed as self-imposed propaedeutic to part three, his poetics of the will. It was as though Ricoeur were exploring every possible development in philosophy of language and linguistics as preparation for the task of speaking – and more definitively than Jaspers – the meaning of the nature and reality of Transcend-

[37] Cf., Don Ihde, *Hermeneutic Phenomenology: The Philosophy of Paul Ricoeur* (Evanston: Northwestern University Press, 1971); David Rasmussen, *Mythic-Symbolic Language and Philosophical Anthropology* (The Hague: Martinus Nijhoff, 1971); Patrick L. Bourgeois, *The Extension of Ricoeur's Hermeneutic* The Hague: Martinus Nijhoff, 1975); and editorial comments by Edward Ballard and Lester Embree in Ricoeur's *Husserl: An Analysis of his Phenomenology* (Evanston: Northwestern University Press, 1967).
[38] *Karl Jaspers et la philosophie de l'existence*, co-authored with Mikel Dufrenne (Paris: Edition du Seuil, 1947); *Gabriel Marcel et Karl Jaspers. Philosophie du mystère et philosophie du paradoxe* (Parris: Temps Présent, 1948).

ence. Therefore given the structure of his magnum opus, Ricoeur will once again have to deal rather directly with the philosophy of Karl Jaspers.[39] His most recent work on symbol and metaphor would appear to be preparation for precisely this reengagement.

To complicate matters further with respect to assessing the earlier Ricoeur's acknowledged debt to Jaspers, we are confronted with criticism bordering on outright rejection and even hostility. For example, in his contribution to the Schilpp *Festschrift* for Jaspers (1957) he contends that philosophizing *aus möglicher Existenz* is both uncritical and, as philosophy of religion, counterproductive, for as the sole "center of reference" the unmitigated "originality" of Existenz in its "moment of choice" does not so much represent the basis of an authentic humanism grounded in the *Ursprung* of freedom as it exemplifies "the invisible cordon of our own vanity."[40] Indeed, it is Jaspers' conception of the self that lies at the heart of Ricoeur's objections, for in Jaspers the self, rationally grounded in freedom, is transparent to itself in the moment of choice. The self, hence, bears witin itself the Unconditional and needs no external grounding such as, one finds in Kierkegaard for example, Jaspers' facile voluntarism, in the eyes of Ricoeur, derives from the fact that he fails to differentiate sufficiently between finitude and fault, contingency and evil, for "Finitude is a condition, a state. Guilt is an event."[41] Because of Jaspers' tendency to fuse ontological and psychological concepts into existential symbols, Jaspers' *Existenzphilosophie* is uncritical as a description of the manner in which the will is operative in *actual* situations of possibility. Ironically, Ricoeur, the French Calvinist, seems to be telling Jaspers, the German Protestant, to pay closer heed to Luther's *de servo arbitrio*. Quoting Marcel, Ricoeur denies the presumed transparency of the ego to itself in the act of willing: "Is not to be free, to choose? And when one loves, does one choose to love? But no doubt one must radically dissociate the notions of choice and freedom. To what extent can I say 'I'? That is the real problem."[42] The *real problem*, indeed,

---

[39] See *Interpretation Theory: Discourse and the Surplus of Meaning* (FortWorth: Texas Christian University Press, 1976), esp. "Metaphor and Symbol," pp. 45 ff.; and *La metaphore vive* (Paris: Editions du Seuil, 1975). Both studies are far more attendant to theoretical considerations regarding the nature of metaphor and symbol than anything Jaspers ever wrote. Nevertheless, Jaspers' insistence that mythic-symbolic language has "an intrinsic claim to validity" continues to undergird Ricoeur's reflections on the subject, especially the question of metaphoric *reference*.

[40] Schilpp, *op. cit.*, p. 636.

[41] *Ibid.*, p. 632.

[42] *Ibid.*, pp. 635-636.

and it is the matrix of Ricoeur's project in *Philosophie de la volonté* as the necessary consideration prior to any statement whatsoever regarding the nature and reality of Transcendence.

Second, Ricoeur finds troublesome Jaspers' "reverential love for the hidden Transcendence."[43] In fact, the lyrical obscurity of his views leads to a "disquieting aestheticism" that does not result in the salvation of Eternalization, but to the "disaster" that is concomitant with endless reflection on "the finally supreme, though silent, cipher of Being."[44] Like a "don Juan courting all the gods," Jaspers' *"philosophie a deux foyers"* is unable ultimately to withstand the assaults of either rigorous theism or atheism. Consequently, it is finally unable to get "beyond tragedy," and it is *amor fati* and not Transcendence that has the final word.[45]

These caustic remarks should not, however, be construed as an outright rejection of the entire Jaspersian project, nor should they be attributed to Ricoeur "the theologian," as some have suggested.[46] On the contrary, it was Jaspers' bold affirmation of the reality of Transcendence amidst the despair of atheistic existentialism, on the one hand, and the *hubris* of positivism, on the other, that initially attracted Ricoeur to Jaspers. Furthermore, it is clearly Jaspers' dialectic of Existenz and Transcendence that Ricoeur seeks to delineate further in his own philosophy of will. "Transcendence," Ricoeur states, "is what liberates freedom from the fault."[47] Like Jaspers, it is Ricoeur's intention to elucidate the "drama of the divided man," taking his cue from the boundary situations of Jaspers as well as some of the intrinsic structures of subjectivity delineated in his *Existenzphilosophie*. In fact, so closely is Ricoeur's yet-to-be-completed project patterned after that of Jaspers' *Philosophie*, that he has, in some ways, been entrapped by it. The question for Ricoeur also is how to move from world, to self, to God and still avoid the certain genetic aspect we have found so troublesome in Jaspers' formal modalities of transcending-thinking. How can the facile voluntarism of Jaspers be ameliorated and still preserve the reality of freedom? How can one best prevent the "Cartesian generosity" intrinsic to a philosophy of reflection from becoming license? And how, above all, can one best elucidate both Fault and Transcendence without assuming, *a priori*, their ver-

---

[43]   *Ibid.*, p. 617.

[44]   *Ibid.*, p. 633.

[45]   *Karl Jaspers et la philosophie de l'existence*, p. 387.

[46]   Cf., Leonard Ehrlich, *Karl Jaspers: Philosophy as Faith* (Amherst: University of Massachusetts Press, 1975), pp. 72-77.

[47]   *Freedom and Nature: The Voluntary and the Involuntary*, trans. Erazim V. Kohak (Evanston: Northwestern University Press, 1966), p. 29.

idicy as ontological realities? In sum, the fundamental task of Ricoeur is that of making an even stronger case for the reality of Transcendence than we find in Jaspers.

For this task, I am suggesting, Jaspers, Marcel and Husserl make separate but complementary contributions to Ricoeur. Using the dialectical corrollary that Jaroslav Pelikan terms "Protestant Principle – Catholic Substance," one might suggest that for Ricoeur Jaspers' philosophy of Freedom represents as a primary source the *principle* and, insofar as both the origin and goal of freedom is Transcendence, also the goal of Ricoeur's project. Gabriel Marcel, by contrast, represents the *substance* apart from which any philosophy of will is quite destitute; that is, the sacramental-incarnational particularity of *le corps propre* in Marcel provides the "consistency of world" that serves as the counterbalance to Jaspers' philosophy of reflection. Husserl, of course, represents for Ricoeur the *method* whereby the complementarity of Jaspers and Marcel, the voluntary and the involuntary, might best be elucidated in a formal and rigorous manner. It is to these respective sources, we suggest, that the following introductory in *Freedom and Nature* are directed: "This is the function of descriptive phenomenology; it is the watershed of separated romantic effusion and shallow intellectualism." [48] Eidetic phenomenology, then, will lead Ricoeur to "a *distinctive understanding* of how the subjective structures of the voluntary and an *encompassing sense* of the mystery of incarnation mutually complete and limit each other." [49] Ricoeur therefore affirms as strongly as Jaspers the reality of Transcendence, but is exceedingly wary of reducing its meaning to Existenz and the processes of its self-constitution. Thus, when Ricoeur says that "a philosophy of the subject and a philosophy of Transcendence . . . are both determined in one and the same movement," he does not mean by *movement* merely a noetic process of progressive reification from world, to self, to God. He suggests rather a "vast circular movement" involving a "double decision" in which "the Cogito affirms itself but not as its own creator; where reflection attests itself but not as self-positing." [50] As a movement of double decision Ricoeur's method will necessitate a "second Copernican revolution" in which the ego is "displaced" in the transition from eidetics to an empirics-symbolics and tentative reconstitution in a poetics. It is this methodical displacement of the ego that Ricoeur believes never really takes place in Jaspers.

[48] *Ibid.*, p. 17.
[49] *Ibid.*, p. 15.
[50] *Ibid.*, p. 468.

In sharp contrast to Jaspers' analysis of the formal modalities of transcending-thinking, then, Ricoeur provides detailed descriptions of "the bottom limits" of human experience: the involuntary, fallibility and fault, the servile will, the indefinite matter of the unconscious – all of which are as central to the incarnate matrix of being human as reason. Whereas Jaspers devotes his attention to *transcending*, Ricoeur, as it were, attends to the subject as *transcended* not only from above and from without, but also from below and within. Indeed, it is Ricoeur's acute awareness of human reality as "bounded" that informs his keen sensitivity of the fact that any comprehension of the meaning of ciphers of Transcendence is far more the result of processes of mediation than any direct intuition. "We clearly reject," Ricoeur asserts, "the pretensions of an overly zealous apologetics which would pretend to derive God from nature or from subjectivity by a simple rational implication." Indeed, throughout his work Ricoeur is frequent to mention his abiding suspicion of idealism however concealed it might be in philosophies of reflection. Thus he warns of the dangers of going straight to the existential project and "arriving too quickly" at meaning for the self. The weakness of *Existenzphilosophie*, he suggests, is its blurring of the rigorous functions and operations of philosophical analysis into a kind of "indistinct existential monism." Ricoeur is suspicious, as he puts it succinctly, of "the Promethean character of all forms of idealism." [51]

Prometheanism, of course, has particularly to do with the defiant will. Let us then look briefly at Jaspers and Ricoeur on the nature of the will and freedom, and how conflicts on these fundamental issues extend to the problem of hermeneutics.

"The will," Jaspers asserts, "originates in *Existenz*, receives the grandeur of its content from the *idea*, is mobile in the service of *passion* and vital *ends*, and is machine-like as the *final form* of long-standing *discipline*." With Kierkegaard, Jaspers agrees "the more will, the more self." The will "in league with reason" has the capacity of "relating the self to itself" and, as such, the power to intervene between fantasy and reality, "the only place where magic, so to speak, is real" inasmuch as the will has the capacity to actualize potentialities in *Lebenspraxis*. While the will is frequently in the service of the *passions*, its higher purpose is service to the *idea* inasmuch as the will, according to Jaspers, has the capacity of taking "instant aim at coherent *entireties*." The will, then, is that which draws the self to that which mere cognition cannot know, viz., Tran-

---

[51] *Ibid.*, p. 464; see also *Husserl*, p. 215. The same mood pervades Mikel Dufrenne's *The Notion of the A Priori* (Evanston: Northwestern University Press; 1966).

scendence. This drive to unity, intrinsic to the dynamics of *mögliche Existenz*, is what Jaspers terms "grand volition." [52]

Thus, far more significant than the *what* or even the *how* of the will is "*that I will*." "It is always I who will," he states, "even when it is for the weakest possible psychological motive." It is not surprising, then, that Jaspers in contrast to Ricoeur pays scant attention to the phenomenology of motivation. "There can be," he says, "no adequate motivation for the will in original choice – in the choice which no longer lies between things but serves to manifest the self in Existenz." As such the essence of will "defies phenomenological description and psychological cognition, though in reality we are certain of its performance." Consequently, Jaspers sketches with conspicuous brevity the dialectic of the voluntary and the involuntary suggesting summarily that "as the encompassing of man's intrinsic power in his Existenz, [the will is] infinite and dark as the involuntary side, and finite, definite and clear at each moment as the voluntary side." [53] Implicit to Jaspers' definition is the notion that the more the will is attuned to "the grandeur of its content in the idea," the more it is attuned to Transcendence. Also implied is the notion that while the bottom limit of the involuntary has the power of subsuming the will and rendering the subject schizophrenic, its upper limit is, as in Plato and Hegel, virtually unbounded.

But what is the source of the power of the will? The will "originates in Existenz," Jaspers states, but this tells us little. Existenz, as in the case of Transcendence, is but a cipher, a symbol, and hence has no reality apart from the experience of the individual subject. As a nonobjective reality, it goes without saying that the will needs no objective source or ground by which it can or should be authenticated. In fact, the opposite is true, for if Jaspers were to provide a material ground for the will, he would perforce revert to the faculty psychology that he left far behind with the publication of *Allgemeine Psychopathologie*. The closest Jaspers comes to providing a ground for the will is to say that it "remains embedded in something Encompassing." [54] Indeed, this is central, for the Encompassing is that which, as in Anaximander's *Boundless*, is not only the origin and goal of Being but its "*between*" known only in freedom. And freedom for Jaspers, as we have seen, is not some state of being where necessity will no longer impinge on me. It is the ground of the very possibility of Existenz and, indeed, Transcendence as well. Because freedom is the

[52] *Phil.*, II, pp. 133-141.
[53] *Ibid.*, pp. 135-140.
[54] *Ibid.*, p. 140.

underlying condition of possible Existenz, the will is understood as "the lever by which Transcendence acts on Existenz" in the moment of original choice.[55] Confronting the mystery of freedom, the subject may experience himself sinking as into a bottomless void. In this state of foundering or "shipwreck," as Nietzsche termed it, one becomes aware of the "possibility of unfreedom" whereupon one is "shaken at the roots of one's being." One may, at this juncture, "be swallowed up by the protective night of madness," as Heidegger said of Hölderlin, or, as in Kierkegaard, venture the leap of faith staking one's claim on the reality of freedom even though one is unsure that it exists.[56]

For Ricoeur the self-grounding of Jaspers' philosophy of freedom on a ground so obscure sounds like sheer mystification. Part of this obscurity, as we have seen, is that Jaspers' understanding of freedom and will has a double set of informants. On the one hand, there is the voluntarism of Kant and the idealist tradition generally, where the ego is transparent to itself in the act of reflection. On the other hand, however, one finds a mystical and ontological conception of freedom not unlike the notion of freedom espoused in Jacob Boehme and Rhineland mysticism generally. Here freedom is not so much the *Urgrund* as the *Abgrund* of Being. As the Encompassing of *die Gottheit* its essence is utterly nonobjectifiable; "a silence that knows no break" as in Plotinus. Moreover, Jaspers stands in the lineage of German romantic philosophy where these abstruse psychological and ontological components are mixed in such a way that it is nearly impossible to sort them out. The same problem, of course, confronts us in Heidegger. It is in view of this peculiar admixture of informants that Ricoeur asks, we suspect, whether Jaspers has not "juxtaposed a philosophy of *unreconciled tragedy* with a *lyric* philosophy that leads towards a disquieting aestheticism."[57] It is the mystical aspect of this "aestheticism" especially that informs Ricoeur's critique of Jaspers and also the primordial conception of Truth we find in Heidegger, for in Ricoeur's view "romanticism of the always anterior" glosses the critical questions in epistemology, ontology and above all ethics.

Within this lyrics there is also, Ricoeur notes, a curious kind of Hegelianism. But it was Hegel who saw also that it is precisely through the "incarnate origins of negativity"[58] that one begins to realize that those as-

[55] *Ibid.*, p. 155.
[56] *Ibid.*, p. 164.
[57] Schilpp, *op. cit.*, p. 638.
[58] *Freedom and Nature*, p. 444.

pects of my being providing me with the capacity for freedom and Transcendence are also those aspects weighing me down as the marks of my limitation and death. Negation, then, derives its force not only at the noetic-conceptual level but also at the level of the passions. Again, it is the lower limit that is not given sufficient development in Jaspers' notion of "qualified negativity," and it is this that prevents Jaspers, in Ricoeur's view, from comprehending the nature of evil as both suffered and willed.

It is not, of course, that idealism's affirmation of the reality of freedom is wrong in the eyes of Ricoeur. What is erroneous is the "positing of the self as sovereign" in the process of the delineation of its meaning; "to be altogether free of the shadow," as he puts it eloquently, "in absolute transcendence of the cave." [59] Thus Ricoeur would probe more deeply into the essence of freedom by attending to its rootedness in the passions in order to establish clearly both its possibilities and its limits, thereby adumbrating the Promethean character of Existenz while preserving its reality and even its centrality. This is effected in Ricoeur's eidetic analysis of the *pathétique* of misery in *Fallible Man*, and his mythics-symbolics of the fault in *The Symbolism of Evil*, works that parallel structurally Jaspers' *Existenzerhellung*. Ricoeur takes his cue, as does Jaspers, from Plato's injunction concerning the wisdom of "lingering in the between" (*Philebus*, 17e-18b) in order to elucidate properly the nature of the soul. But contrary to those who, like Descartes and also Jaspers, place man midway in the ontological symbolism of Being and nothingness, transcendence and immanence, Ricoeur develops the participatory boundary of *metaxu* in terms of "feeling" (*thumos*). The matrix of the soul, then, is not for Ricoeur best understood immediately in terms of the eidetics or rationality but in terms of the affects of "desire," as in Aristotle. [60] Ricoeur believes that a phenomenology of desire can correct reflective-speculative philosophy that "overvalues the movement of choice" in its placement of the self at the center of reflection. Ricoeur, in this analysis, shows that man is an "affective fragility" which, as the "zero point" or "luminous center" of being human, is also matrix of inclination towards either good or evil. [61] This tendential locus is not in and of itself considered either good or evil. The self is rather the "synthetic unity of intentions" and has no intelligibility apart from its intentions. What speculative-reflective philosophy fails to recognize is that one cannot obtain an

---

[59] *Ibid.*, p. 464.
[60] *Fallible Man*, pp. 78-79.
[61] *Ibid.*, pp. 224 ff. A similar approach characterizes Karl Rahner's analysis of *Potentia Oboedientalis* in *Hearers of the Word* (New York: Herder, 1969); i.e., man's "luminous" capacity for Being is rooted in the will.

accurate understanding of the self only through a consideration of the rationality and irrationality of the will. Such descriptions, according to Ricoeur, are second and not first level differentiations that make sense only when one first attends to the phenomenology of motivation. Thus myth, and especially the Adamic myth of the fall, for Ricoeur elucidates what pure reflection can never achieve, namely, a sense of the "affective fragility" that the will represents in the concrete situation of choice. Here man finds himself in the situation of possibility and freedom. Yet the primordial reality of chaos is also present in the form of the serpent; a cryptic reminder of the reality of violence and death from the deicidal cosmogonies of Sumero-Akkadian literature. Thus even here in the Edenic paradise, freedom for man – created in the image of God" – is *bounded*, and evil is both suffered and willed. [62]

Ricoeur's notion of freedom as *bounded*, then, is what differentiates his conception of the self from that of Jaspers more than any other single factor. From within, freedom is bounded by the particular shape of one's decisions, actions and choices. One can never, as in Jaspers' "grand volition," will totality even as an idea. One can only will particulars and then only in proportion to one's ability to attend to that which is willed. One must remember that what appears to be purely cognitive in the act of willing is really conative, and that "to will," as Ricoeur insists, "is not to create." [63]

From without, freedom is bounded for Ricoeur as for Jaspers by Transcendence. But in Ricoeur Transcendence is not viewed primarily as a noetic limit. It is also an eschatological limit that vitiates all unmitigated forms of voluntarism. Indeed, it is precisely the eschatological limit or Transcendence that constitutes its "alterity," as Levinas insists; i.e., that aspect of Transcendence which defies methodological reductions of the "Other" to the "same." [64] And this can be documented on a very practical basis whenever a given Existenz willfully manipulates reality to conform to noetic designs. Within the province of meaning, such reductions are oblivious of the fact that all meaning *pro me* has an origin that is *extra nos*. Failure to recognize this results in a kind of semi-Pelagianism that Ricoeur, and indeed, Bultmann and Gadamer as well, would avoid on both philosophical and theological grounds. This is what Ricoeur means when he says that in the "double movement" of reflection the "cogito

---

[62] *Symbolism of Evil, passim.*
[63] *Freedom and Nature*, p. 486.
[64] Levinas, *op. cit.*, p. 281ff.

reaffirms itself but not as its own creator." Thus, only when these internal and external limits of freedom are clearly established is one in a position, for Ricoeur, to begin speaking about Transcendence.

It is this double dialectic that also informs Ricoeur's assessment of Jaspers' hermeneutic of ciphers and the fashioning of his own hermeneutic phenomenology. On the one hand, Ricoeur agrees with Jaspers' insistance that the mythic-symbolic enjoys an "intrinsic claim to validity" and that one must be very cautious about imposing on any given cipher a prescriptive method of interpretation. To this end he supports Jaspers' views regarding the need for "remythologizing" religious language: "We must never speak of demythicizing but strictly of demythologizing, it being well understood that what is lost [that is, *suspended* by way of the phenomenological reduction and the eidetic description] is the pseudo-knowledge, the false logos of myth, such as we find expressed, for example, in the etiological function of myth. But when we lose the myth as immediate logos, we rediscover it as myth." [65] Such a "rediscovery" is cognizant, it would seem, of Jaspers' distinction between the *deutbar* and the *schaubar* aspect of the cipher, i.e., that the explanatory approach violates a deeper level of meaning that can only be appropriated existentially through a kind of intuitive participation. However, Ricoeur's "logic of double meaning" does not imply, as we sometimes find in Jaspers, an intuitive penetration to the definitive essence of any given symbol or myth. What it effects is "second level *naiveté*" that is still *naiveté*. Ricoeur's hermeneutics, then, and contrary to all forms of allegorical interpretation, does not have as its goal the "purification of mythical vision" that results in a kind of "eternalization" rendering superfluous the radical particularity of any given myth. Just as the anthropological voluntarism of Jaspers can be ameliorated through attention to the "obscurity limit" of the self, so also the hermeneutical hubris of a speculative reading of ciphers can be abated only through attention to the "ideality limit" of reflection.

Both of these limits inform Ricoeur's cogent delineation of the hermeneutical circle. In keeping with the symbol of the circle, and from a standpoint of both religious avowal and a certain Jungian aspect, Ricoeur begins not with transcending-thinking but with descending-thinking. [66] The downward arc of the circle, then, represents descent of analysis into what Clifford Geertz terms "the dense thicket of particulari-

---

[65] *The Symbolism of Evil*, p. 162.
[66] Cf., "The Hermeneutics of Symbols and Philosophical Reflection" in *The Conflict of Interpretations*, pp. 287-334.

ty" [67] that the profound symbol or myth represents. Quick interpretations are immediately renounced as the hermeneut assumes the role of
the archeologist plummeting, as it were, into the hidden depths of the
myth, and, as phenomenologist, without prescriptive notions as to
what the myth must mean. This archeological moment, however, does
not bring one to the *Urgrund* of the mythic-symbolic either in the epistemological sense that we find in Cassirer, or in the romanticism of the
primordial that we find in the Jungians and to some degree in Heidegger.
What it eventuates, rather, is an awareness of the obscurity limit of the
mythic-symbolic through (*a*) the implementation of the technique of *distanciation* similar to that of Gadamer, and (*b*) the necessity of *avowal* as
the restorative moment of the hermeneutical circle.

Distanciation for Ricoeur, as for Gadamer, is a technique that
renounces *a priori* any notion that the horizon of the mythic text or symbol is identical with one's own. [68] As such, it is a technique that recognizes
the alterity or fundamental difference between the other and the same
and hence a notion that prevents the obscurity of limit from coming
into view, paradoxical as that may sound. This is totally different than
either the quantifying procedures of the *Wissenschaft* proponent or the
romantic effusion of *Erlebnisausdruck* in which the hermeneut understands intuitively the meaning of a text and indeed even the author better
than the author understood himself. Another way of putting it would be
to say that only when through distanciation, or whatever similar method,
the interpreter has fully appreciated the alterity of the text precisely as
extra nos, is he in a position to hear what it says and accept the challenge
to say what it means or "let speak the text," as Gadamer puts it.

Sensing the obscurity limit one realizes that one cannot, as it were,
descend any deeper or the meaning of the text will dissolve in the silence
of the archaic. This, then, represents the necessity for a transition from
descending analytic to an ascending dialectic or transcending-thinking,
as in Jaspers; from archeology to teleology in which the interpreter *risks*
interpretation through avowal. And it is always, for Ricoeur, a cautious

---

[67] Cf., *The Interpretation of Cultures* (New York: Basic Books, 1973), pp. 3-30; and *Islam Observed* (Chicago: University of Chicago Press, 1971), pp. 27ff. The semantics of "thick descriptions" in Geertz, however, always stops short of the speculative leap based on avow-al that we find in Ricoeur's "restorative hermeneutics." It represents quite strictly a social anthropological analysis of "symbol systems."

[68] Cf. Two lectures by Ricoeur entitled "The Task of Hermeneutics" and "The Her-meneutical Function of Distanciation" printed in *Philosophy Today*, Volume 17, Summer, 1973, where he acknowledges Gadamer but would develop a technique of distanciation that would also acommodate dialogue with the semiological and exegetical disciplines.

transition, a transition in which faith is still conditioned by doubt but now an informed doubt. It is precisely in this sense that Ricoeur's movement from a "hermeneutics of suspicion" to the "restorative hermeneutics" of "sympathetic reenactment" represents a transition from the interrogative to the indicative mood that is still tempered by the subjunctive. This is necessarily the case because the hermeneutical speaking of meaning must, for Ricoeur, remain fully conscious of the ideality limit of speculation. Philosophical hermeneutics is informed by philosophical anthropology at each step. This is why Ricoeur maintains the hermeneutical circle precisely as a circle in what he terms "the dimming of speculation and a return to the tragic;" [69] a view that is closely tied to Jaspers' insistence that we must never "break out of the hermeneutical circle," but rather strive to make it more "encompassing," and also similar to Gadamer's notion concerning the "fusion of horizons" as a never ending task.

In summary, the basic similarity between Jaspers and Ricoeur is the development of a philosophical anthropology that can better elucidate the nature and reality of Transcendence. What is fundamentally different in their respective projects is the deployment of a method that can adequately elucidate the nature of the self and its relatedness to Transcendence. For Ricoeur such a task necessitates not one but several methods. He proceeds initially through an eidetic description of *le corps propre*, a notion that is at once informed by Merleau-Ponty's *le corps vécu* and phenomenology of perception, and Gabriel Marcel's reflections on the mystery of being incarnate. In this analysis both the upper and the lower limits of being, viz., Transcendence and the Fault, are rigorously suspended in order to bring to light the manner in which the will is operative as embodied. Secondly, Ricoeur moves to an empirics-symbolics of the will. In this analysis the symbols of fallibility and the Fault are released from the dispassionate bracketing of eidetic description and encountered in their mythical instantiations where there is always a surplus of meaning, i.e., a density that resists eidetic analysis and which calls for sympathetic reenactment through a restorative hermeneutics. In the final part of his project, Ricoeur will presumably release from suspension the symbols of wholeness and Transcendence. But what is of major consequence in these methodological shifts, in contrast to Jaspers, is Ricoeur's attention to the mediation of meaning and the curtailment of a philosophy of reflection based on intuition. It is precisely in this respect

---

[69] See "The Hermeneutics of Symbols and Philosophical Reflection," *op. cit.*, and *The Symbolism of Evil*, pp. 360 ff.

that Ricoeur insists that "truly reflective philosophy must be mediated by the ideas, actions, works, institutions, and monuments that objectify it. It is in these *objects*, in the widest sense of the term, that the Ego must lose and find itself. Thus we can say in a somewhat paradoxical sense that a philosophy of reflection is not a philosophy of consciousness if by consciousness we mean immediate self-consciousness." [70] We would, therefore, strongly agree with Patrick Bourgeois that we are of late witnessing merely the "extension" in Ricoeur of concerns that have been fundamentally hermeneutical throughout. "All reflection is interpretation," Bourgeois cites Ricoeur, "for we only have indirect access to the meaning of our acts and to the meaning of ourselves." [71] It is also, we would add, the rigorous extension of Jaspers' intention that authentic philosophizing has to do with determining the meaning of the concrete situation of being-in-a-world squarely into hermeneutic phenomenology.

Because the mediation of meaning is a fundamental *Leitmotiv* in Ricoeur, it was inevitable that he would, sooner or later, have to come to terms with the contention of Heidegger and Gadamer that *Sprachlichkeit* and not *Geschichtlichkeit* is the *fondement* of Being; or better, that historicity is a possibility only when it is mediated by the linguisticality of Existenz. Such a move also expands the scope of the question concerning Transcendence far beyond the mere elucidation of the subject. This is well evidenced in the following statement by Wolfhart Pannenberg, one of Gadamer's more influential students in the domain of theology, where he rejects Bultmann's contention that the existential question is the only legitimate question that can be put to mythic-symbolic texts: "Hermeneutical obscuring of the *intentio recta* of the statements about God, the world, and history in favor of the meaning of the text as an expression of an understanding of human existence evidences an anthropological constriction in the formulation of the question . . . The understanding of the world and of God are not merely the *expression* of man's question concerning himself, but, on the contrary, the relationship to the world, to society, and to God is what first *mediates* man to himself. Only by means of these relationships does he obtain self-understanding." [72]

There can be little doubt that Jaspers' insistence on the centrality of the mythical, the symbolic, and the poetical to philosophy and religion

---

[70] *Freud and Philosophy*, pp. 44-45.
[71] Bourgeois, *op. cit.*, pp. 129 ff.
[72] *Basic Questions in Theology*, I, trans. George H. Kehm (Philadelphia: Fortress Press, 1970), pp. 110-111.

persists in both Gadamer and Ricoeur. The work of Gadamer and Ricoeur, however, can be viewed as the attempt to delineate more precisely just how the mythical, the symbolic and the poetical are instrumental in the *mediation* of philosophical and religious meaning. Since these aspects and/or expressions of experience are primarily linguistic, it is to an analysis of language that Gadamer, following Heidegger, turns his attention in the period following the Bultmann-Jaspers debate and up to the publication of *Wahrheit und Methode* in 1960. Indeed, it is Gadamer's contention that one does not begin merely in the situation of being-in-a-world, as Jaspers and the existentialists generally contended. One's situation of being-in-a-world is preeminently "linguistic being," for the moment the event of reflection takes place leading to the emergence of the *question* as to what it means to-be-in-a-world, language is presupposed as the agency whereby this question is possible in the first instance.

We turn now to a consideration of Gadamer's hermeneutic philosophy within the context of Jaspers' understanding of Transcendence, and to a brief consideration of the manner in which Ricoeur is extending Gadamer's pioneering work in this field.

THE QUESTION OF LANGUAGE: JASPERS AND GADAMER

Hans-Georg Gadamer, Jaspers' successor at the University of Heidelberg, is generally complimentary of his predecessor's work. But he is also quick to note that the larger potential impact of Jaspers' thought was eclipsed in a "single stroke" with the publication of Heidegger's *Sein und Zeit* in 1927, "before Jaspers' *Philosophie* even appeared in print."[73] This is not to say that the periechontology of Jaspers and the fundamental ontology of Heidegger do not share a great deal in common, especially the intention of opening a new era of *humane* philosophizing. Nor does he fail to recognize that Jaspers in many ways anticipated philosophical thematic that was to be later identified with other thinkers. It is rather to suggest that Jaspers' position was never developed with the same degree of intensity or precision as Heidegger's, nor was it, for Gadamer, as radical in critique of neo-Kantian idealism. Thus while Jaspers' *Existenzphilosophie* is hermeneutical in the general sense of the term, hermeneutics is never perceived as the primary *ontological* mode of one's

[73] Cf., Gadamer's marvelous account of "The Phenomenological Movement," in *Philosophical Hermeneutics, op. cit.*, p. 138.

being-in-a-world as is the case in Heidegger. Ontology, as we have seen, is rejected by Jaspers in favor of an existentialistic metaphysics, whereas Heidegger, by contrast, seeks to rehabilitate ontology through an analysis of *Dasein* that eventually encompasses *language* as the *fondement* of *Dasein*. In sum, Heidegger's move to *Sprachlichkeit* provides philosophical discourse about *Geschichtlichkeit* with a concreteness and specificity that is missing in Jaspers' notion of *Existenz*.

Gadamer's hermeneutic philosophy, then, takes its orientation from Heidegger and not Jaspers for two basic reasons. First, Gadamer perceives in Heidegger's focus on language an effective way of displacing the primacy of the subject and with it the subject-object dichotomy as it is understood and maintained by Jaspers concerning the nature of reality. Thus while Gadamer shares Jaspers' contention that all philosophizing originates from the situation of finding oneself in a world, it is not just the *idea* of world but finding oneself in a *worded-world*. In Gadamer, therefore, the meaning of being-in-a-world is made possible in and through language and, as such, language and not Existenz is the "middle ground" of philosophizing. [74] Alluding to Jaspers, but obviously taking his cue from Heidegger's notion of "language as the house of Being," Gadamer asserts that "language is the all-encompassing." [75] Indeed, it was Gadamer who perceived, far more clearly than many commentators, that Heidegger's fundamental interest from the outset was not existentialism and the historicity of the subject but ontology and the linguisticality of Being.

Second, Gadamer's hermeneutic philosophy stands in a more sympathetic relationship to theology than the *Existenzphilosophie* of Karl Jaspers. While this is due in large measure to his appreciation of the biblical theology of the Lutheran tradition that he avows (in contrast to the rather vague Protestantism of Jaspers), the influence of Heidegger here is also discernible in two quite specific ways. This may be seen, first, in Gadamer's inclination to the *Wortmystik* that is intrinsic to German theology and that is so prominent in the later writings of Heidegger. [76] While Jaspers, in his theory of ciphers, constantly guards against any linguistic "corporealization of Transcendence," Heidegger and Gadamer view the word as not only the symbolic mediator of Transcendence or Being, but

---

[74] *Truth and Method,* pp. 345 ff.
[75] *Philosophical Hermeneutics,* p. 67.
[76] It is ironic, in fact, that it is the so-called "atheist" Heidegger, and not his theological contemporaries, that truly explores the implications of *Wortmystik* through his hermeneutic of ancient texts. In this respect, of course, he stands in a position similar to that of Nietzsche.

as somehow being one with that which is presented. The sacramental overtones of this notion, we suggest, derive in part from the Catholic and Lutheran backgrounds of Heidegger and Gadamer respectively, and therefore it is not surprising that we should find in Gadamer an utterly different interpretation of the "cipher of Incarnation" than what we find in Jaspers. Given this inclination it is, moreover, not surprising that theologians like Gerhard Ebeling and Wolfhart Pannenberg should be so heavily influenced by Gadamer and that Heinrich Ott should find in Heidegger a theory of revelation more consistent with Barth and orthodox theology generally than with the existentialist hermeneutics of Bultmann, with whom Heidegger was initially associated. With the notable exception of Fritz Buri, Jaspers' philosophy, by contrast, has not been readily appropriated by theologians who wish to be fully identified with a consistently confessional form of Christianity.

Heidegger's influence can be discerned, secondly, in Gadamer's truly innovative rehabilitation of the meaning of Tradition, and that tradition like language "bears us along" even as we bear it along by virtue of our being linguistic. This means that tradition is to be taken seriously, not viewed merely as a theoretical problem which may or may not be of concern to the philosopher or theologian. Tradition, for Gadamer, is developed as an ontological problem inasmuch as it manifests a preformative power that is frequently unknown to the subject. Thus the meaning of Heidegger's presumed "destruction" of the tradition, for Gadamer, is completely misunderstood if one sees in the radical engagement and recreation of tradition a kind of capriciousness. The hermeneutical encounter with tradition is rather fundamental in the sense that one must seek to determine not only what tradition says but how it pre-forms both how and what the subject sees it as saying. Because this dialectical feature is intrinsic to interpretation and understanding one can neither ignore tradition, as tends to be the case in many circles, nor should one merely repristinate those aspects of the tradition deemed authoritative out of special interests. One must seek rather to understand more comprehensively that tradition is the inevitable point of our departure by virtue of our being linguistic and that we can never, as it were, transcend tradition either backwards to the so-called "real facts" or forwards to some utopian state that is free from the presumed bondage of tradition.

One must, it seems, find oneself situated in a tradition where "tration" represents more than just an academic question to obtain a full impression of its urgency. Such is the case with Gadamer's Lutheranism and its longer view to the tradition as a primary source of revelation and therefore Being, even though this is not understood clearly by many who call themselves Lutherans. Heidegger, with his Roman Catholic underpinnings, however estranged from them he might appear to be, also evidences similar orientation with respect to Western philosophical tradition in the notion that the tradition is to be effectively confronted in order to effect a transformed understanding as to what *it gives*. "There is," as Jaspers was fond of putting it, "no way around history, but only through history." We might add to this, by way of Heidegger and Gadamer, that the reason we find ourselves so inextricably bound up with history and tradition is because they are imbedded in us in and through language.

On the other hand, and here very much in tune with Jaspers' insistence that philosophy has primarily to do with *communication* and *Lebenspraxis*, Gadamer develops his hermeneutic philosophy as *practical* philosophy. Contrary to Jaspers, however, Gadamer develops the practical dimensions of his position through Aristotle and not Plato, thus absolving in part the dichotomy between theory and practice that frequently results from a Platonist orientation. Focussing on the Aristotelian notion of *phronesis*, where moral knowledge consists of the fusion of theory and practice, Gadamer insists that transcending within and through language has primarily to do not with absolute, theoretical knowledge concerning the nature and reality of Transcendence, but with the actual occasions of self-transcendence in day to day living. It is *praxis* and not just *theoria* that underlies Gadamer's seemingly abstruse notion of "the effective-historical consciousness" (*Wirkungsgeschichtlichen Bewusstseins*) which, when combined with his notion of "the linguisticality of Being," removes completely the extrinsicism present to Jaspers' understanding of Transcendence; i.e., our feeling that in spite of his denials and qualifications to the contrary, Jaspers' notion of Transcendence still retains a sense of a spatialized "out-thereness."

Let us now focus a bit more directly on the question of language as the *fondement* of Being, paying special attention to Gadamer's "rehabilitation of the concept of prejudice" as it relates to tradition and the mediation of the meaning of Transcendence.

"Language," Gadamer insists, "is the universal medium in which understanding is realized. The mode of realization of understanding is interpretation."[77] In a similar vein, Ricoeur maintains that "There is no symbolism before a man speaks, even if the power of the symbol is grounded much deeper."[78] Against the intuitionist both Gadamer and

[77] *Truth and Method*, p. 350.
[78] *The Conflict of Interpretations*, p. 13.

Ricoeur maintain, therefore, that there are no wordless meanings and no epiphanies of Being apart from language. The private languages so common to eastern philosophy and to all maintaining metaphysical immediacy to Being transcending language are fictions, as Wittgenstein suggested. But this does not mean that there is no experience apart from language. It rather means that the meaning of experience is unintelligible apart from language; i.e., language is the agency that renders all experience consciously intelligible and, in that very process, conditions the intelligibility we find. This is why Ricoeur insists, as we have seen, that philosophies of reflection are also hermeneutical, for it is language that undergirds the possibility of reflection on the meaning of experience. While the Jungians and others insist that there is a dark, subterranean, archetypal unconscious antecedent to all experience, this, too, is a notion that can be articulated meaningfully only through language. And the moment one refers to language, one refers to a given; that is, one refers to something that is not one's invention no matter how creative one's use of language might be. Thus the question is not whether language, but what kind of language and how to speak most effectively the meaning of that which language gives. [79]

Gadamer sees his notion of language as the "middle ground" of Being strengthened through the insights of Joannine Christology and the medieval mystics. What is unique to "the Word become flesh" formulation of Christianity, according to Gadamer, is a radical despiritualization of the Platonistic conception of *logos*, for in the New Testament the word is consubstantial with that which it presents. It is a view which, in line with Heidegger's reflections on pre-Socratic philosophy, presents *logos* as bringing into the "open" that which is hidden. This insight, Gadamer maintains, is developed richly in Aquinas where the dialogue of the soul with itself and the fusion of the "inner word" and "language" is not to be understood as a "temporal relation" but in terms of an *emantio intellectualis*; that is, an event in which the word is "simultaneous with the formation (*formatio*) of the intellect." [80] For hermeneutic philosophy this means that "the inner mental word is not formed by a reflective act." [81] Rather, thought and word are coextensive with respect to the objects they intend; objects which, as in Husserl, do not have to be real as entities. To be sure, reflection on what is thought is both possible and necessary, but

---

[79] Cf., Heidegger, *What is Called Thinking?* and his discussion of *es gibt* throughout.
[80] *Truth and Method*, p. 383.
[81] *Ibid.*, p. 385.

one must remember that this is a secondary level operation. What takes place initially, according to Gadamer, is the "word expressing . . . " an intended object just as in phenomenology generally, consciousness is always "consciousness of . . . " an intended object. Within the context of kerygmatic Christianity this means, obviously, that in the proclaimed Word there takes place the "presencing of the presence" of that to which the word is incarnate, namely, the work and person of Jesus as the Christ.[82]

Thus there is continuity between Gadamer's theory of language and the Christian doctrine of revelation and not the radical discontinuity we noted in Jaspers' theory of ciphers and the incarnation.

In Cusanus, Gadamer finds further evidence for the consubstantiality of language with that which it intends. Cusanus, as we have seen, views word and mind as identical with respect to representing a *complicatio*, for "it is the human mind that both gathers together and unfolds." But this *complicatio* is not merely noetic but linguistic; that is, the unfolding of the enfolding is a process that takes place only in living speech. Here the more traditionally idealistic interpretations of Cusanus, including Jaspers', are adumbrated in Gadamer. Under the influence of nominalism and freed from the constraints of conceptual realism, Gadamer suggests that it was Cusanus who first saw the multiplicity of language lends credence to and does not detract from the possibility of meaning, and not the reverse as the enemies of nominalism insisted. In other words, it is precisely due to the infinite horizon of living speech that infinite meaning is possible. Because of the intrinsic relationship between living speech and the natural (inner) word, an "unfolding of the single unity of mind" is possible, not, to be sure, in terms of a kind of Pythagorean pre-established harmony, as is sometimes suggested in Cusanus, but as the primordial possibility of language. [83]

In Gadamer, therefore, man's capacity for Transcendence is identical with his capacity for "living speech" [84] because living speech is an unfolding of the meaning of what language has gathered. "It is not that the world becomes the object of language. Rather the object of knowledge is already inclosed within the world horizon of language" [85] and therefore all possible *worlds* are the disclosures of language and not the victories of conceptual totalism. This is what Heidegger, for Gadamer, discovered in going back to the pre-Socratics: that it is the "finiteness of the lunguistic

[82]   *Ibid.*, p. 397.
[83]   *Ibid.*, p. 397.
[84]   *Ibid.*, p. 403.
[85]   *Ibid.*, p. 408.

event" that effects understanding precisely as an "event" in which Truth "appears" (*aletheia*) out of its concealment. Such events, however, are not the result of objectifying thinking; that is, the eventfulness of Being does not take place when the knower presumes himself to exist independently of the known. On the contrary, the self-disclosure of Being takes place *only* as a linguistic event whereby the subject-object structure of Experience is momentarily displaced. Being appears only within the mediative context of the primordial possibility that language itself represents and within which the subject is already both a hearer and a speaker of the word.

Now the mediative context that the world horizon of language as primordial possibility represents, for Gadamer, is best illustrated through "play" of sport. In the game well played, there is no longer a distinction between the players and that which is played. [86] Playing, however, presupposes a game to be played. That is, one does not invent a game every time one plays. One rather plays the game that is given and mutually agreed upon by the players. Apart from this givenness, there would be no play but only chaos. As such, the game as given enjoys a tradition. So it is with language, and it is here in Gadamer's "rehabilitation" and transformation of the concepts of "prejudice" and "tradition" that we find the critical notions forming his understanding of the "effective-historical consciousness" and the "fusion of horizons," notions that run wholly contrary to the *pro me* preoccupation of transcending-thinking in Jaspers and his wholly antagonistic assessment of Catholicity.

There were two kinds of prejudice Gadamer reminds us to which the Enlightenment reacted negatively: the prejudice of being "overly hasty" and hence precipitous in one's judgements, and also the prejudice of "tradition" and its constraining authority. The former type, quite obviously, is wholly inimical to good scholarship and is usually detrimental in the general situations of life. The second type of prejudice based on tradition, however, is not always negative but "can also be a source of truth, and this is what the Enlightenment failed to see when it denigrated all authority" [87] except, of course, the authority of science.

---

[86] *Ibid.*, pp. 444 ff. See also the introduction to "Primitive Mythology", volume one of Joseph Campbell's *The Masks of God* (New York: Viking Press, 1959), for discourse on *Homo ludens* as an intrinsic aspect of interpretation. Campbell's comments are obviously more psychologistic than Gadamer's and aimed at what Ricoeur would term a kind of "first level naiveté." Nevertheless, Campbell clearly recognizes that the "playfulness" intrinsic to mythic-poetic language is what critical science fails to accomodate under the pretense of "rigor."

[87] *Ibid.*, p. 247.

What the rationalist fails to see in this and all other instances is that prejudice in some form or another is inevitable, and that it has, in fact, a preformative function, for apart from some kind of prejudice, there can never be judgement. Thus the task is not to free oneself from prejudice (which is impossible), but to differentiate true from false prejudice. Furthermore, the strict rationalist fails to recognize that one never stands outside tradition but always within it even when it is a tradition against tradition. One's task, therefore, is not to abandon tradition and thereby presume that one is free of both tradition and its prejudices, but rather to "nurture" tradition as that within which we both stand and to which we contribute. Just as we do not so much speak language as language speaks us, and just as history does not so much belong to us as we belong to it, so also "Tradition is not simply a precondition into which we come, but we produce it ourselves inasmuch as we understand, participate in the evolution of tradition and hence further determine it ourselves." [88] Indeed, the circle of understanding is precisely "the interplay of the movement of tradition and the movement of the interpreter. Thus the anticipation of meaning that governs our understanding of a text is not an act of subjectivity, but proceeds from the communality that binds us to the tradition" and, as such, represents "an ontological, structural element in understanding." [89]

Thus Jaspers' hermeneutical intention of "purifying ciphers" through his vitriolic attack against "Catholicity" as merely the heteronomous imposition of meaning on the transcending-subject is, for Gadamer, utterly misguided. [90] To be sure, the authority of Catholicity or any other tradition can be negative in its effect if it is merely a substitute for clearheaded judgement. But it is sheer foolishness to presume that one can ever reach Truth unaided by tradition on the grounds that one stands in a direct, "unmediated" relation to its reality as Jaspers tends to suggest repeatedly.

Gadamer's views on tradition also clearly inform his understanding of the "effective-historical consciousness" (*wirkungsgeschichtlichen Bewusstseins*). Now this troublesome term has been variously translated. Richard Palmer renders it as both "the historically operative consciousness" and "the consciousness in which history is ever operative." [91]

[88]   *Ibid.*, p. 261.
[89]   *Ibid.*
[90]   Ibid., p. 248. Cf., *Von der Wahrheit*, pp. 766 ff.
[91]   Richard Palmer, *Hermeneutics* (Evanston: Northwestern University Press, 1969), pp. 193 ff.

Ricoeur translates it as "consciousness of the history of effects." [92] Barden's translation as "the effective-historical consciousness," however, seems to be the one that Gadamer most prefers inasmuch as it manifests clearly both the active and the passive aspects of historical consciousness. "True historical thinking," Gadamer says, "must always take account of its own historicality." [93] Now of what does this "taking into account" consist?

It consists, first of all, in realizing that all truth claims are historically conditioned and therefore time bound. This was the great discovery of critical historical science in its origin. As Lessing put it, "The accidental truths of history can never become the proof of necessary truths of reason." [94] The great error of the historicist was the assumption that one could rationally reconstruct what really happened thereby spanning the historical separation between the past and the present, and that the proper development of *method* could transcend historical prejudice and extricate the true meaning otherwise hidden.

But what is even more important concerning the historicality of understanding, for Gadamer, is the fact that we are also the "effective" agents in its development, for history and its relativities not only effect us but we effect them. The effective-historical consciousness is, therefore, dialectical in the fullest sense of the term. Once this is understood, then the interpreter no longer has to assume that time is a "yawning abyss" that must somehow be "bridged," but can receive it as "filled with the continuity of custom and tradition in the light of which all that is handed down presents itself to us." [95] To use Ricoeur's terms, an historicist "hermeneutics of suspicion" can be replaced by a "restorative hermeneutics" through the implementation of a type of questioning that permits the subject himself to be questioned and in this manner "discover the question for which the text is an answer," as Gadamer puts it. [96]

Thus, the effective-historical consciousness, in Gadamer, moves beyond what we moderns have grown used to understanding as critical-historical consciousness. It moves beyond the historicist model tha assumes the past to be full of errors and that we, through the implementa-

er,

[92] Paul Ricoeur, "The Task of Hermeneutics," *Philosophy Today*, Vol. 17, Summer, p. 127.
[93] *Truth and Method*, p. 267.
[94] G.E. Lessing, *Theological Writings*, ed. Henry Chadwick (Stanford University Press, 1954), p. 53.
[95] *Truth and Method*, p. 264.
[96] *Ibid.*, pp. 326 ff.

tion of scientific methods, can get to the bottom of things. Moreover, it moves beyond the existentialist model which, believing that the past can never be known objectively, merely appropriates the meaning that can be appropriated *aus möglicher Existenz*, to use Jaspers' phrase, as meaning for the self in the moment of self-elucidation and disregards the rest. In either case, the primacy of the subject is uncontested for it is the subject that here always dictates what must be or not be the case. Because time, for Gadamer, is no longer viewed as the great villain forever obfuscating the meaning of history, the attainment of the wholly objective method of investigation is no longer viewed as the key to meaning and truth. Rather temporal distance is reconsidered as the greatest ally for interpretation inasmuch as it permits the superficial prejudice to disappear and the authentic prejudice to appear. In other words, the prejudices that are intrinsically rooted in the "fore-structures" of understanding are frequently reinvigorated with the passage of time whereas prejudices of the moment disappear. Gadamer insists, moreover, that the meaning of a text does not "occasionally" but "always" goes beyond what the author intended. Therefore tradition is not merely "reproductive" but "productive" every time an interpretation takes place. [97] With respect to the notion of Catholicity, there is indeed the aspect of gradualism which, when properly understood, enables tradition to filter out prejudices of the moment "whose grip on understanding is too much for us to comprehend." But there is also the aspect of the development of dogma which, while insisting on contiguity, also recognizes that this development is not merely repristination but also growth, in the cautious sense of relevancy to the situation.

The recent writings of Ricoeur may be viewed as the attempt to both integrate and move beyond the work of Jaspers, Heidegger and especially Gadamer, in order to challenge more effectively the reductionistic tendencies in linguistic and structuralist interpretations of the mythosymbolic.

In *The Symbolism of Evil* (1960), for example, Ricoeur moves away from the abstractness of pure eidetics into a mythics-symbolics of the will by means of which he intends to recover a sense of "the fullness of language." [98] Ricoeur recognizes, following Heidegger, that there has taken place in the modern scientific age a profound devaluation of language. Under the technological mandate of univocity those aspects of language that are equivocal and resist reduction to a single meaning are simply

[97] *Ibid.*, p. 264.
[98] *The Symbolism of Evil*, p. 348.

ignored. Logic is reduced to a series of mathematical signs and knowledge to information retrieval systems modelled on linear conceptions of objectivity and meaning. Discourse on "the ancient name of Being," therefore, becomes impossible since such talk is riddled with ambiguity and seeming circularity. Thus the task for Ricoeur, as in the case of Heidegger, is to return to the "pre-philosophical fullness" of mytho-symbolic language in order to obtain a more adequate point of departure. In this respect, however, Ricoeur is somewhat different than Heidegger in that he does not intend to cultivate a kind of mystic connaturality with Truth in and through primordial linguistic expressions. Ricoeur's movement to the archaic is rather propaedeutic to the development of a "logic of double meaning" that can (*a*) move beyond objectifying thinking to a more productive level of naiveté, in order to (*b*) return to basic questions of epistemology and ontology at a more constructive level. [99] It is Ricoeur's firm belief that if hermeneutic philosophy is to have credence among the empirical sciences and thereby make its unique contribution, it simply cannot forsake critical questions for that most "unhappy of situations" when philosophy simply abandons the sciences for the kind of primordial romanticism he finds in Heidegger.

Ricoeur orders his inquiry under the axiom "the symbol gives rise to thought." [100] Taking his cue from the Heideggerian *Wiederholen* he asks the question, "just what is it that the symbol gives?" What it gives, according to Ricoeur, is something to think about other than thought itself, for mythic-symbolic language tends to break the solipsistic pattern in pure philosophies of reflection. Jaspers, in his theory of ciphers, had an inkling of this but did not go far enough in disengaging the bondage of thought over language. It is precisely in this context one must understand the statement of Ricoeur that "philosophy which begins and ends with the *cogito* remains as empty and abstract as it is invincible." [101] This is why the mythic-symbolic *invites* reflection, as I put it, inasmuch as it provides or "gives" a density or what Ricoeur terms a "surplus of meaning" that transcends considerably what noetic reflection can provide on its own, as it were. Ricoeur's descent into the mythic-symbolic language of evil, then, provides him with a more encompassing conspectus of the will as *embodied*. Because the mythical language of good and evil resists the

---

[99] *Freud and Philosophy*, pp. 7 ff.
[100] *The Symbolism of Evil*, pp. 347 ff.
[101] *Freud and Philosophy*, p. 43. See Heidegger's extensive treament of this in *What is Called Thinking?* trans. Fred D. Wieck and J. Glenn Gray (New York: Harper and Row, 1972).

pure eidetic description, it is the perfect occasion for the extension of phenomenology into a hermeneutics of culpability.

Now Ricoeur's restorative hermeneutics of "sympathetic reenactment" is not to be perceived as the attempt to return to what he terms "first level naiveté." One simply cannot re-enter the dreaming innocence of myth through a kind of childlike fantasy as though the critical-historical sciences never happened. "We are in every way," Ricoeur insists emphatically, "the children of criticism" and cannot, therefore, escape the challenge of interpretation and its risks. Our only alternative is "to go beyond criticism by means of criticism" [102] whereby we may once again be freed to hear the myth's call to Being.

Ricoeur implements this double intention through a methodology closely modelled on the hermeneutical circle – the movement from whole to part and part to whole – with its antecedent underpinnings in the medieval dialectical conception of faith as *credo ut intelligam, intelligo ut credam*. Ricoeur develops four basic operations in this movement: the transition from speaking to writing, the structures of language and the text, unfolding the world of the text, and finally perceiving oneself before the world of the text. The first two operations can be viewed in terms of the downward or archeological arc of the circle, that is, as the analytical descent to the obscurity limit of the text. The latter two operations, by contrast, may be viewed in terms of the upward or teleological arc of the circle, that is, as the dialectical/dialogical ascent to the ideality limits of the meaning of the text. [103] While we cannot here delineate in detail the implications of each operation, suffice it to say that it is Ricoeur's notion of Transcendence as "eschatological limit" that informs this double movement. [104] In other words, unless the subject moves from the statics to the dynamics of the text, one remains merely a textual obscurantist and pendant. It is therefore the call of Transcendence that moves the subject into a position whereby he is ready, as Gadamer puts it, to be questioned by the text and its claim on Being. Only in this manner can the subject appropriate the meaning of the text as a coherent unity. On the other hand, it is also Ricoeur's understanding of Transcendence that forces the

---

[102] *Symbolism of Evil*, p. 350.

[103] See Ricoeur's essay on these operations entitled: "Philosophical Hermeneutics and Theological Hermeneutics," *Philosophy of Religion and Theology*, The American Academy of Religion, 1975, compiled by James W. McClendon, Jr., pp. 1-17.

[104] I have given this subject more extensive treatment in an essay entitled "Unfolding the Enfolding: Hermeneutics and Mysticism" to be found in a forthcoming collection co-edited by Walter Brenneman and Stanley Yarian called, *The Seeing Eye: Essays in Phenomenology of Religion*.

hermeneut to "the dimming of reflection and the return to the tragic" as the ideality limit of the text is approached. Because the definitive interpretation is impossible, one's only recourse is to begin anew. This is analogous to Jaspers' notion that one never escapes from the hermeneutical circle; one can only attempt to render it more encompassing. If Transcendence did not at once provide this invitation and this limit, one would be guilty of either a material or a formal reduction of its meaning.

But there is an important difference between Ricoeur and Jaspers on this matter. Because "Transcendence," for Ricoeur, "erupts from above downward in reverse," [105] it can never be identified with Jaspers' mystical conception of the Encompassing. Indeed, he firmly abides by Transcendence understood as an eschatological limit that precludes utterly the postulation of any kind of absolutes, even those concealed metaphorically in ciphers and the immanentalistic monism such a notion suggests. Ricoeur therefore continues to resist what he terms "an absolute transcendence of the cave" through an aesthetic resolution of what, in both the Judaic and Christian traditions, has always been unresolvable "from below," as it were. Thus, while Jaspers speaks of the knowledge of Transcendence as a "gift," and while Heidegger speaks about the "eventfulness of Being," Ricoeur, it would seem, wishes to solidify the *extra nos* character of this gift or happening more definitively than Jaspers, Heidegger, and even Gadamer. This can be seen in Ricoeur's recent discourse regarding the "textuality of Being" in which, it appears, he wishes to disavow somewhat earlier movements in the direction of Heidegger and Gadamer concerning the linguisticality of Being. It is an intriguing notion for two basic reasons. First, the notion of *textuality* provides a new basis for discussion with the linguistic sciences and literary criticism in the broad sense. This is what concerns Ricoeur at a very intense level this writing. [106] But secondly, the notion of *textuality* also provides

---

[105] *Freedom and Nature*, p. 469.

[106] See "What is a Text?" in David Rasmussen, *Mythic-Symbolic Language and Philosophical Anthropology* (The Hague: Martinus Nijhoff, 1971), pp. 135-150, and Ricoeur's most recent major studies including, *Interpretation Theory: Discourse and the Surplus of Meaning* (Fort Worth: Texas Christian University Press, 1976), and *The Rule of Metaphor: Multi-disciplinary Studies of the Creation of Meaning in Language*, a translation of *La métaphore vive* (Paris: Editions du Seuil, 1975), by Robert Czerny (Toronto: University of Toronto Press, 1977). This most recent work on metaphor may certainly be viewed as formal preparation to Ricoeur's long awaited *Poetics of the Will*. It also seems to me that in this most stunning recent work the Jaspersian theories of *Grenzsituationen* and *Chifferschrift* hover in and about Ricoeur's tensive theories of metaphor. The "semantic impertinence" and "innovation" effected by metaphorical usage, Ricoeur suggests, produce in the hearer a kind of "shock" that is concomitant with the opening of new horizons of meaning through imaginative philosophical speculation. These "shocks" or jolts, so recollective of the "recoils" in Jaspers' "boundary situations," are caused by what Ricoeur terms the "split

a space for the insights Ricoeur has gleaned from Gadamer, and perhaps most importantly the Protestant theological conviction that it is not just language but very specific language in the form of the "eminent text" called the Bible that mediates to us definitively the meaning of Transcendence.

It is precisely here, we suggest, that Ricoeur refers to Pascal in maintaining that "philosophical faith" can be coherent with its intention to "revelation" only when it is preceded by a *wager* in which it surrenders its autonomy to a theonomous ground that is nonidentical with Existenz. This, it would seem, is the ultimate meaning of Ricoeur's injunction to Jaspers: "Only he who can address God as Thou can speak of God as Transcendence." [107]

---

reference" of metaphor and the reorientation of consciousness through linguistic disorientation. While this split reference can be viewed strictly at the formal level of semantics, this is not sufficient for Ricoeur inasmuch as it is his intention, as stated in "Freedom and Nature, to reconnect ontology with poetics while insisting on their formal separateness. In order to do this it would appear that Ricoeur must develop further his theory of symbol inasmuch as the split reference of symbol consists of a linguistic and a non-linguistic reference, and it is the latter that is decisive vis-à-vis the problem of Transcendence. In these explorations it would appear that Ricoeur will have to deal not only with Heidegger, who looms so large at the end of *The Rule of Metaphor*, but also Karl Jaspers' philosophy of Transcendence.

[107] Schilpp, p. 640.

AFTERWORD

It was Meister Eckhart who said, "I have spoken of an agent in the soul whose primitive function it is *not* to reach God as He is good, or to apprehend him as he is the truth, but go further, to the foundations; to seek him and apprehend him in his uniqueness and abstraction, in the desert of his solitude, in the essence of his Being." While the mystical quest implicit to Eckhart's confession is more subdued in recent philosophy of religion, it is decisive for all who would respond to the call of Transcendence. Certainly it is in this aspect of *eros* that underlies the "restless heart" of Augustine, and it is the "longing" that will always make God *the* problem in philosophy and theology.

As we have attempted to show, it is precisely this quest that represents the central motivational force in the philosophy of Karl Jaspers. Whenever this is the case, one's philosophy will be hermeneutical inevitably, for if one is going to deal with Transcendence one must begin, as Jaspers has shown, with one's personal situation of being-in-a-world. And if one begins from the immediacy of one's situation seeking in it the "traces of Transcendence," one must accept the challenge of interpretation.

Therefore, and without pretending to be conclusive on the meaning of a cipher so protean and evanescent as Transcendence, we offer the following comments by way of summary.

First, we conclude that Jaspers rehabilitates the language of Transcendence by delineating carefully how the possibility of Transcendence is rooted formally in the nature of experience. Through his phenomenological analysis of experience Jaspers demonstrates that what we call Transcendence is a dynamic structure that consists in the movement of the self to higher and more encompassing levels of meaning. Only when this process has been clearly articulated is one in a position to ask reasonably the question concerning the ultimate meaning of Transcendence-Itself, and even then, only qualifiedly. What distinguishes this dynamic structure of transcending from that of all other organisms, of course, is the power of reflection. It is a power which can be permitted to stagnate, in which case the question of Transcendence in its ontological aspect is lost, or it can be cultivated, in which case the self, as possible Existenz, is awakened to the meaning of Transcendence as the cipher of Being-Itself. Transcendence, then, is in some sense isomorphic with the capacity for reflection on the meaning of experience and is, moreover, the antecedent condition of this possibility. Once this is understood it is possible to move from mere cognition to transcending-thinking.

Second, we conclude that Jaspers' philosophy of Transcendence also conveys a sense of "being Transcended," even though we have criticized him for the vagueness inherent in his notion of the Encompassing. "To philosophize is to transcend," Jaspers puts it following Plato. But one knows that transcending is real only when one knows simultaneously that one is transcended. An awareness of the reality of Transcendence, then, derives from the experience of *Grenzsituationen* and the curious paradoxical awareness that with the knowledge of limits one has gone beyond the limit itself. Such was the discovery of Kant and before him Cusanus. Such limits, of course, are not physical boundaries even though in metaphor they appear to be. They are rather events. Once this is understood, one can forever rid oneself of the notion that God or Transcendence-Itself is some kind of object. This is the reason why we have emphasized rather strongly Jaspers' familiarity with and his philosophical dependence on the mystics, for it is the mystics who are most immediately familiar with the language of boundaries. This is also why we have suggested repeatedly, especially in Part III, that it is the mystical impulse that undergirds the hermeneutics of Ricoeur and Gadamer and that this is necessarily so whenever hermeneutic philosophizing is more than just an academic game.

Third, even though we have criticized Jaspers for being excessively rationalistic in his elucidation of the meaning of Transcendence, and while we have pointed out the presence of idealistic presuppositions that are in some cases uncritical, we also recognize that the philosopher and the theologian have quite separate tasks. Therefore, even if Jaspers had attended more carefully to the mediation of meaning (as we find this problem illumined in Gadamer, Ricoeur and Lonergan, for example, and in a manner more consistent with a Christian interpretation of the Incarnation and a doctrine of Grace) one cannot ultimately overcome, thereby, the hiatus between knowledge and faith. Therefore we must confirm Jaspers' insistence that one cannot speak meaningfully about Transcendence apart from reason. Indeed, we hope that we have shown effectively that it is not reason that stands between man and God as a kind of insurmountable barrier. The question is always "what kind" of reason is being identified as a barrier. Is it the rationalism of the egoic self or is it a rationality that transcends rationalism by displacing the ego as one's center of reference? It is precisely the latter understanding of reason that we have located in Jaspers' notion of "the moving center of possible Existenz." Thus the cognitive and the affective, essence and existence, Transcendence and immanence are not, for Jaspers, contraries, but the dialectical foci of transcending-thinking grounded in Freedom. When Jaspers says that the reality of Transcendence is "perceptible in its traces," he is, therefore, not invoking empty poetics. Transcending in the ciphers of speculative metaphysics, for Jaspers, is always a hermeneutical exercise that presupposes an exhaustive phenomenological description of ordinary experience. Transcendence, therefore, far from being the emptiest of terms, becomes meaningful only when the transcending-subject is continuously engaged in the task of the interpretation experience. And the term *continuous* is here decisive, for if one concludes that hermeneutic philosophizing will lead the subject to the wholly comprehensive point of view, then one will be forced to conclude that Transcendence is a mere chimera. It is the dynamic character of the hermeneutical task, then, that is presupposed in Jaspers' notion that "Eternalization" is the philosophical analogue of "redemption." Far from exhausting the meaning of Transcendence, Eternalization has to do with rising unto that sublime state of knowing that we do not know and in that *ignorantia* "knowing," as Saint Paul put it, "that we are known" even when we do not name that knowing Presence.

Finally, and in conclusion, there will always be those who believe that words like Being, Transcendence, and God are meaningless and uncoinable fictions because their referents cannot be demonstrated to exist. For such persons the philosophy of Karl Jaspers and hermeneutic philosophy generally will have nothing to say.But for those who sense in experience a luminosity informed by the hidden depths of the within *and* the of meaning and to the enigmatic dialectics of Being and non-Being, as will be powerful and irresistible. Indeed, if it is said that faith in our time has foundered in the face of the silence of God, it has not foundered so much as floundered on the shoals of objectifying thinking. Only when one moves from the semantic surfaces of sensation to the deep structures of meaning through the enigmatic dialects of Being and non-Being, as Nietzsche reminded us, is something so sublime as foundering possible.

APPENDIX

INTERLUDE: SCHEMATIC DIAGRAM OF BEING*

To be sure there is the greatest disproportion between the meaning of the idea of the Encompassing and the tangible security of a spatial likeness. But it is also a psychological fact that our thinking needs to cling to a framework of visual clarity in order to ascend to its goal. When an idea is deprived of every perception, then in its non-objectifiability one needs all the more some kind of psychological support for so strange an intuition. The psychological binding of all one's thinking to representations and especially spatial representations, we cannot deny. If we use it as a framework we obtain a technical facility, an abstract for our way of speaking and for the ordering of ideas which we reject after it has served its purposes for memory.

Philosophical thinking has made use of spatial images at all times. These images have also been frequently drawn. There is, to be sure, the danger of making ideas themselves suspicious through such philosophical barbarisms. And there is the further danger of promoting misunderstandings which are connected to such sketched images which can only be factually worked out through verbal exposition. Such dangers, however, originate only if the image is taken as a fact and also if some kind of validity is attributed to the image itself. A schematic diagram of Being is no necessary element in the sequence of ideas as such.

Spatial schemata therefore, insofar as they stand in the service of truth, are a mere play. As such we playfully fix our thinking about the modalities of the Encompassing and its lines of references in a momentary image. The image is the most concise language. I never hide the fact that for me such schemata originate in the spirit of play.

There were many possible schemata. Before me lie several out of which I select one. To place several next to one another would have the advantage of preventing fixation on just one but the disadvantage of confusing matters. When one uses technical aids for reflection, one must follow

---

Diagram and text from *Von der Wahrheit*, pp. 141-147, trans. by the author, and printed by permission of R. Piper Verlag Co.

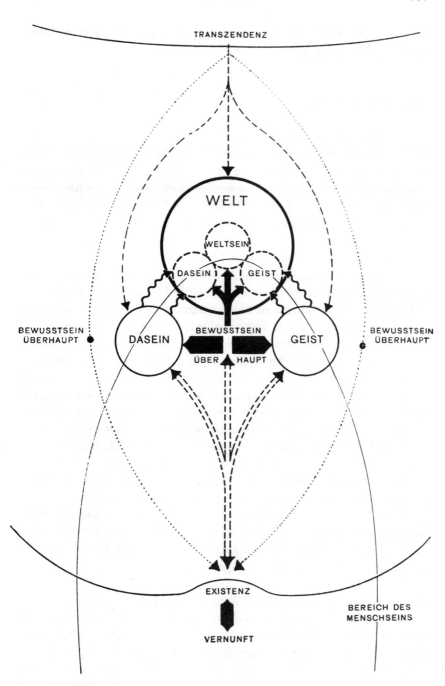

Diagram of Being (Source: *Von der Wahrheit, p. 142*).

their rules and expect that even though misunderstanding may be avoided through this, one also makes it drastically near.

Interpretation of the Diagram

(*a*) We will first consider the *fields* (*Felder*):
In the middle of the diagram lies the world as the totality of the immanent; above, the unbounded space of Transcendence; below, Existenz connected with Reason comprehensively opening up (*der umfassend aufgeschlossenen Vernunft*). The world hovers (*schwebt*) like a sphere between Transcendence and Existenz.

The fields signify modalities of the Comprehensive or Encompassing. The names of the Encompassing are listed within.

The fields of Transcendence and Existenz (next to reason) are separated from one another by the world. Their fields flow into infinity.

The fields of immanence are characterized as circles, the world-sphere as the circle of circles with consciousness-in-general as a point.

The world is characterized as the largest circle which signifies the Encompassing of world-Being. Within it lie smaller circles that mean to-become-object (*Zum-Gegenstand-werden*); in the middle, the world-Being-we-are-not as it becomes an object for consciousness-in-general; next to it, the Encompassing-that-we-ourselves- are, belonging to the world, as world-Being as it likewise becomes an object for consciousness-in-general. The names of these smaller circles which have become-objects-for-us (no longer Encompassing) are printed in smaller letters.

"World" is therefore drawn twice, as a greater circle encompassing the smaller circle within it; world-Being having become object.

Existence (*Dasein*) and spirit (*Geist*) are likewise shown twice. In addition to appearing as smaller circles next to world-Being, they also lie as independent Encompassings – as larger circles – outside the world circles at the points of consciousness-in-general.

(*b*) Secondly we consider the relationship of the fields to one another.

Between the fields, wavy lines are drawn which indicate the references of the modalities of the Encompassing with one another. The lines are drawn in different ways conforming to the essence of each reference.

Strong, fully drawn lines signify the relationship of consciousness-in general to objects (the ways of world-Being, existence and spirit having become objective).

The connections through *wide* masses of lines: the being-with-one-an-other and the being-towards-one-another of the modalities of the En-compassing that we are (of consciousness-in-general with existence and spirit; reason with Existenz).

Wavy lines: world-Being as the objective appearance of the Encom-passing that we are (Dasein and Geist).

Hyphenated lines: the active-itself in the world; existence, conscious-ness and spirit becoming phenomena for the self-Being of Existenz.

Dotted lines represent the languages of Transcendence in the phenom-ena of the pure thinking of consciousness-in-general and the cipher-lan-guage of the world, existence and spirit.

There are three ways from Existenz to Transcendence.

The *first way* leads through the world, through the vitality of existence (*Dasein*), the spirituality of mind (*Geist*) and through knowledge of World. Existenz lies contemplatively in all world-Being as cipher lan-guage.

The *second way* leads through the speculation of consciousness-in-gen-eral (indicated through the points outside of the world, through the dot-ted lines which connect Transcendence and Existenz apart from the in-terference of the world): in a formal transcending of pure thinking, Exis-tenz becomes aware of transcending in foundering-thinking (*scheitern des Denken*).

The *third way* is a meeting and a coincidence of Existenz and Tran-scendence in *unio mystica*, which is not drawn in the diagram and is indi-rectly expressed: Transcendence and Existenz are above and below the borders of the figures indicated by sections of the arcs of greater circles but in a way suggesting that the larger curve (Transcendence) would at-tract the smaller curve (Existenz). In the world, the meeting of Tran-scendence and Existenz always happens in ambiguous language that never completely bridges the distance between them. In formal tran-scending, a becoming-aware takes place but always in general and with-out specific content. In *unio mystica* a becoming-One happens but with-out reality or immediacy in the world.

(*c*) *The Diagram as a Whole* is able to indicate certain characteristics of Being for our consciousness of Being:

While all other modalities of the Encompassing are characterized as fields, consciousness-in-general is characterized by a point. This con-sciousness, in which all of world-Being is summarized for us, itself has no content of its own. It is for us the center of the world but it is empty in itself. It *is* only when filled by that which is not itself.

The entire immanent Being hovering between Transcendence and Existenz is indeed represented as a sphere or circle, however not as a simple circle in its entirety. This has the following meaning:

The Encompassing world-Being is more than that which is accessible to us in the natural sciences and cosmological knowledge (in consciousness-in-general). What we have before our eyes and think of as cosmos is an image having become objective in a way which cannot be perceived. Research and thinking transform these images (the world-Being as a smaller circle within the encompassing "World").

World-Being encompasses that which we are as Dasein and Geist. However, existence and spirit are at the same time independently comprehensive vis-à-vis the cosmos, being more than that which is never objectifiable in our knowledge (therefore the circles of Dasein and Geist occur twice, inside and outside the World).

So the immanent Being present to our experience is an intertwining (*Verschlungenheit*) of our being and world-Being, of the world which originates in us and which independently originates apart from us. We are part of the world insofar as we are Dasein and Geist. However, we are not to be explained by the world independent of us any more than the world is to be derived from us.

The immanence of our being and the being of the world in the middle of the diagram (through its concentration in the close configuration of the circles in the sense of a wide distance from Transcendence and Existenz) expresses that which continually misleads man to see the world and immanence as his entire Being, permitting the world to be sufficient in itself hovering as a sphere in nothingness before the Deity itself.

However, because of its relative compactness, its asymmetry and its reference to others, this figure does not permit the world to become a circle freely hovering in itself. It indicates that the world must be penetrated by the Ground of Being.

Transcendence and Existenz in general are not included in the figure but only at its edges. The infinity of Transcendence, the boundless unfathomable origin of Existenz in its freedom, created through Transcendence and all the comprehensive possibilities of reason are indicated by these configurations. The wideness of the distance between Existenz and Transcendence from the middle of the world indicates the leap (*der Sprung*) that exists between them.

Although Transcendence and Existenz are separated by the world lying between them, they still have direct approach to one another even apart from the world, but then without expansion into form and tangible reality; in emptiness so to speak. That this relation exists makes Existenz and all the intricacy of the world (as its way to Transcendence) simultaneously independent of the world through a knowing that is prior to all worlds and an occurrence (Finden) beyond all worlds.

(*d*) A line drawn through the whole in the arc limits the *realm of being human* (*Bereich des Menschseins*). Man is not everything. Perhaps man can have reference to everything, but he is not everything.

The line indicates what lies beyond man's possibility, what can lie only in man and also what is attributed to man as being outside man. Transcendence and a tremendous realm of man lies beyond man. Existenz and reason are only within man. Consciousness-in-general is possible perhaps in animals but then only latently, disappearing without any development. Ultimately man is more than being human. As a body he is matter and hence part of the cosmos. He is in existence as are all living things. And he is mind which is also outside man in the living and in the world. Only a fraction of possible matter is present in man. As Dasein and Geist he is, however, distinguished from all other beings. It is yet to be determined the extent to which all living things are Dasein and to what extent they are Geist.

All living things are Dasein as living in the world, but we are able to comprehend existence only insofar as we find ourselves as Dasein. Seen from that standpoint, all existence becomes increasingly strange. When Dasein is measured, it seems less, as if arising by an abstraction from character which in us belongs to existence in its entirety: however it is also more and other through character which we are not able to interpret from within.

Are living things, insofar as they are extant, also Geist? Not, in any case, as they are Dasein.

If Dasein and Geist are contrasted to Existenz, then in both something seems to coincide. Geist seems to speak in living nature, not only in man. In man himself there is always the beauty of singing, dancing, movements and expressions of vital spirituality (*Geistigkeit*), as life is a moving form of endless reference appearing as a spiritual vitality. Spirit seems to be present in living nature not only as a likeness to the language of creation in ciphers, but really as the fantasy of the living. Perhaps, in fact, life produces more forms in adaption according to the conditions necessary to life and the necessities of life for the surrounding world, than at any time are expected.

But the mind of natural life is deprived of so much of its fundamental character as Geist, that, at best, it could be considered as a fragment of spirituality. This natural spirit is without the inner movement of understanding. It misses enlightening development due to consciousness-in-general. The alternatives of true and false, beauty and ugliness, good and evil as the moment of decision which Existenz accomplishes in the spirit are lacking to it. Spiritual vitality alone remains innocent, unprejudiced and without consciousness for it is beyond such distinctions. The beautiful and the ugly happen equally without prediction or reliability. It does not know itself and therefore does not determine its own movement.

It is a question, therefore, whether simply an understanding of behavior is meaningful for determining the relation of living things to the mind. Is there a meeting point halfway out of the realm of nature where the mind recognizes itself? Can there be a nature-philosophy which not only reads ciphers but forcefully interprets spiritual reality? The radical differences between Dasein and Geist which have been contrasted by us makes any possible coincidence of spirit and natural life beyond man to appear questionable indeed. But the question remains open.

BIBLIOGRAPHY

WORKS BY KARL JASPERS

JASPERS, KARL. *Chiffren der Transzendenz*. München: R. Piper, 1970.

_____ .*The Future of Mankind*. Trans. E.B. Ashton. Chicago: University of Chicago Press, 1961.

_____ .*The Great Philosophers*, Two Volumes. Trans. Ralph Manheim. New York: Harcourt, Brace and World, 1962, 1966.

_____ .*Man in the Modern Age*. Trans. Eden and Cedar Paul. New York: Doubleday, 1951.

_____ .*Nikolaus Cusanus*. München: R. Piper, 1964.

_____ .*Nietzsche and Christianity*. Trans. E.B. Ashton. Chicago: Regnery, 1961.

_____ .*Nietzsche: An Introduction to the Understanding of His Philosophical Activity*. Trans. Charles Wallraf and Frederick J. Schmitz. Tucson: University of Arizona Press, 1965.

_____ .*The Origin and Goal of History*. Trans. Michael Bullock. New Haven: Yale University Press, 1959.

_____ .*The Perennial Scope of Philosophy*. Trans. Ralph Manheim. New York: Philosophical Library, 1949.

_____ .*Philosophical Faith and Revelation*. Trans. E.B. Ashton. New York: Harper and Row, 1967.

_____ .*Philosophy Of Existence*. Trans. Richard Grabau. Philadelphia: University of Pennsylvania Press, 1971.

_____ .*Philosophy*, Three Volumes, Trans. E.B. Ashton, Chicago: University of Chicago Press, 1969, 1970, 1971.

————. *Philosophy and the World.* Trans. E.B. Ashton. Chicago: Regnery, 1961.

————. *Psychologie der Weltanschauungen.* Berlin: Springer Verlag, 1931.

————. *Reason and Anti-Reason in our Time.* Trans. Stanley Godman. New Haven: Yale University Press, 1952.

————. *Reason and Existenz.* Trans. William Earle. New York: Noonday Press, 1955.

————. *Schelling: Grösse und Verhängnis.* München: R. Piper, 1955.

————. *Three Essays: Leonardo, Descartes, Max Weber.* Trans. Ralph Manheim. New York: Harcourt, Brace and World, 1964.

————. *Tragedy Is Not Enough.* Trans. Harold Reiche, Harry T. Moore and Karl W. Deutsch. Boston: Beacon Press, 1952.

————. *Truth and Symbol.* Trans. Jean T. Wilde, William Kluback and William Kimmel. New Haven: College and University Press, 1959.

————. *Von der Wahrheit.* München: R. Piper, 1947.

————. *Way to Wisdom.* Trans. Ralph Manheim. New Haven: Yale University Press, 1959.

JASPERS, KARL and BULTMANN, RUDOLF. *Myth and Christianity.* Trans. Norbert Guterman. New York: Noonday Press, 1958.

AUTOBIOGRAPHICAL ESSAYS

JASPERS, KARL. "On My Philosophy," *Existentialism from Dostoevsky to Sartre.* Trans. and ed. by Walter Kaufman. New York: Meridian, 1956.

————. "Philosophical Autobiography" and "Reply to My Critics," *The Philosophy of Karl Jaspers.* Schilpp edition. New York: Tudor, 1957.

RECENT MAJOR STUDIES OF JASPERS IN ENGLISH

Ehrlich, Leonard. *Karl Jaspers: Philosophy as Faith.* Amherst: U. Mass. Press. 1975.

Samay, Sebastian. *Reason Revisited: The Philosophy of Karl Jaspers.* South Bend: University of Notre Dame Press, 1971.

Schrag, Oswald. *Existence, Existenz, and Transcendence.* Pittsburgh: Duquesne University Press, 1971.

Wallraff, Charles F. *Karl Jaspers: An Introduction to his Philosophy.* Princeton: Princeton University Press, 1970.

NAME INDEX